Jeff W...

Brendan Gribben

TWR Jaguar Prototype Racers

Andy Buehly

Dave Hawk

M...

G. R...

M. Blackwell

Dedication

This book is dedicated to Tom Walkinshaw and the many drivers, designers, engineers, mechanics, team members and all other TWR and Jaguar personnel whose skills and unceasing dedication helped to make the 1980s and early 1990s one of the most interesting and rewarding periods in Jaguar's long and illustrious history.

TWR Jaguar Prototype Racers

Group C and GTP XJR Cars 1985-93

By Leslie F Thurston
with an introduction and additional material by Ian Norris

To Steve
with Best wishes
Leslie Thurston
8-11-03

JAGUAR DAIMLER
Heritage Trust

Published 2003 by
Jaguar Daimler Heritage Trust Limited
Browns Lane
Allesley
Coventry CV5 9DR

Designed by Bruce Aiken

ISBN 0-9541039-1-2

Printed in China

Contents

Foreword

**by Roger Putnam,
Chairman, Ford of GB and Chairman of
Trustees, Jaguar Daimler Heritage Trust**

In 1981 John Egan asked me to join Jaguar, then still part of British Leyland. I was at Lotus at the time, having joined Colin Chapman and his team at the end of 1965, the year Jimmy Clark won his second Formula 1 World Championship and the Indianapolis 500. Of the many jobs I had at Lotus, launching the hugely successful Lotus 49 Cosworth with Colin and Graham Hill sticks firmly in my mind.

One of the first tasks we tackled at Jaguar as we were floated away from BL was to re-establish the Brand Equity that had been so strong in the 1950s and '60s. John Egan asked me, as Sales and Marketing Director, to add the Motorsport programme to my other responsibilities because 'You're the only one who knows anything about motor racing'.

From the European Touring Car Championships won with the TWR XJ-S cars we soon focused on the Group C Sports Prototype programme, which of course included the tremendously important Le Mans 24-hour Race, where so many Jaguar triumphs were achieved in the 1950s. Le Mans, along with Monaco, Indianapolis and Daytona, is one of only four races worldwide which are known in almost every household.

Following a tentative start with Bob Tullius in 1984 we moved into an arrangement with Tom Walkinshaw and his Oxford-based TWR team, and the Silk Cut Jaguar Team first appeared in 1986, racing at Le Mans and around the world. In 1988 we saw the TWR-run Castrol Jaguar team start racing in the IMSA series in North America.

There is no doubt in my mind that the victories at Le Mans and Daytona, and the World Sportscar Championships in 1987 and '88, made the Jaguar brand complete again - so much so that Ford Motor Company purchased Jaguar in 1989. By then we had achieved what we had set out to do and the race programme was scaled down over the next two years.

However, it would be remiss of me not to pay huge tribute to Tom Walkinshaw and his team. The drivers, the sponsors – major and minor – and my own motor racing department, the late Ron Elkins and Alan Hodge.

Of course, the foreword to this book must pay tribute to the effort, dedication and detailed knowledge of Leslie Thurston. Whether it be naval shells, heavy artillery weapons or Jaguar memorabilia, this man's knowledge and private collection are unique and I thank him for his perseverance with this book, which adds so much to the history of the Jaguar marque.

Roger Putnam, September 2002

Foreword

by The Author

My interest in all things Jaguar began long ago as a schoolboy, in the days before the historic XK engine and XK120 first saw the light of day. I have always enjoyed collecting as a hobby, with a special interest in Jaguar memorabilia, particularly mascots, badges and any interesting company artefacts. Several years ago, while visiting a sports car show, I bought a number of ex-TWR prototype race car panels in the autojumble section, intrigued by the thought of owning actual components from these very historic machines. On examination, some panels had three-figure numbers on the backs: 186, 187, 288 and so on. What did they mean?

Although I have owned Jaguars as personal transport for many years, while engaged in business totally unconnected with the motor trade, lack of time prevented me from enjoying Jaguar's motor sports activities or getting to know much about the cars involved. Nevertheless, curiosity got the better of me; I had to know what the numbers meant. The discovery that each one referred to a particular car, and was in fact its unique chassis number, soon had me well and truly hooked. To cut a long story short, I acquired mountains of books, racing magazines, press packs, photographs and collections of material from writers and enthusiasts who followed the teams wherever they raced, and eventually I gained a reasonable knowledge of these remarkable machines and their racing activities.

While researching it became apparent that outside the circle of people directly involved, few could tell the different models apart and were unaware of the tremendous following Group C and IMSA GTP racing had in certain countries. Many wanted to learn more, and as this historic chapter recedes into the past, it is most likely that future generations will take an even keener interest than is perhaps the case today.

I am far from being a professional writer, and this text is not intended as a detailed technical treatise on the cars or an in-depth biography of the personnel involved, neither of which I am qualified to attempt. Instead it represents my own simple introduction and identification guide to the machines, along with brief descriptions of the races they competed in.

Leslie F Thurston, January 2003

Introduction

The Jaguar Racing Legend

by Ian Norris

This book is the result of one man's enthusiastic devotion to a subject that fascinated him. Leslie Thurston's desire to find out everything he could about Jaguar's activities in the field of sports-prototype racing has uncovered a depth of detail that is staggering. His collection of data and artefacts, which ranges from complete Group C cars to team clothing, makes him the greatest authority on the second great period in Jaguar's racing history. The main body of this book lists details of every car and every race during the period in which TWR and Jaguar were one of the strongest forces in sportscar racing. The purpose of this introduction is to give an overview of Jaguar's racing history and to place Leslie's detailed analysis of the collaboration between Jaguar and Tom Walkinshaw in an historical context.

It is natural that a company such as Jaguar, whose reputation was built on sporting and performance cars, should take part in motor sport. Jaguar is unusual, however, in that when it has participated as a factory-backed team, the reason behind taking to the track has been commercial, not the expression of a deep-seated urge to compete as part of a company philosophy. Jaguar's approach to racing – for it is only in racing that the factory itself has competed, rally successes having been achieved by customers – is directly influenced by the company's founder, Sir William Lyons. His support of racing was determined by the effect it would have on the image of his products, and the effect that an improved image would have on sales.

It was for that reason that in pre-war years Lyons would take company demonstrators to club events and drive them himself in tests and sprints. Seeing the latest model performing well would encourage club members, already Jaguar (or in those days SS) enthusiasts, to upgrade, thus helping the young company to sell more cars. If a Jaguar was to appear in competition it had to be successful, and there is evidence that on occasion Lyons and the management would actively discourage owners from competing in high-profile events where their SS cars were unlikely to shine.

The factory itself did not enter cars in competition. Instead it helped those private owners who were likely to succeed. In the days before the Second World War broke out, SS 100 cars driven by private owners with factory assistance earned good results and valuable publicity. Success came more often in rallying, for the SS 100 was not a racing car on the same level as some continental models of the period. However, when it was prepared by the factory, the SS 100 could do great things on the track. The car owned by motoring journalist and racing driver Tommy

Wisdom, whose preparation benefited from his close relationship with the factory, proved this in the years immediately before and after the war. A similar arrangement greatly assisted up-and-coming young rally driver Ian Appleyard, son of a Jaguar distributor and soon to become William Lyons's son-in-law.

After the war, Lyons was faced with the unexpected commercial success of the XK120. The car had been conceived as a limited-production attention-getter for the new XK engine, but the demand created by its style and performance potential meant it had to be turned into a profitable mass-production reality. But if it was to achieve real commercial success it had to surmount one hurdle – it had to justify the claim that the '120' in its name did actually refer to its top speed in miles per hour. This was a task that had to be undertaken by the factory, and a car prepared by the company's experimental department proved the XK120's credentials comprehensively at Jabbeke in Belgium in May 1949.

Lyons was persuaded that while the XK120 was still in short supply, it could be kept in the public eye by competition successes, and the experimental department began to prepare cars. They would be owned and campaigned by the factory, but would still be driven by private entrants. Wins came in races, notably at Silverstone in August 1949, and rallies, and soon private owners across the world were competing in their own XK120s. Among them was a group of three that ran at Le Mans in 1950. Two out of the three finished, and the one that retired ran as high as second before succumbing to clutch failure.

Lyons and his service manager, the great 'Lofty' England, together with William Heynes, Jaguar's engineering director, had taken great interest in how the cars performed in the most prestigious sportscar race in the world. In view of their reliability, and the reports of the works mechanics that had accompanied them, it was decided that the XK120 should be turned into a car capable of winning the 24-hour classic.

The car that the Jaguar design team created was the XK120C, with the 'C' standing for 'Competition'. It soon became known as the C-type, and it won at Le Mans on its first outing in 1951, driven by Peter Walker and Peter Whitehead, starting a period in which Jaguar was the dominant force in the French classic. Five wins in seven years have been recorded in sufficient detail and in so many publications as to require no repetition here. However, for the reader who wants the definitive story there can be no better source than the two volumes of Jaguar's racing history written by

the late Andrew Whyte, a Jaguar man to his fingertips and a painstaking historian.

From 1951 to October 1956, Jaguar competed as a works team, with the racing section of the experimental department building and developing not only the C- and D-types, but also preparing road cars such as the Mark VII for saloon car racing. But in the autumn that followed Jaguar's fourth Le Mans victory, Sir William Lyons decided to withdraw the works team from competition. The main motivation for Lyons to approve the racing programme had always been his realisation that success in motor sport brought additional publicity which helped to sell the standard cars, particularly in the now all-important American market. The series of wins at Le Mans captured everyone's imagination, and ownership of a Jaguar took on a new meaning. Ever the canny businessman, Lyons pulled out of racing when he felt that his car was becoming less competitive against new opponents featuring costly technological improvements which elevated the sport to a higher plane than probably he considered worthwhile pursuing.

Furthermore, at Jaguar racing had always been a responsibility of the experimental department, and the work that was being carried out on new road cars, which would culminate in 1961 with the E-type, meant that there were insufficient resources to do both. Racing activities came back into the care of the service department, where work was carried out on behalf of customers. It is a tribute to the quality of the cars, the enthusiasm of the service department under Lofty England and the dedication of the customers that a fifth Le Mans win, a whole era of domination by Jaguar of Touring Car racing and a run of successes for the E-type all took place while Jaguar was not officially engaged in motor sport.

The first major victory of the 'client' era was the 1957 Le Mans race, where Ecurie Ecosse scored its second victory. The Scottish team had won the 1956 race when the works cars hit trouble, and it was naturally well supported by the factory, receiving the works cars when Jaguar withdrew. However, 1958 saw the end of the D-type's domination of Le Mans, as new regulations limited engine size to three litres. The XK engine wasn't happy at the lower capacity, and Jaguar faded from the international sportscar racing scene.

The name did not fade from racing, however, for a group of private teams, including Tommy Sopwith's Equipe Endeavour and John Coombs in Britain, made the compact 3.4 and 3.8 saloons the cars to beat in Touring Car racing. Jaguar saloons won Championships across the world, and in British saloon car racing Jaguars driven by such as Mike Hawthorn, Graham Hill, Tommy Sopwith and Jack Sears provided entertainment and excitement that enlivened many race meetings of the late 1950s.

There was a tentative return to racing at Le Mans in 1960 with E2A, a prototype that combined D-type chassis construction with the independent rear suspension that was to make the E-type a world-beater. However, it was all very much 'under the counter' with the car being entered by one of the greatest of Jaguar's competition clients, the American Briggs Cunningham. E2A was not successful, and with the E-type getting ever closer to production, there was no temptation to split the experimental department's energies, or to dilute the efforts of the Jaguar engineers involved in the development of the new sportscar.

It must have been frustrating for the development team under 'Bill' Heynes, for there was great enthusiasm for racing among his group. There was, however, the satisfaction of knowing that what had been learned on the track was directly applicable to such a high performance car as the E-type. Nowhere was this truer than in the field of aerodynamics. Body designer Malcolm Sayer used his aircraft industry experience to shape the C- and D-types and passed the lessons learned on the Mulsanne straight at Le Mans directly on, in the form of the E-type. This was one of the few Jaguar body designs that did not come from the styling ideas of Sir William, but almost straight from the wind tunnel, via Sayer's unrivalled eye for a shape. The E-type was infinitely superior to its XK predecessors and set new standards in sports car motoring. With a 150mph top speed, its racing potential was pounced upon, although most successes came in club-level racing for production cars. In 1963 Jaguar did built a small series of 'lightweight' models for racing. They performed well but were not capable of winning a race such as Le Mans, despite the efforts of the Cunningham team in 1963.

Despite the fact that there was no works team involved in racing, the engineers could not be dissuaded from pursuing thoughts of competition cars. Thus, in 1964, came about the construction of XJ13, a mid-engined racer that could have challenged Ford and Ferrari at Le Mans. Powered by a newly designed twelve-cylinder engine and with a body designed by Sayer, XJ13 was effectively a spare-time project for the engineering and experimental departments. Designed to follow the latest trends in racing car design, it suffered from its 'unofficial' status, which limited the budget available. In addition, Sir William did not want his engineers spending their energies on a racing programme when their efforts needed to be directed at the creation of the XJ6 saloon. As in most things, the boss was right. To have entered sportscar racing at that time would have brought Jaguar up against the bottomless budgets of Ford and the 'racing comes first' philosophy of Ferrari. Jaguar, racing on a budget limited by Lyons's requirement for everything to be done in the most economical way, would not have been able to compete. And would Jaguar have followed Porsche's example of building 25 of the phenomenal 917s to qualify it as a 'production' sports car for the 1969 Le Mans?

XJ13 was developed to a degree, with test driver Norman Dewis and the engineers giving up their Sundays to track test the car. But in the end it was put aside, until the fateful day in 1971 when, during filming for a publicity campaign to announce the adoption of its twelve-cylinder power unit for the E-Type, a wheel collapsed while Dewis was driving it at the MIRA test track. The car rolled end over end, with the diminutive driver crouching under the dashboard and switching off the ignition while the car was in mid-air, to emerge with nothing more than bruises. The car was more seriously damaged, but two years later it was rebuilt, to appear in public for the first time.

By this time, however, Jaguar had lost its independence. First had come a merger of equals, in the shape of a link with the British Motor Corporation to form British Motor Holdings. This took place in 1966, but in 1968 BMC's failing profitability forced it into a merger with Leyland, incorporating Standard Triumph and Rover, to form British Leyland. Encompassing so many brands, BL had plenty of people who were eager to show the flag in motor sport. Unfortunately, the sporting activities were controlled by a centralised group that did not have the single brand loyalty shown

previously by the constituent companies. Jaguar, BMC, Triumph and Rover had all achieved successes in races and rallies with their own competition departments, but BL's competition policy seemed to be to pick and choose marques that appealed to the centralised policy makers on a somewhat random basis. So it was that after winning the British Saloon Car Championship with the small Triumph Dolomite Sprint, Ralph Broad, a tuner working under contract to BL, proposed that his company's next project should be to turn the much larger Jaguar XJ12 coupé into a race winner in the European Touring Car Championship.

Jaguar engineering, isolated in a group that it felt did not understand the luxury and performance car business, was not happy about being a secondary partner in turning one of its products into a racing car, but there was little that could be done to change the decision. The XJ12 programme was announced in March 1976, but it was indicative of the way things were in British Leyland that the car did not appear on the track until September, when it completed just over one-third of the RAC Tourist Trophy. Two cars ran a full season in 1977, but with only partial success, leading races but rarely finishing them. The project was dropped for the following year, as BL's motor sport planners turned their attentions to fresh fields. To the relief of Jaguar engineering, they were not involved, while Jaguar purists were deeply insulted by the red/blue/white Leyland livery and badges, with no reference to Jaguar.

Across the Atlantic, the BL influence was also at work, but with greater success. Mike Dale, an amateur racing driver who had come to the British Leyland sales department via BMC, had added Jaguar sales to his responsibilities in 1969. Through BL links, Dale the race driver had met Bob Tullius, another racer whose speciality was Triumphs. A former salesman for Kodak, Tullius had prepared his own TR3 and made it a winner. Noticed by BL, he had been encouraged, and had set up his own race preparation business to race a TR4 and won the Sports Car Club of America's Championship in his class for four successive years.

British Leyland's venture into racing with the V12 Broadspeed Coupé might have proved a success had it been given more time. (JDHT)

In 1974 the V12 E-type was losing its showroom appeal, and race fan Dale proposed a racing programme to brighten its image. When he got approval to take to the tracks he gave the job to Tullius's operation Group 44, a name that came from his regular racing number. Because of the size of the United States, Tullius, based at Winchester in Virginia and sponsored by Quaker State Oil, was to be Jaguar's racing arm on the East Coast, while the Western representative would be Huffaker Engineering of San Francisco. Both teams were successful from the start, but by the end of 1975, and the end of the E-type's production life, Tullius had established Group 44's position as BL's tuner of choice in the United States.

In 1976 the team was preparing MGs and a Triumph for BL, but it was also working on a private venture, preparing one of the then-new XJ-S coupés for racing. Tullius had to do all his own development on the car, but the team's experience paid off, and by the end of the 1976 season the XJ-S was a winner. Between 1977 and 1981, Tullius raced it so successfully that the car became an official Jaguar entry with full support from BL's operation in the USA.

In April 1980, an event which was to have the greatest influence on Jaguar's racing policy took place. John Egan was appointed to head Jaguar, with the task of either making the company work, or closing it. Egan knew that there was more to putting Jaguar back on its feet than re-organising the factories and sorting out quality problems. One of Jaguar's strongest points, in the view of its new boss, was the pride of its workforce, based on the unique position that Jaguar occupied and on the company's achievements. Part of that pride came from Jaguar's racing heritage. Racing success was a good morale-booster as well as good publicity, so Egan was in favour of it. What he was not in favour of was success at any price – for him, racing had to be cost-effective, like everything else in the new Jaguar organisation. One of the first budgets Egan approved was for Group 44's activities with the XJ-S in 1981. After building a new car to comply with the new rules for the Trans-Am Championship, Tullius won three races out of the nine in the series to finish as runner-up in the Championship.

While Tullius and Group 44 were campaigning the XJ-S in America, racing driver and entrepreneur Tom Walkinshaw had been looking at the possibilities of racing Jaguar's GT coupé in Europe. Scottish-born Walkinshaw operated from a base in Oxfordshire and had already become British saloon car champion. One of his greatest skills lay in reading and interpreting the language of motor racing regulations. He could see the best ways of being ultra-competitive while staying within the letter of the law, and it was this that brought him into contact with John Egan and Jaguar. From 1982, cars eligible for the European Touring Car Championship would have to look like standard cars, with no wings and no oversize wheel-arch extensions. Walkinshaw realised that in production form the XJ-S could accept the widest possible tyres and wheels, while its two-plus-two format brought it within the touring car regulations (even if Jaguar did not quite at first meet the stipulation for minimum annual production of 5000 units of the type!). He decided to approach Jaguar with a proposal.

John Egan undertook to support Walkinshaw's Jaguar entry with cars and a certain amount of technical help, but sponsorship was to be on a basis of payment by results – no wins meant no money. An agreement was reached to field a single car in 1982, driven by Walkinshaw with Chuck Nicholson as his co-driver, with a second XJ-S available later in the season, starting with the important Spa 24 Hours. The cars would be raced in the colours of Motul, the French oil company, and hi-fi manufacturers Akai; the Jaguar name would appear only on the badges. In 1981, Roger Putnam, formerly of Lotus and with experience of motor sport, became Jaguar's Director of Sales and Marketing, and Egan soon asked him to head up Jaguar's new motor sports involvement.

In America, more ambitious plans were afoot. Dale and Tullius had been looking at the new IMSA (International Motor Sports Association) series for Grand Touring Prototype (GTP) cars, which promised to be well promoted and to have wide media exposure. Tullius was convinced that a Jaguar V12-powered car could be competitive, and now that Jaguar was more independent, there was an argument to be made for a car which would publicise the company name, rather than one particular model. Persuaded by Dale's conviction and rationale for a Jaguar prototype, the board of directors approved the switch to IMSA and a pure racing car.

The announcement was made early in January 1982, with a target date for the first race of 19 March at Sebring. Despite the efforts of Group 44 and their designer Lee Dykstra, there was no chance of achieving this somewhat unrealistic goal with a completely new design. XJR-5 – so named because it was Tullius's fifth racing Jaguar – took Group 44 into areas its previous experience with production-based cars had not, and progress was of necessity slow. The new prototype finally made its bow at Road America in August, where it finished a creditable third in front of an audience that included John Egan.

When the Jaguar Chairman returned to Coventry, he came back to news of further racing successes; Walkinshaw's TWR team had achieved two wins in nine races. September was to bring even better results, with Jaguar finishing first and second in both the Tourist Trophy at Silverstone, and the final championship round at Zolder in Belgium. A Jaguar had last won the TT in 1951, when Stirling Moss had taken the historic trophy with his C-type; the TWR win was seen as a reminder that Jaguar was on its way back. Walkinshaw and Nicholson finished third and fourth in the ETC Drivers' Championship.

And so 1982 ended with high spirits on both sides of the Atlantic. Sales were up, reaching record levels in the USA, and morale was up too; the success of the two race teams was seen as an important element in maintaining that morale, and both looked forward to another season of progress. On 4 March 1983

In the TWR Group A XJ-S, outwardly almost unchanged in general appearance from standard production models, Tom Walkinshaw took four European Touring Car wins and one non-Championship victory during 1982. (JDHT)

at the Waldorf Hotel in London, Jaguar Cars announced to the assembled media representatives the company's intention to become fully involved in motor racing in Europe. Present at the reception was one of the XJ-S cars, now repainted in the new 1983 livery of green and white, although outwardly little changed in general appearance from the standard production vehicle. Sitting alongside Tom Walkinshaw, Jaguar's technical chief Jim Randle and other directors, was John Egan, who explained Jaguar's complete faith in TWR's ability to make their mark in Europe as a prelude to moving on to greater glories.

ETC racing at that time was dominated by BMW, with Austrian Dieter Quester as Tom Walkinshaw's principal rival for Championship honours. The first 1983 round at Monza saw 10 of the new BMW 635 CSi cars entered against the two XJ-S cars. Walkinshaw and Nicholson's Jaguar came second, only 3.5 seconds behind the Quester/Rossi BMW. Had the XJ-S not been delayed by of all things a troublesome bonnet fixing, the race would certainly have been Jaguar's.

For Bob Tullius and Group 44, the high spot of 1983 came at Road Atlanta in April, with the XJR-5 taking Jaguar's first victory in what had come to be called sports-prototype racing. After another win, at Lime Rock in Connecticut at the end of May, Tullius's team packed up the XJR-5 and shipped it to Britain. The success of the prototype had naturally created an interest among the management at Jaguar in Coventry, and it was decided to have Derek Bell, Britain's foremost sportscar driver, test the car and give Jaguar the benefit of his opinion. There were close relations between IMSA and the Le Mans organisers, and XJR-5 was eligible for the French race; could it be, the press speculated,

that Jaguar were contemplating a return to the scene of their greatest triumphs?

Along with the Jaguar top brass at Silverstone when Derek Bell carried out his tests was Tom Walkinshaw, freshly returned from Zeltweg. Just two days earlier he and an eager young driver called Martin Brundle had led home a Jaguar one-two on the Austrian circuit, making the TWR XJ-S team's score three wins in the seven races run so far in the Touring Car Championship, with a Jaguar in the top three at every race. The battle between Walkinshaw and Quester for the Championship was not decided until the final race. The first 11 races had seen five wins each for BMW and Jaguar, with the Silverstone TT won by Rover. Of the Jaguar victories, four were taken by Walkinshaw and Nicholson, while Martin Brundle took the fifth with co-drivers Fitzpatrick and Calderari. The final race went to BMW, leaving Walkinshaw runner-up to Quester in the Drivers' Championship. However,

1983 was even more successful, with five Championship and one non-Championship win. A change of livery to dark green in 1984 was accompanied by seven Championship wins to take the ETC title, and one non-Championship victory. (JDHT)

Walkinshaw's second place in the European Touring Car Championship was an improvement on his third in 1982, and the racing team was now seen as a reflection of Jaguar as a whole – improving all the time.

The performance of Bob Tullius and Group 44 was also improving. After his mid-year visit to Britain, Tullius had gone back on the IMSA trail and taken two more victories at Mosport and Pocono Raceway. At the end of the season he mirrored Walkinshaw's performance in Europe by taking second place in the Camel GT Drivers' Championship. For a first full season, the Jaguar team had put up an excellent performance, and looked forward to 1984 with confidence. For Tullius, there was another source of pleasure that was not publicly announced until April; his team had been selected to take the Jaguar name back to Le Mans again.

The lead-up to Le Mans was enlivened by Group 44's early-season performances. In the Daytona 24 Hours Tullius, teamed with David Hobbs and 'Doc' Bundy, came third, and in the Miami Grand Prix 'Doc' Bundy and veteran British driver Brian Redman led home a Jaguar one-two. Group 44 set off for Le Mans with high hopes and put on their usual immaculately presented show. They raced here in the GTP class but were also up against a formidable array of Porsche 956s and Lancias in the Group C category. Bundy and Redman co-drove with Tullius in car number 44, while the other car (number 40) was crewed by John Watson, Le Mans veteran Claude Ballot-Lena, and Tony Adamowicz. They retired early after a spin, but the Tullius car lasted until 11.30am on Sunday morning until retiring with engine problems, having run around fifth or sixth position for much of the time.

Although neither of their cars finished, the reaction to the return of Jaguar to Le Mans was extremely positive. The British media had latched on to John Egan's success in turning Jaguar around as a company, and the return to the scene of the company's earlier triumphs was seen as much more than just a motor racing story. The Jaguar/Group 44 image in IMSA was one of the brave little guys going out and giving their best, and this translated directly to the European – or more correctly, British – situation. The cars looked good and they tried damned hard, and one could not ask for much more. The short period at the end of the first hour, when a Jaguar actually led the race as the thirstier Porsches made their first pit-stops, struck a strong patriotic chord in the media, the British fans, and most importantly, Jaguar's management.

Unfortunately, the trip to Le Mans had a detrimental effect on Jaguar's IMSA championship campaign; the team's resources had been stretched and some races had been missed. Tullius and his fellow Jaguar drivers finished the championship behind Randy Lanier and Bill Whittington – who had competed in every round in their March/Chevrolet and won nine of them. The one consolation was the fact that after the Le Mans performance, Group 44 had an enthusiastic Jaguar commitment to their return in 1985.

For 1984, Walkinshaw's regular co-driver in the European Touring Car Championship XJ-S car was German Hans Heyer. Martin Brundle and Win Percy were also among the TWR team drivers this year. Between them they won seven Championship victories and one in a non-championship race. The TWR XJ-S cars thus dominated the Championship, with a particularly emotional win for Walkinshaw, Heyer and Percy coming in the Spa 24 Hours, which was run the weekend before Jaguar was privatised. At the end of the season, Tom Walkinshaw was the

After three successful years in European touring car competition, the TWR team were well equipped to face the more challenging prototype racing. (JDHT)

new European Touring Car Champion, with Chuck Nicholson as his runner-up. By now, the green-liveried cars were racing as a Jaguar team, and racing was an integral part of the newly-privatised company's image. With the championship target achieved, Walkinshaw and Jaguar could have gone on to defend the title in 1985, but that was not the style of John Egan or Tom Walkinshaw. They both wanted new challenges and new victories. After the reception which the Group 44 Jaguars had received at Le Mans, they both knew that there was only one possible next step, and that was where Jaguar had made its name the first time. Sportscar racing and Le Mans had to be as much a part of Jaguar's renaissance as it had been of its original rise to prominence.

Although no public announcement had been made, the decision had been taken at the end of 1984 that Jaguar would race sportscars on a world-wide basis. TWR would be handling the European operation, with a view to competing in the World Sports-Prototype Championship, while Bob Tullius and Group 44 would go after the IMSA GTP Championship. The first intimation which outsiders had of TWR's new activity was when the Le Mans entry list was issued in the spring of 1985, showing two sets of Jaguar entries. Since both categories were eligible to race at Le Mans, both teams would be competing in the most important race of the year.

The theory was that TWR would race a Europeanised version of XJR-5, and TWR did have a Tullius car in Britain during the winter of 1984-85, repainted in British racing green and tested at Donington and Silverstone by Martin Brundle. It was fitted with an experimental four-valve engine but both this and the car were rejected. There was never any thought in Tom Walkinshaw's mind that he would campaign the IMSA car in the World Championship.

World Championship cars could be adapted to be competitive in IMSA, but the reverse was not feasible. Walkinshaw now began to assemble a first-class team with his famous knack of choosing the right man for the right job. His choice for team manager was Roger Silman, who had previously been involved with TWR in the Toleman Formula 2 project. Silman began working with the Northamptonshire-based racing car designer Tony Southgate on TWR's first Group C Jaguar prototype.

Walkinshaw was determined that they should start with a clean sheet of paper, the only common factor between Group 44 and TWR being the V12 engine. TWR's engine division manager, the New Zealander Allan Scott, set about developing a much-improved two-valve unit, radically different in many ways from the standard V12 production engine. In addition to increasing power output while keeping weight to a minimum, the engine was designed to be a fully-stressed member, carrying the entire transmission, axle and suspension assemblies. Southgate came up with a package far in advance of the Group 44 car. Having been constructed for IMSA racing, this was never likely to have performed well in Group C competition.

Although entries had been made at Le Mans on behalf of both teams, the TWR car was nowhere near race readiness by June, so once again the Jaguars in the race were bearing the white and two shades of green colours of Group 44. The Jaguar presence at the race was even stronger than it was in 1984, with supporters from the company itself, its importers and the public. Jaguar's return to *Le Circuit Permanent de la Sarthe* in 1984 had revitalised the race, which was beginning to be seen as a Porsche procession. The organisers – and even Porsche – welcomed the new element in the competition and the additional interest it brought.

Group 44 were well prepared for Le Mans in 1985; they had two 'Le Mans' cars which were quite separate from their IMSA XJR-5s, so the trip to France did not interfere with the already hectic IMSA season. Although there had been only one win in the period leading up to Le Mans – at Atlanta – it had been a one-two result, and in other races the Jaguars had been steadily recording

finishes in the top three. Group 44's teams of Le Mans drivers were Bob Tullius with Chip Robinson and Claude Ballot-Lena, Brian Redman with Hurley Haywood and Jim Adams. The emphasis was on finishing, for although Tullius was confident, he was not so over-confident as to think in terms of outright victory.

In the event, the XJR-5 of Tullius did finish. But it was a typical Le Mans display of dedication and spirit on the part of the mechanics as much as the drivers that enabled car 44 to complete one final lap on 11 cylinders as the clock ticked round to 4.00 pm on Sunday afternoon. Nevertheless, the car was classified, in 13th position, and it did win the prize for the best IMSA entry. Unfortunately, Group 44's result was not enough to earn them a return to Le Mans as Jaguar's standard-bearers; from 1986 that was to be the role of TWR.

TWR's car for the World Sports-Prototype Championship was nearing completion as Le Mans approached, but there was never any question of it being ready to start its competition career with the toughest race in the calendar (unlike the C-type in 1951!). There was a false start at Hockenheim in July, when the car was expected but did not appear because of a lack of sufficient spares to race it properly, but the problems were overcome for the next round, and it first raced at Mosport in Canada on 11 August 1985. Continuing the pattern set by the Group 44 cars, the new racer

Group 44's XJR-5s were the centre of attention at Le Mans in 1984 and 1985. (JDHT)

was designated XJR-6, although the American side of Jaguar's racing activities did not wholeheartedly welcome the use of the naming system they had invented. Two cars started, painted in Jaguar racing green with white stripes, and for a few glorious laps at the start of the race Martin Brundle led the two factory Porsches. It was too good to last, of course, and soon the German cars were past and Brundle's car had retired with a ruined wheel bearing. Nevertheless, the second car was still running, and Brundle took it over, together with his team-mate Mike Thackwell. By the end of the 1000-kilometre race the Jaguar was third, behind the two works Porsches, and the world knew that Jaguar was back.

The XJR-6s ran in three more races before the end of the season and finished the year on a high note, with a second place for Thackwell and Jan Lammers in Malaysia. The Tony Southgate-designed cars were obviously very competitive, and the TWR organisation ensured that the team was a credit to Jaguar. It was therefore not surprising that sponsorship was found relatively easily for the company's return to World Championship racing in 1986 from Gallaher International's Silk Cut cigarette brand. Although it may have saddened the purists to see the British Racing Green of the team's early races replaced by Silk Cut's mauve and white, there was no arguing the business sense of offsetting some of the extremely high costs of an international race programme with support from a brand with the world-wide recognition of Silk Cut.

In America, Jaguar remained Group 44's major backer, and although there must have been disappointment that Le Mans was

not in the team's schedule for 1986, it did not show. The closing races of the 1985 season had been a walk-over for the factory-backed Holbert Porsche team, but the Jaguars had been the only cars to challenge them seriously, and the XJR-5 design was obviously a basis on which to build. Evidence of that principle came at Daytona in December; for the last race of the season Tullius had his new XJR-7, a lighter, more efficient car than XJR-5. An advantage of the XJR-7 was that it no longer had to be a dual-purpose car, suited to both Le Mans and the shorter IMSA races. Unfortunately, the development of the car was slowed by the departure in early 1986 of Lee Dykstra, the engineer who had designed both it and XJR-5. Unfortunately this loss came at a time when Group 44 was losing high-level sponsorship and, in the

Photographed by Essex-based Jaguar restorer and enthusiast Alan Collins at Monterey in 1993, Group 44's XJR-8 can truly be described as stunning. (Alan Collins)

opinion of some, car development and morale suffered as a result. The team felt it had been snubbed by Jaguar's Coventry management over Le Mans, and Porsche's 962 was presenting a daunting challenge in IMSA. The biggest challenge of all, however, came not on the track but from TWR; it was a challenge as to who would represent Jaguar on the tracks of the world.

Therefore 1986 was a tough season for both teams, with Porsche providing the main opposition on both sides of the Atlantic. TWR and Group 44 both finished the season with one win; in IMSA it came at the end of the year in the last race on the calendar, the Daytona Three Hours, while TWR's victory was in the Silverstone 1000 km race. Unfortunately for Bob Tullius, most of Jaguar's board-members were at Silverstone to share the champagne after the TWR victory. For the decision-makers, Jaguar racing was more and more seen as the Silk Cut Jaguar Team, with Walkinshaw's hand on the tiller.

Le Mans was, as it had been in the 1950s, the most important race of the year and the prize that Jaguar most wanted to win. They did not, however, entertain any realistic hopes for a victory in 1986. Tom Walkinshaw had impressed upon the company's representatives as they discussed TWR's contract in late 1985 that winning Le Mans was a three-year programme. 1986 was for learning about the race in terms of cars and team organisation; a good result would be a bonus and a win would be a miracle. Three cars were entered and three failed – but the third car to retire was lying second after 16 hours' racing and had been a strong challenger throughout the race. The fans who turned out in their thousands to cheer the Jaguars may have been disappointed, but the team went back to their base with notebooks and computer disks full of data which would bring them back in 1987 much better prepared. The TWR mechanic who spray-painted the message 'We will be back' on the team's timing desk as he cleared up the pits knew what he was talking about.

The turning point for both Group 44 and TWR came in 1987, with TWR consolidating its position as Jaguar's racing team at the expense of the Americans who, through the enthusiasm of Mike Dale, had taken the company back into active competition. The *coup de grâce* came at Silverstone in May, where it was announced that from the beginning of 1988, Jaguar's IMSA programme would be in the hands of a team to be run by TWR from a new base in the United States. This became TWR Inc, based at Valparaiso in Indiana, managed by Englishman Tony Dowe with his fellow countryman Ian Reed as chief engineer. Both had considerable experience in racing activities, at home and in the US. To get the feel of sportscar racing, they joined the Silk Cut team at Spa Francorchamps in September 1987. For this race they took charge of the Boesel/Brundle/Dumfries XJR-8 and enjoyed the great satisfaction of seeing it take a convincing victory – the only victory for this particular chassis, number 387 – one lap ahead of the second-placed Jaguar of Watson/Lammers.

TWR underlined the announcement by going on to win the Silverstone 1000 km for the second year in succession. The fact that this was the team's fourth win in four World Championship races was not lost on the Jaguar executives who once again toasted their company's victory. Neither was it lost on the thousand or so Jaguar employees who had gone to the race to cheer on 'their' cars.

The rest of the year was no different, for the Silk Cut Jaguar Team went on to win eight of the ten World Sports-Prototype Championship races, taking the Team Championship and the Drivers' title for Raul Boesel. Only Le Mans and a sprint race at the Norisring in Germany fell to Porsche, and ironically the Norisring victory came on the weekend when Porsche confirmed that it was withdrawing its factory entries from the Championship in the face of the Jaguar onslaught.

The second year of the Le Mans programme was right on target – this time there was a survivor of the three-car team and it finished in fifth place. There was also more information and experience, and Win Percy had even subjected one of the cars to the ultimate crash test when a rear tyre blew out at full speed on the Mulsanne straight. Despite the severity of the impact, the car's construction stood up perfectly and Percy was unhurt. In the context of the three-year Le Mans target, it was encouraging.

Frustratingly for Bob Tullius, a mid-season farewell party at the Watkins Glen IMSA race to mark the end of his team's curtailed relationship with Jaguar came at a time when they were showing their best results for two years. Despite the fact that a reduced budget meant only one car was being run, the Group 44 team already had two outright victories to their credit. The team made one more appearance in the championship, when the local Jaguar dealer in San Diego, Performance Jaguar, sponsored an entry in the last race of the season at Del Mar. Unfortunately, the car retired, writing a sad final chapter in a relationship that had seen the enthusiasm of two men – Bob Tullius and Mike Dale – lead Jaguar back to the forefront of international racing.

Walkinshaw's operation started 1988 with a bang. The sixteen week-old American team, operated by TWR Inc from a base in Valparaiso, Indiana, and with major sponsorship for a three-year period from Castrol, won the Daytona 24 Hours, the first race for the three IMSA specification Jaguar XJR-9s. The victory fulfilled all the fears that had run through IMSA about the arrival of the new big-money professionalism that had replaced the underdog image of Jaguar. In fact, the fears were exaggerated; the threat to IMSA's private Porsche teams lay not in the professionals from Britain, but in an up-dated version of what had happened with Jaguar and Tullius. The big winners in the 1988 IMSA season were not TWR and Jaguar, but an American team, Electramotive, running with importer's money from Nissan. Electramotive had been racing Nissans for some years and had followed the Jaguar path from production cars to a GTP prototype. Their sportscar's turbocharged engine had been awesomely powerful but unreliable until the end of 1987, but in 1988, perhaps thanks to the restrictors which had been made obligatory for that year, it was suddenly a little less powerful and a lot more reliable. Jaguar, who the IMSA establishment had feared would dominate the series, won only one more race, the season's finale at Del Mar.

In the World Championship, however, it was a different story. Silk Cut Jaguar took the Team title for the second time and Martin Brundle, who had been lead driver for both the IMSA and World Championship teams, was Champion driver. More important, however, was the culmination of the three-year assault on Le Mans, which ended in a magnificent win for Jan Lammers, Andy Wallace and Johnny Dumfries in the XJR-9. Playing the 'strength in numbers' card, TWR entered five cars for the 24 Hours, using its American arm to prepare and crew two of the cars. At the end

of the race three of the five were still running, giving Jaguar fourth and 16th places in addition to the company's first Le Mans win for 31 years.

Although Jaguar had won the Drivers' and Teams' titles in 1988, it had been against strong opposition from a new force in prototype racing, the Sauber Mercedes team. Swiss-based Peter Sauber had been building Mercedes-powered prototypes for some years, but it was not until 1986 that the team won their first World Championship race. The professionalism of the Sauber operation and the higher profile of sports-prototype racing which followed Jaguar's entry made the Mercedes factory more supportive, and in 1988 there was official involvement from Stuttgart for the first time. The team won five races to Jaguar's six in the 1988 season, and 1989 saw them dominate the World Championship with seven wins in eight rounds. Le Mans was not a championship race that year, but it too saw a Mercedes victory, with the best Jaguar finishing in fourth place.

It was obvious that something had to be done on both sides of the Atlantic, for in IMSA Nissan continued to be the team to beat. TWR introduced new turbocharged cars in IMSA and the World Championship, the XJR-10 and XJR-11, but neither made a real impression on the opposition. The American XJR-10 took two victories, to which was added a final win for the most successful TWR Jaguar, the XJR-9. This gave three wins against Nissan's ten in a series of 15 races. In Europe the XJR-11's turbocharged power unit was its weak point, and the team's fourth position in a Championship which it had won for the past two years underlined the problem.

The team saw a mixture of 'good news/bad news' in 1990, but on balance the good news – wins in the Daytona and Le Mans

Bob Tullius's reputation for immaculate turn-out is well illustrated in this shot of the Group 44 workshop. The unmarked XJR-8 lines up ahead of an XJR-7 and three XJR-5s. (Ken Wells)

24 hour classics and another Silverstone 1000 km victory – outweighed the bad news of a Sauber Mercedes domination of the World Championship and another IMSA Championship for Nissan.

The World Championship rules for 1991 outlawed turbo engines in favour of 3.5-litre normally-aspirated units. Mercedes and newcomers Peugeot developed their own engines, while Jaguar were able to draw on the resources of its new parent, Ford, and adapt the Cosworth Formula 1 engine for sportscar use. The engine was mounted in a new car, the XJR-14, which owed much to Formula 1 technology and the skills of designer Ross Brawn, who was to go on to Formula 1 success with Benetton and Ferrari. The Jaguars were almost unbeatable in the season's early races, but by the end of the season Peugeot was in the ascendancy. Nevertheless, Jaguar took three outright wins to win the Team Championship, while team driver Teo Fabi became World Champion driver.

At Le Mans, the machinations of the World Championship meant that the XJR-14s were entered on the understanding that they would practice but not take part in the race. Politics had no impact on the result, however, and Mazda scored the first-ever Japanese win, ahead of three V12-powered Jaguar XJR-12s. It was a result that emphasised how far the most important endurance race of the World Championship had moved from the mainstream of the Championship – or perhaps, given the political forces at work through the FISA, the reverse was true.

In IMSA, the new XJR-16 won its first-ever race and gave TWR Inc and Jaguar, together with its new sponsor, Bud Light beer, six outright victories, five to Davy Jones and one to Raul Boesel. Despite this success, the IMSA championship went to Nissan for the fourth successive year. The Jaguar team had every reason to feel it had been robbed, for in terms of wins they were far ahead of Nissan, but the Japanese company's consistency, which saw two of its cars in the top four on a regular basis, racked up the points that mattered.

So, 1992 saw Jaguar withdraw from the World Championship, as the company balanced the costs of competing against the returns in publicity terms at a time of economic recession. Jaguar was going through a hard time financially, cutting back in every aspect of its activities, and an expensive racing programme would not sit well with Ford's shareholders when the workforce was being cut back severely. In America, the IMSA programme continued, and in order to counter the threat from Toyota and Nissan, it was decided to use the XJR-14 that had proved so successful in the World Championship. The XJR-14 was not considered suitable for the Daytona 24-hour race, and an XJR-12 took second place to give Davy Jones a good start in the Championship standings. However, although he was always well-placed, Jaguar's sole runner Jones could not withstand the challenge of the two-car Toyota team. Arie Luyendijk was drafted in to help Jones for some mid-season races, but it was to no avail and Juan Fangio II became IMSA GTP Champion. Apart from a one-off entry in the 1993 Daytona 24 Hours, this was the end of Jaguar's activities in sports prototype racing.

There were two footnotes to the collaboration between TWR and Jaguar that have their place in the company's racing history. In 1990, word filtered out that TWR was preparing a road version of the XJR-9 race car for sale in limited numbers. Such was, in fact, the case, but in view of the fact that Jaguar – in collaboration with TWR – was also working on a high-performance, limited-production 'supercar', the XJ220, it was felt that the two partners should not compete with each other so obviously. The TWR car was therefore announced as a race car, with its own race series that would run in concert with Formula 1 at a number of circuits. The car was badged not as a Jaguar but as the 'JaguarSport XJR-15', taking its name from the joint-venture company set up by Jaguar and TWR to build performance versions of Jaguar road cars. Although it is commonly referred to as a Jaguar and it follows the Jaguar 'XJR' numbering scheme, the XJR-15 was not legally a Jaguar.

The XJR-15's contemporary, the XJ220, was a Jaguar, having been designed and built in a similar manner to XJ13, by Jaguar engineers operating in their own time. By the time it was unveiled at the 1988 Birmingham Motor Show it had become an official project, and its rapturous reception effectively forced Jaguar to put it into production. The task was sub-contracted to TWR, and it was not surprising, in view of the pedigree of the companies and people involved and the car's performance, that the XJ220 should appear on the race track. A number of owners raced their cars independently, but the car's only official factory-backed outing in a major event was at Le Mans in 1993, where it won its class. However, after an argument over the car's eligibility, it was disqualified on a technicality. Although it was not a sports prototype but a true road car, XJ220 in production form did use the turbocharged V6 developed by TWR for the XJR-10 and 11 prototypes. Its appearance at Le Mans was, therefore, effectively the end of a sports prototype era.

It had been a period in which the collaboration between Jaguar and TWR had won four classic 24-hour races and three drivers' and three team world titles. All the races in which the TWR Jaguar prototypes featured are briefly described in the Race History chapters. From start to finish, these historic races had great prestige value for Jaguar and TWR, and sales were boosted each time another win was announced, but all good things have to end some time. Group C and GTP racing saw some of the most impressive grids in motor racing history, but the sport eventually relied far too much on the input of the major manufacturers. As spectator numbers dwindled and media interest slumped, the top names began pulling out. What the C- and D-types had done for Jaguar in the 1950s, Tom Walkinshaw's XJR prototypes repeated in the 1980s and '90s. It was a worthy continuation of the Jaguar tradition. Jaguar was now once again a firmly established world-class motor manufacturer with sporting credentials equal to the very best.

Chapter 1

An Overview of the XJR Cars

There were effectively three generations of Jaguar sports racing cars during the period between 1985 and 1992, when TWR was responsible for operating teams on Jaguar's behalf in the FIA/FISA and IMSA championships. The first cars were powered by developments of the V12 engine that had been introduced in Jaguar road cars in 1971, and which had established itself in touring car racing championships on both sides of the Atlantic. It was natural that the engine should be used for sports prototypes built by Group 44 in the USA and TWR in Europe. The V12 was a proven racing unit, and it enabled Jaguar to show a direct connection between its racing and road cars.

The second phase began in 1989, when TWR was operating both the British and US-based race teams. It was felt that to counter the opposition a lighter, more modern power unit was needed, preferably with turbocharging. Using experience gained when it bought the rights to the turbocharged V6 engine developed by Austin-Rover for Group B rallying (used in the ill-fated MG Metro 6R4), TWR created an engine that was suitable for racing use and for the road-going XJ220, the supercar that TWR was turning into a production reality for Jaguar.

Finally, in 1990 it was announced that in 1991 the FISA sports-prototype championship would no longer allow turbocharged engines and that capacity would be limited to 3.5 litres. The engines were similar to the existing Formula 1 units, and there was a suspicion that the major manufacturers who were now involved in sportscar racing, such as Peugeot, Mercedes-Benz, Toyota and Nissan, were being edged towards building engines that would be eligible for Formula 1. The aim, it was surmised, was to persuade them to move their racing efforts from endurance racing to Grand Prix. Ford, which already had a competitive Formula 1 engine in the shape of the Cosworth V8 unit, gave Jaguar the opportunity to hit the ground running from the beginning of the 1991 season, and the final generation of XJR cars was one of the most successful. There were no links to Jaguar road cars, but by now sports racing cars were little more than Formula 1 cars with bodywork, and links to production models had become so tenuous as to be invisible – indeed irrelevant.

V12-engined cars
XJR-6, XJR-8, XJR-9 and XJR-12

From the summer of 1985 to early 1993, the Kidlington-based TWR Racing Organisation, joined later by its American counterpart at Valparaiso, developed and fielded three very different generations of Group C and GTP prototype racing cars. The first of the series was constructed around the well-proven, normally-aspirated Jaguar 24-valve V12 stock block engine, with which the team and Tom Walkinshaw personally had already amassed an impressive catalogue of successes, racing the XJ-S in the European Touring Car Championship for three years before entering Group C racing.

The new Tony Southgate-designed car, designated XJR-6, first saw the light of day on 2 July 1985 at Snetterton, Norfolk, during an initial shakedown in the hands of Tyrrell Grand Prix driver Martin Brundle. Chassis number 185 was the first of many V12 cars progressively upgraded year by year, becoming XJR-8 in 1987, XJR-9 in 1988 and 1989, and finally XJR-12 in its most potent form from 1990 onwards.

Why XJR-6? For the answer, we need to cross the Atlantic. Bob Tullius's American-built Group 44 Jaguar XJR-5 GTP prototypes had already completed nearly three years of competition with notable success in the IMSA Camel GT series. He adopted XJR-5 after discussions with Mike Dale of Jaguar North America, in which the XJR-1 to XJR-4 designations were retrospectively assigned to earlier Group 44 Jaguar production car-based racers. The 1975 Group 44 E-Type became XJR-1. The 1976, 1979 and 1981 series of XJ-S racers, in which Tullius won the 1977 and 1978 Trans Am Drivers' Championships, and came second in the 1981 Camel GT Drivers' standings, became XJR-2, XJR-3 and XJR-4 respectively.

Having gained much valuable experience in the last five World Endurance Championship races of 1985, the TWR team returned to Kidlington to put lessons learned into practice. The winter of 1985-86 saw considerable improvements to the XJR-6 chassis, to such an extent that the 1986 cars might well have been re-numbered there and then instead of waiting until 1987.

There was no TWR-built XJR-7 since Group 44 had already adopted this number for their Lee Dykstra-designed, much revised XJR-5, first raced in the Daytona three-hour race in December 1985. Driven by Bob Tullius and Chip Robinson, it came fourth, only two places behind team-mates Hurley Haywood and Brian Redman in the second-placed XJR-5.

The 1987 season was the most successful for Jaguar in the whole WSPC series, when comparing the number of starts to podium places. In ten races, they had eight wins, four seconds, and several third, fourth and fifth places. The much improved re-numbered XJR-8 achieved everything except the coveted Le Mans win. With Group 44 now sidelined, TWR was the only team enjoying Jaguar's full support and seemed unstoppable.

Group 44 still had one unexpected surprise up its sleeve in the shape of a third beautiful prototype, also sharing the XJR-8 nomenclature. Jaguar race fans were not to become confused though, as this single chassis never raced in any championships in America or elsewhere - just as well in view of TWR's declared intentions to contest the 1988 IMSA Camel GT Championship from brand new facilities set up at Valparaiso, Indiana.

Chassis re-working for the 1988 season involved considerable alterations to bodywork, suspension and mechanics, although the new up-numbered XJR-9 appeared little changed. The 1988 season kicked off in spectacular fashion with the Castrol-sponsored Jaguar XJR-9s winning the Daytona 24-hour race. In June, the Silk Cut Jaguar team completed the double with a tremendous win in the Le Mans 24-hour race, Jaguar's first win at the Sarthe circuit since 1957. This impressive double was repeated two years later, but the 1988 XJR-9 will always remain synonymous with Jaguar and Le Mans in modern racing parlance.

Further changes were made to the XJR-9 bodywork in 1989, mainly involving new engine covers with revised air intakes. With other very important new car developments in progress at Kidlington during 1989, the XJR-9 designation was retained for the V12 chassis for the remainder of that year. Another series of modifications to existing and newly built V12 chassis occurred in 1990, when they became XJR-12s, the next available numbers 10 and 11 having already been assigned to the 1989 new-generation V6 turbo cars.

V6 Turbo Cars
XJR-10 and XJR-11

TWR Jaguar's entry into international sportscar racing came at a time almost totally dominated by the all-conquering Porsche 962Cs and their lookalike predecessors the equally successful Porsche 956s. Race after race saw a high percentage of the top ten grid positions commandeered by these stylish cars, powered by 2994cc flat-six turbocharged engines. Without question the acknowledged leaders of the pack were the formidable pairing of Britain's Derek Bell and Germany's Hans Stuck in the Rothmans-supported works team. Becoming joint 1985 World Champions, they swept to victory at Le Mans in 1986 and finished the year with another World Championship.

Yet 1987 was not to be Rothmans-Porsche's year as they were soundly trounced by Jaguar in eight out of the ten World Championship races. Of the two non-Jaguar wins that season, the victors at Norisring were Mauro Baldi and Jonathan Palmer in the Britten Lloyd Porsche 962. Also disappointing for Jaguar was the very creditable win at Le Mans for Derek Bell and Hans Stuck, making it five times in all for Bell, who was unanimously acclaimed the greatest British sportscar racing driver of the period, if not of all time.

The Porsche 962Cs' supremacy might have waned a little with the strong Jaguar opposition, but they were still a force to be reckoned with. There were other promising turbo-powered rivals waiting in the wings to take over. The V12 Jaguars were enjoying their day for the present, but time after time they were out-dragged by the phenomenal power of the turbos when it really mattered, so development work on a brand new Southgate-designed V6 turbo car commenced during the latter half of 1988. Two versions would be necessary to comply with different Group C and IMSA regulations, one with a 3-litre engine for IMSA racing, while for the WSPC championship the engine size would be increased to 3.5 litres.

Track tested for the first time on 8 February 1989 at Donington Park by 1988 Le Mans winner Jan Lammers, the first car bore the chassis number 189. This particular chassis was the first of two XJR-11s programmed to race in the latter part of the 1989 season WSPC, the other being chassis 289. Early pre-launch press photographs show them in Silk Cut colours, correct for WSPC XJR-11s, but mistakenly described as XJR-10s - quite understandable though as no announcement had been made at that particular time regarding which of the two types was going where. The first 3-litre XJR-10 IMSA car, chassis number 389, was in fact shaken down by Andy Wallace at Silverstone on 31 March 1989.

XJR-16

These superb, highly competitive machines, developed at Valparaiso, were the ultimate incarnation of the forced-induction turbo racer, and were streets ahead of their XJR-10 and XJR-11 predecessors. Raced for less than a season in the 1991 IMSA series, they notched up four impressive wins, including on their first outing at Road Atlanta. One qualified second in the 1992 Daytona 24-hour endurance race, but engine problems forced its withdrawal. It clearly showed what the V6 turbos could have achieved had their time span been longer.

XJR-17

Converted from an XJR-16 chassis, this one-off car was basically a turbo car with the turbochargers removed. With a normally-aspirated version of the 3.5-litre V6 engine, it was aimed at private customers following Jaguar's withdrawal from Group C championship racing. This, however, came to nothing. No further XJR-17s were built and, as far as is known, the single prototype was never raced as an official Jaguar team car.

XJR-14 Non-Turbo V8s

Perhaps the most radical changes to Group C sportscar prototype racing occurred at the end of 1990. For 1991 turbo cars were to be outlawed, as were unlimited engine sizes. The new formula dictated exclusive use of normally-aspirated 3.5-litre engines. Designed by Ross Brawn, the new XJR-14, powered by Jaguar's version of the race-proven Cosworth V8 HB engine, was a complete departure from the previous XJR generations. Frequently described as a two-seater fully-enclosed Formula 1 car, it was so light that ballast needed to be added to bring it up to the minimum permitted weight level.

Raced in the now re-titled Sportscar World Championship for the 1991 season only, before Silk Cut's sponsorship ended, these superfast cars gained one more Manufacturers' Championship for Jaguar and a drivers' title for Italian Teo Fabi: a fitting finale for the home-based team, and one from which Jaguar derived great satisfaction. The XJR-14s were then shipped to the USA, where they raced a further season in the 1992 IMSA Camel GT series in Bud Light colours and produced two good wins at Road Atlanta and Mid Ohio.

Two numbers missing from these lists are 13 and 15. Twenty years prior to Jaguar's entry into Group C racing, a one-off prototype mid-engined Jaguar racer fitted with the original experimental four-camshaft V12 engine was produced as a possible Le Mans contender. Given the title XJ13, it was indeed rather unlucky. While showing great promise, Jaguar's return to endurance racing in the mid-1960s was shelved for a number of reasons. Some years later XJ13 was dusted off and was filmed at MIRA as part of the publicity for the launch of Jaguar's new production V12 engine. Driven by Jaguar test driver Norman Dewis, after a long day's filming the car suffered a disastrous wheel failure, left the track and was badly damaged. This unfortunate incident may have prompted TWR to avoid using the XJR-13 designation.

No such qualms for number 15. XJR-15 was reserved for a limited edition super-sports road racer produced by JaguarSport, and badged as such, rather than as a Jaguar. Evolved from the 1988 Le Mans winning XJR-9 chassis complete with the 6-litre

Jaguar's prototype sportscar racing programme gained new momentum with the introduction of the XJR-14 in 1991. (JDHT)

24-valve V12 engine, and with a half-million pound price tag, owners of these beautifully designed cars were invited to contest the International Continental Challenge one-make three-race series, with a $1million purse for the winner.

TWR's last prototype XJR-17 was part XJR-16 and part XJR-14 but was unlikely to have matched either. (Ron Russel)

Chapter 2

XJR Identification

Chassis numbers are the fingerprints of cars. Allocated at birth, they accompany the car throughout its life, enabling it to be identified and traced. Under modern regulations, the VIN, or Vehicle Identification Number, has to be on a plate that is easily seen from outside the car, as well as stamped into the structure of the vehicle. In the future, the VIN will no doubt be recorded on a microchip, ensuring the car is 'electronically tagged' and universally recognisable and traceable.

Racing cars, however, are different, and have been throughout their history, as a number of legal decisions over historic racing cars have demonstrated. Built to racing regulations rather than road car legislation, their construction is less regimented. Although they may be identified by a chassis number when they are 'fresh out-of-the-box' new, as their life and racing career progresses their identity becomes less defined as parts are replaced or modifications introduced.

This procedure is even more noticeable in the case of endurance racing cars. Their races are longer and more eventful, and they will often be built in greater numbers than single-seater formula cars. It is a fact of sportscar racing that, in major events like Le Mans, the more starters a team has – including, if necessary, those of its customer teams – the better are its chances of having a respectable number of finishers. In long races, damage or mechanical failure on one car is often repaired by cannibalising another, with the result that components from one chassis number finish up on another, making the task of identifying both cars more difficult. Identifying and recording individual chassis numbers for a marque such as Jaguar over a period of eight years has therefore been no mean task.

XJR-6
Chassis numbers 185, 285, 385, 186, 286, 386

Many race car manufacturers incorporate year dates into their chassis numbers. TWR was no exception, even if the last 1985 chassis listed here was not constructed until January 1986. Chassis 185 and 285 were somewhat hastily built in the late spring and summer of 1985, as the team was anxious to gain as much practical experience as possible by contesting the last five races of the season in what at that time was the World Endurance Championship.

The first two Tony Southgate-designed 1985 XJR-6s, powered by Allan Scott's new 6.2-litre engine, were a far cry from what their World Championship-winning successors would become. From the start, the basic high-downforce bodywork and aero wing

The first 1985 XJR-6, chassis 185. Note the absence of rear wheel covers and front brake ducts. (Author's collection)

Allan Scott's superb V12 Jaguar Group C engine, winner at Le Mans, Daytona and numerous Championship races. (Jaguar)

configuration would remain relatively constant in general appearance throughout the V12 bloodline. Each year modifications were carried out, dictated by different cooling and engine air intake requirements, changing wheel sizes and, last but not least, unique bodywork and wing assemblies to suit the special conditions encountered during 24-hour endurance racing.

No other V12 XJR chassis was more noticeably different than the embryonic 1985 XJR-6. Its beautiful streamlined, slippery bodywork lacked the profusion of ducts, apertures, extra downforce aids and attachments found on later models. That these were added in the course of time illustrates the improvements it was necessary to make to the successors of that first season.

The two 1985 cars were the only ones raced in traditional British racing green livery, enhanced by white panelling on the engine cover and nose, with double stripes around the bottom edges. In its earliest form, the nose radiator intake above the forward-projecting splitter was rather shallow. Front-brake cooling ducts were not installed until the third race at Brands Hatch in September. When fitted, these flanked the radiator intake and

were also quite shallow compared to what they would become two years later.

Unique to XJR-6 models only were gull wing doors, opened from the inside by an elaborate latch arrangement, and from the outside with sliding catches. Cockpit cooling ducts would be grafted into the horizontal door panels as part of later XJR-6 improvements but were absent in the early stages. The one-piece monocoque external surfaces were devoid of noticeable ducting. The engine cover or tail panel, with its square-cut rear end, gave the rather distorted impression that the car was shorter than it actually was. Two slotted openings provided the engine air intake, positioned directly above the double banks of inlet trumpets.

Lack of fully effective rear brake cooling on the 1985 XJR-6 resulted in serious overheating of axles and bearings - problems which led to early retirements. Eventually periscope brake cooling ducts fixed to the top of the hollow uprights became standard. Over the years the rear brake cooling periscopes would become larger, and would change to suit different track conditions. Small side panels between the monocoque and the rear wheel arches were subject to considerable alteration and re-design throughout

Five-spoke sandcast Speedline wheels with flat-faced spokes were standard fitments on all XJR-6s. (Author's collection)

During a miserable wet and windy session at Estoril, Portugal in February 1986, chassis 285 suffered severe rear end damage while driven by Gianfranco Brancatelli. Panels borrowed from the green-liveried sister car made for an unusual combination. (Malcolm Bryan)

the V12 development. At the beginning those on the 1985 XJR-6s were almost blank, except for a single scoop or forward facing louvre at the front edge, both sides being identical. As the V12 was developed, the side panel ducting became multi-functional, directing air to the engine and transmission oil coolers, as well as cooling the starter motor and more.

For sprint racing, all V12 and most V6 turbo cars had double element rear wings carried on a pair of alloy support plates bolted vertically to the gearbox end casing. Several patterns of wing endplates would be tried. Those fitted to all XJR-6s were tapered towards the front with a vertical back edge, rather similar in appearance to dart flights. There were slots near the top, so the trailing edge of the upper wing could be raised or lowered to

adjust downforce levels.

All XJR-6 chassis ran on sand-cast one-piece five-spoke magnesium Speedline wheels, of 17in diameter at the front and 19in at the rear, fitted with Dunlop Denloc tyres. These wheels are readily identifiable by having flat-faced square-sided spokes. The one remaining feature exclusive to the early XJR-6s was the front corner headlamp recesses. Not to be confused with the larger double headlamp recesses seen on the special Le Mans bodywork, or on the 1986 noses, these accommodated a single headlamp and indicator light only.

In 1985, main sponsorship came largely from Jaguar Cars, with Castrol Oil as the second sponsor. The Jaguar name, in white, was emblazoned along the side and across the nose. TWR

Lack of periscope rear brake ducts on early XJR-6s led to overheating problems. Note the gearbox oil radiator and the torsion bar fixed along the rear of the suspension beam. (Author)

1985 XJR-6 in 1986 Silk Cut livery. The half-length engine intake scoop was first tried at the end of the 1985 season. (Jaguar)

initials, quite prominent in the test stages on wing endplates and across the windscreen, gradually migrated to join Dunlop, Champion and other parts manufacturers' names around the lower bodywork. From the first race at Mosport the Castrol name was found on wing endplates. From Spa onwards, JAGUAR always appeared across the windscreen sunvisor in various bright colours, a valuable aid to timekeepers and pit crews in identifying each particular car as it streaked by. Car 52 used red lettering while on 51 it was usually white.

Chassis 185 and 285 were not raced after 1985 but both were taken to Estoril, Portugal, in February 1986 for winter testing, 185 still in green livery, while 285 appeared in full 1986 Silk Cut paintwork. Chassis 185 is believed subsequently to have been converted into a show car. Chassis 285, restored back to its 1985 specification and livery, is currently active in Group C Revival racing.

The 1986 season XJR-6

Great changes were made to the XJR-6 chassis during the 1985-86 winter closed season, including a long list of mechanical and bodywork improvements together with a larger 6.5-litre engine. A new three-year sponsorship deal, brokered by former Grand Prix and Sportscar driver Guy Edwards with Gallaher International, was announced in February. The car's livery would change from British racing green and white to Silk Cut corporate mauve and white. The latter became the dominant colour with mauve panels

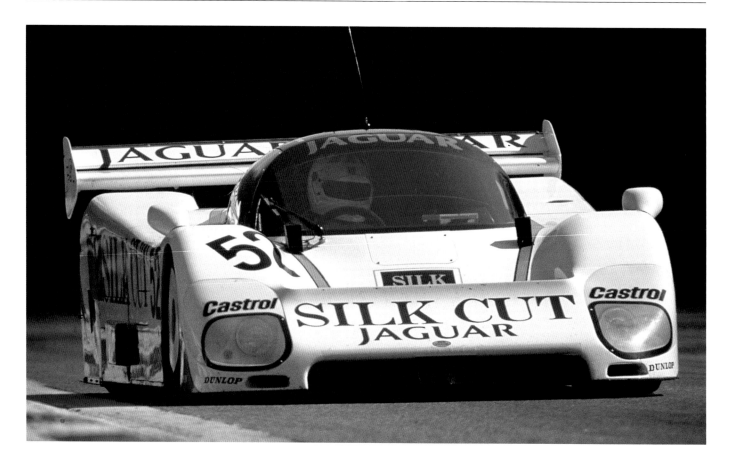

Front view of the 1986 Silk Cut XJR-6 livery, dubbed 'the white car' by some. Note the pronounced flip-up along the top of the nose panel to improve downforce, and the lack of cockpit air duct. (Malcolm Bryan)

in diminishing sizes down the engine cover, and a fairly narrow band at low level along the sides, sweeping upwards at the rear. The two-tone side colours were separated by a 1⅜in gold stripe with black edging. Similar black-edged gold stripes extended from the radiator well to the tail, skirting around the base of the Perspex door windows and engine bulge. Gold stripes without edging were used to surround the mauve panels on the engine covers, giving the top a multi-striped appearance.

The wings and endplates were all-white, as was most of the nose. Viewing the car from the front, very little mauve paintwork could be seen. It became dubbed 'the white car' by some, and was subject to rather unfair levels of criticism by purists, who felt British racing green was the only appropriate colour for Jaguar race cars. This particular colour scheme was to last only one season before another radical re-styling.

Several bodywork changes, combined with the new livery, transformed the car's appearance, making it appear longer than the last year's model, although overall dimensions remained unchanged. At the front, the radiator air intake was deepened, but the shallow brake duct intakes remained the same. On sprint noses, the panel above the radiator exit featured a more pronounced flip-up to increase downforce. The two side panels had double forward facing louvres, the left one for cooling the engine oil heat exchanger, while the battery was located behind the right side panel. The flow of air through both sides made a useful contribution to engine bay cooling, and this was further

aided by NACA duct cut-outs in the new flush-fitting rear wheel covers. The new angled tail was more pleasing in appearance, but the wings and endplates remained unchanged in general appearance.

Easily the most noticeable new feature on 1986 XJ6s was the roof-mounted engine air intake scoops. These evolved in stages, commencing with a half-length scoop riveted over the forward end of the 1985 intake slots. A second much longer riveted-on scoop covered the slots completely. Finally the scoop became an integral part of the engine cover moulding. Group C regulations stipulated scoop intakes must be kept below roof level. A large NACA duct situated near the left rear wheel arch at the rear of the engine cover served to cool the gearbox oil radiator.

The year 1986 saw the first Le Mans special from Tony Southgate's drawing board. Cars prepared for this event featured lengthened aerodynamic tails and low-set single-element wings with long, narrow matching endplates. The high-downforce bodywork of sprint cars was not suited for prolonged maximum-speed running down the Mulsanne straight, so lower downforce was the order of the day. Endurance nose panels lacked the pronounced flip-up next to the radiator exit, and the front wheel arch louvres were sealed over. To cater for prolonged night driving these specials were fitted with much larger twin-headlamp recesses. The splitter was shortened, closely following the contours of the nose. In addition to the streamlined tail, the engine cover featured NACA ducts either side of the engine bulge near

the front end. These were clearly different on car 53 (chassis 385) in being wider than those on the other two Le Mans chassis.

On the track there would be no mistaking the main sponsors. Silk Cut in large mauve capital letters featured on both sides and across the nose. Jaguar, Castrol, TWR, Dunlop and Champion all appeared in one place or another at lower levels. The Jaguar name across the windscreen appeared in white on car 51 (chassis 286), red on 52 (186), and yellow on car 53 (385). The 1986 Le Mans was the latter car's one and only race. The corporate logo (or 'mortise') of the tobacco company, SILK CUT in gold on a square mauve panel, was situated on the nose below the windscreen. Two different sizes were seen, initially a small version, later becoming much larger. The logo also appeared in varying sizes everywhere the cars raced, as well as on team-wear, pit equipment, stationery and wherever appropriate to give maximum exposure for the sponsors. Jaguar's 'leaping cat' logo was used in the same way, the two being inextricably linked throughout the entire sponsorship period.

In some countries, displaying any form of cigarette advertising was already then illegal, as it still is. Cars competing around British and German circuits nearly always raced unbranded, with all the smoking-related graphics blanked over or substituted with secondary sponsorship advertising. Unbranded Group C Jaguars nearly always used Silk Cut corporate mauve block panels along the sides, decreasing in width toward the tail. Similar treatment was applied across the white noses of the 1986 XJR-6s.

From the beginning the intention was to race only two cars at most events, with a third car as a spare, although in the earlier seasons three cars were entered in some races. Chassis 385, first shaken down at Snetterton on 3 March 1986 by Derek Warwick, incorporated much of the close season development work. It was taken to Monza in April and Silverstone in May, serving only as a T car on both occasions (The term 'T car' is used to denote a car used to set a best time in qualifying, or which is only used in practice). After its appearance at Le Mans in full Le Mans specification it was never raced again.

Chassis 186 raced as car 52 in the first five races of 1986, then became 53 at Jerez and Nürburgring. It finished the season as car 51T at Spa, and then went on to win the Nürburgring Supercup non-championship race as car number 51. Chassis 286 remained as car number 51 throughout the 1986 season, giving Jaguar its first-ever Group C win at Silverstone in May, driven by Derek Warwick and Eddie Cheever. Chassis number 386 was shaken down for the first time at Silverstone by Win Percy on 23 June. Three weeks later it appeared for the first time at Norisring, racing as car 53.

1987 – The year of the XJR-8 supercar
Chassis numbers 187, 287, 387 and the reworked XJR-6s

New season, new car, re-styled livery: 1987 brought results beyond all expectations, repaying two years of dedication, frustration and disappointment but never defeat.

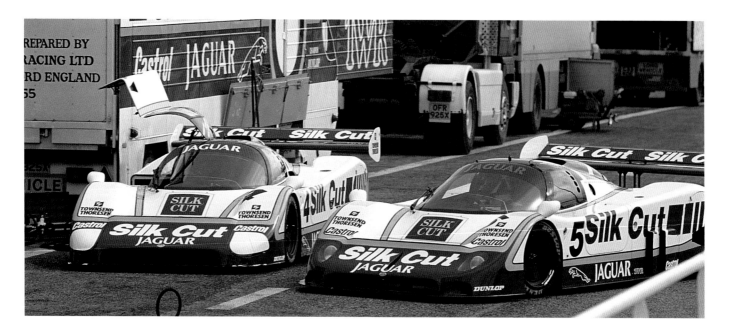

An interesting study of XJR-6 (386) with gullwing doors alongside XJR-8 (187), both in full 1987 Silk Cut livery, taken at Paul Ricard during testing in February 1987. (Malcolm Bryan)

While in appearance basically similar to the previous season's XJR-6, the new up-numbered chassis reappeared with 64 important improvements, most of them mechanical changes including an enlarged 6995cc engine. Externally, starting at the front end, the nose came with a deeper radiator intake, with matching height brake duct openings. Cockpit cooling was catered for via narrow teardrop ducting through the centre of the front and rear nose panels, crossing above the radiator. Sprint noses came with new-style single headlamp recesses, just large enough to accommodate one light unit and an indicator lamp. Endurance noses retained the much larger twin-headlamp corner recesses.

The most important change to the monocoque came in the shape of forward-opening doors, replacing the gullwing doors used on XJR-6s. The left-hand twin-louvre side panel remained as before, but a new elongated single-scoop duct panel became

The superb lines of XJR-8 187, on test at Paul Ricard in February 1987, are clearly shown in this overhead shot. Designer Tony Southgate (seated) is in conversation with driver Eddie Cheever while John Watson stands by. A particular point of interest is the gearbox oil radiator duct next to the left rear wheel arch, carried over from the XJR-6. (Malcolm Bryan)

standard on the right-hand side for the full 1987 season. On top, the engine air intake was revised, being wider and faired down to a taper near the tail, quite different from the rounded-end scoop on XJR-6s. To improve airflow into the scoop, the monocoque roof was redesigned with a cutaway to provide a NACA duct lead into the intake. The rest of the engine cover panel remained largely unaltered, as did the rear wheel covers. There was a different shape to the wing endplates, which were larger, well rounded and with a distinct angled trailing edge. These were exclusive to the XJR-8 and were never seen on any other Group C model, although similar endplates featured on IMSA Jaguars long after they disappeared from the Silk Cut cars.

To the casual observer the XJR-8's general appearance hardly differed from the preceding XJR-6 or for that matter any other Jaguar Group C car; they all seemed to look identical. However, with the two models side by side the differences become obvious, mainly because of 1987 livery changes and new supporting sponsorship decals. To begin with, a greater level of Silk Cut corporate mauve was introduced, including on the nose and front end up to the top of the headlamps. There was a larger area of mauve on the monocoque roof, and the wings also changed colour to match. The former gold stripes on the XJR-6 now became deep yellow. Those along the sides widened sharply across the rear wheel covers, continuing around to cover all the rear tail panelling. Instead of black edging, all yellow paintwork was lined with half-inch green striping, except the yellow box striping surrounding the engine cover mauve panels. The larger

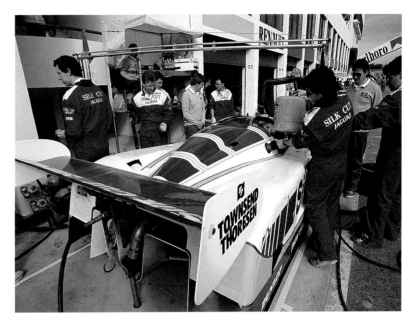

Silk Cut logo became standard on the scuttle panel below the windscreen, but now the Silk Cut name was yellow.

Take a good look at the front end of an XJR-8. What do you see? It's plain enough: the radiator intake is the mouth, the headlamps the eyes, and last but not least, two ears depicted by the unusual up- and downswept yellow stripes extending to the wing mirrors. At least this is what the race car graphics designer Ian Hutchinson intended when re-styling the XJR-8 livery. It was

Rear view of an XJR-8 at a pit stop. Note the deep diffuser tunnels. (Malcolm Bryan)

An unusual feature of the 1987 XJR-8 LM racer is the one-off siting of exhaust pipes below the suspension beam. Note also the shallow Le Mans-spec lower-downforce diffuser tunnels shaped specially to make room for the exit pipes. (Malcolm Bryan)

designed to represent a cat's face, but in the oft-quoted words of a certain well-known Cockney actor, 'not a lot of people know that!' This aside, the striking new livery was a great improvement, and because of the level of success the cars attained in 1987 they became instantly recognisable as the cars to look out for.

Throughout the season the main sponsorship names remained unchanged but the colours were reversed. Letters which had been mauve on white now became white on mauve, for instance on the nose and wings. What distinguished a 1987 car was the appearance, for one year only, of Townsend Thoresen as a supporting sponsor. This company's name and logo appeared on both front wings and on the wing endplates.

The year 1987 also saw new race numbers 4, 5 and 6. Number 4 would be used again later in the Group C programme, but 5 and 6 were unique to this year. Throughout the season, chassis 187 carried race number 5 while 287, which scored the most championship points, always appeared as car number 4. Chassis 387 twice raced as 4, once at Le Mans where 287 did not compete, and again in the non-championship Wurth Supercup race at Hockenheim, where it came home in third place. It was taken to Brands Hatch in July and Nürburgring in August as the spare car, in both cases listed as 4T. In its last appearance at Spa-Francorchamps in September it was car number 6, one of three cars entered in this particular race. Here it romped past the chequered flag to yet another convincing 1987 win, one lap ahead of the second-placed 187.

The only other race to attract the entry of three Silk Cut cars that year was Le Mans. Two of the previous season's chassis, 186 and 286, had been specially prepared and upgraded to XJR-8LM specification for this race. Chassis 186 ran as car 6, while 286 was the ill-fated car number 5. Both of these cars fell by the wayside, 286 in a most devastating incident. Fortunately, driver Win Percy walked away unscathed. XJR-8LM bodywork differed in detail from the regular sprint cars in having the usual lower downforce nose complete with short splitter, but without wheel arch louvres.

In order to reduce pit stop times, 1987 Le Mans XJR-8 chassis were raced without rear wheel covers. Tests had shown a slight loss in downforce resulting from their absence, but this was compensated for elsewhere. This was the only year at Le Mans in which the rear wheels were not covered. For night-time identification a small aviation light unit was mounted on the monocoque roof above the passenger side. Each car had a different coloured lens, a common feature on many Jaguar 24-hour endurance race cars.

Throughout the season car number 4 (chassis 287 in sprint racing, but chassis 387 at Le Mans) ran with white Jaguar lettering on the sunvisor, while on car number 5 (chassis 187 in sprint racing but chassis 286 at Le Mans) had red Jaguar lettering. Whenever a third car raced as number 6 the Jaguar name appeared in yellow lettering.

Another important 1987 change was to replace the sand-cast Speedline wheels with die-cast magnesium Dymag wheels. These were visibly different in having rounded spokes. The sizes remained unchanged at 17in front and 19in rear, but now the latter came with four spokes, not five as on Speedline rears. Dunlop had been working with TWR on developing new improved Kevlar ply tyres, still clearly identified as Dunlop Denloc in yellow on the sidewalls.

1988-89 XJR-9 – on two fronts
WSPC Group C chassis numbers 488, 588 and 688
IMSA GTP chassis numbers 188, 288 and 388

The most important difference between 1988 XJR-9 Group C and IMSA GTP cars was the engine, still 7 litres for the former while GTP normally-aspirated engines were restricted to 6 litres. The

Looking almost identical to the previous year's XJR-8, this 'unbranded' 1988 XJR-9 had been subjected to a long list of detailed chassis and bodywork improvements. (Jaguar)

minimum weight for IMSA cars was set at 900kg for 1988, which made it necessary to replace many components with heavier alternatives. A slight benefit from this was that less expensive materials could be used on American XJR-9s such as steel instead of titanium, which was more widely used on the lower minimum weight Group C cars.

Outwardly the differences between 1987 XJR-8s and the new 1988 season XJR-9s appear so minimal that they could almost be the same car. Not so, for as in previous years a great many significant changes were incorporated, both mechanically and to the bodywork. Some degree of standardisation was introduced to comply with Group C and IMSA GTP regulations within the same

package. IMSA required GTP cars to have same diameter wheels front and rear, so all 1988 XJR-9 variants were fitted with 17in rims all round, still shod with Dunlop Denlocs.

With the smaller rear wheels came reduced-size rear wheel covers and new lower-profile engine cover panels. Whereas previously the 19in rear wheels had been large enough to accommodate the upright damper and spring assemblies, the dampers now sloped inwards, and there were numerous modifications to the floor panels, engine positioning and running gear. The former deep diffuser tunnels had to be reduced in height anyway to comply with rule changes. The double louvred left-hand side panel remained much as before. At least two different

Early showing for the new 1988 season Castrol XJR-9. 88 was never used as a race number. (JDHT)

The 1988 Le Mans winning XJR-9 LM (488) on a recent return visit to La Sarthe. Note the roof cutaway to allow improved airflow to the engine intake, introduced on XJR-8s in 1987. (Author)

side panels would be seen on the right-hand flank during the season. The first panel had a single NACA duct towards the front end. The second was similar but had an additional louvre intake just behind the duct. The NACA duct served to cool the transmission oil radiator, now moved from its former position near the back of the left-hand rear wheel arch. The louvred intake cooled an additional engine oil radiator, needed to cope with prolonged high-speed running at Le Mans. There were also 'feed-offs' to cool the starter motor and to keep the rear tyre sensors cool.

Engine compartment cooling was catered for by two sizeable ducts each side of the bulge at the forward end of the cover, aided by pairs of slots and grille vents spaced down the back. New on the XJR-9 was a small cockpit ventilation duct, fitted into the engine intake cutaway at the back of the monocoque roof. From time to time cars would be seen racing with various ducts partially or fully blanked over to suit different track and weather conditions. The wings remained as before, but new endplates on Group C cars now had a vertical back edge. Later in the season, extra deep endplates appeared on Silk Cut and Castrol XJR-9s. They were designed to increase downforce but seem to have

lasted only a few races before being withdrawn, followed by a return to the original plates. Le Mans-style single-element wings were not used in America. All Daytona 24-hour and Sebring 12-hour endurance races were run with sprint-style double wings.

At the front end, the nose differed only in minor detail. Some time before Le Mans new stalk-mounted driver-controlled wing mirrors were introduced; until then the standard mirrors were housed in pods fixed directly to the wings. The latter remained in use on GTP V12 chassis for another two years. There was a significant bodywork change at the start of the 1989 season involving the re-design of the engine air intake system. The engineers thought that hot air from the radiator exit travelled over the monocoque roof directly into the engine intake, with a detrimental effect on performance. The new system involved sealing-over the roof intake, then installing NACA ducts each side of the engine cover. From these air was conveyed to the airbox through box ducting moulded to the underside of the cover.

Two types of revised engine covers were introduced, the first with modified existing panels where the roof intake duct was sealed over and the monocoque indent faired to match. Later, more streamlined covers appeared, with a pronounced hump

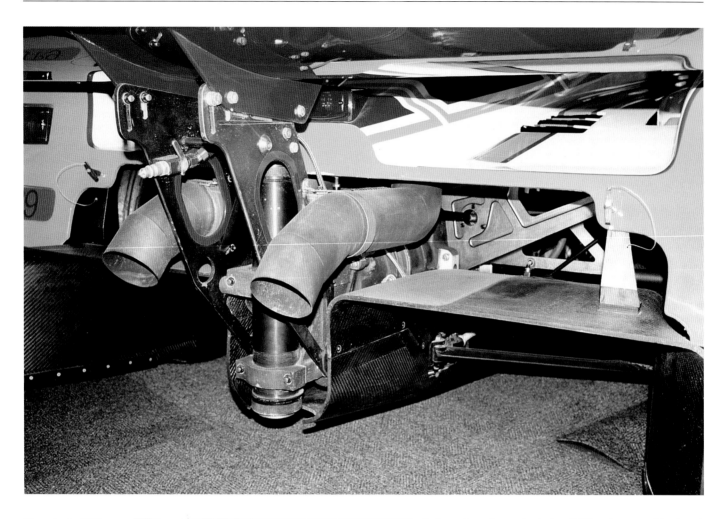

New rules for 1988 required a greater flat-floor area and lower-height diffuser tunnels, as seen here on the Le Mans winning XJR-9, chassis 488. (Author)

Inside the right-hand side panel of the XJR-9 LM. The top two braided hoses feed and return engine oil to and from the larger radiator while the smaller unit cools the transmission oil. The black hoses cool the starter motor and keep the tyre sensor at an even temperature. (Author)

halfway down the engine bulge. TWR engineers and bodywork stylists competed with each other to find suitable descriptive names for new components as they were introduced. The hump panels were referred to as 'camels' - not difficult to understand why. IMSA GTP XJR-9s retained modified panels long after Silk Cut cars made general use of 'camel' replacements. In 1989 the rear wheel diameter was increased from 17in to 18in, the fronts remaining at 17in. Another detail bodywork change that year was to much larger grille vents in the front wheel arches.

For IMSA racing a three-year sponsorship contract had been brokered with Castrol Oil, again by Guy Edwards. The three Valparaiso-managed cars would race in the striking Castrol corporate green, white and red livery, also from the drawing board of Ian Hutchinson. Unlike the constantly changing Silk Cut livery, it would remain generally unaltered throughout the sponsorship period.

The livery of the Group C cars throughout 1988 and 1989 changed little from what it had been in 1987. One feature which made a 1988 Silk Cut car readily identifiable was the name change from Townsend Thoresen to P & O European Ferries as a support sponsor for this year only. This name and logo appeared on the front wings and rear wing endplates. Other sponsorship names remained much as before, but for the 1988 Le Mans race three cars were part sponsored by Swiss Jaguar importers Emil Frey AG. This company's name and logo appeared on the front wings and endplates, where P & O featured on the other two cars. This one-off deal was never repeated. Another important change in the XJR-9's livery involved dispensing with the single Silk Cut logo on the scuttle, replacing it with two smaller ones on the front wings. For 1989, Dunlop Tyres replaced the ferry company as support sponsor. Large Dunlop stickers appeared on the nose and the wing endplates displayed the Jaguar leaping cat logo and name in place of P & O.

As 1987 WSPC World Champions, the 1988 Silk Cut Jaguars now proudly raced as car numbers 1 and 2 in all Championship races. Chassis 588 appeared as car number 1 in sprint racing as well as at Le Mans in 1988 and 1989. Chassis 488 raced only as car number 2 before winning at Le Mans in 1988. This historic car never raced after that event and was immediately handed over to the factory, becoming part of the Jaguar Daimler Heritage Trust collection. It is occasionally taken out for demonstrations, driven for the pleasure of the crowds at events such as the annual Goodwood Festival of Speed.

After 488's withdrawal from racing, chassis 688 took over as car number 2 for the remainder of the 1988 season and wherever Group C XJR-9s raced the following year, including Le Mans. Jaguar's five-car assault at Le Mans in 1988 included one former XJR-6, chassis 186, and XJR-8 chassis 287. From America came IMSA chassis 188. All had been especially upgraded to XJR-9 LM specification with identical endurance bodywork and single-element rear wings. For the record, the Jaguar name on the

windscreen sunvisor appeared in the following colours: 1 (588) white, 2 (488) orange, 3 (287) yellow, 21 (188) blue and finally 22 (186) lime green.

Another one-off feature unique to the 1988 Le Mans was the appearance of XJR-9 and V12 lettering in various colours on the rear tail panels, some matching the colour of the Silk Cut lettering on the windscreen. Some but not all the tails had special recessed panels for this additional signwork. After Le Mans, newly-made tails lacked this short-lived modification.

IMSA GTP Jaguars nearly always appeared with the chassis type and engine details clearly displayed at the rear, eg XJR-9 V12, XJR-12 V12 and so on. Chassis 188 appeared first as car 66 but then its race number was frequently changed, to 60, 61 then back to 66, often as the spare car and occasionally racing when one or other of its sister cars was out of action. Chassis 288, the 1988 Daytona winner, raced mostly as car 60 with two changes to 66 in late 1988. Chassis 388 retained number 61 through the majority of its lengthy race career, changing to 60 later in 1989 for two races only.

XJR-12 1990 to 1993 – the last V12s
Chassis numbers 288, 388, 190, 290, 990, 1090, 891, 991 and 193

Now upgraded exclusively for endurance competition only, the XJR-12's racing history was punctuated equally by moments of greatness and frustrating disappointments. Winning Le Mans in 1990, coming home second, third and fourth a year later, and taking both the 1991 Manufacturers' and Drivers' Championships

Front brake cooling changed in 1990 to NACA-style ducts mounted inboard of the headlamps. Wheel arch louvres also became quite prominent, as seen on this Castrol XJR-12D nose. (Ian Norris)

with the XJR-14, Silk Cut Jaguar's departure from Group C racing was not without honour.

In America the new Castrol XJR-12's first appearance at Daytona in 1990 concluded with a stunning one-two finish for 388 and 288 respectively. These were the regular 1988-89 XJR-9s upgraded to XJR-12s, but retaining their original chassis numbers for a while. A few weeks later, 388 came home third in the Sebring 12-hour race. Two years would pass before another good V12 result, when 891 came second overall but first in the GTP category at Daytona in February 1992, concluding a praiseworthy list of successes for the venerable V12s.

Not for the first time, a new XJR appeared which to the average race fan seemed little changed from last year's model, yet under the guidance of the new technical director Ross Brawn the new XJR-12 took to the track with many subtle improvements. With a little explanation, a few obvious differences serve to make XJR-12 identification very easy. The first noticeable change was to the nose, no longer seen with low level brake ducts flanking the radiator air intake. Brake cooling was now fed through a pair of NACA ducts inboard of the headlamps. The former smooth-profile front wheel arch louvres were replaced by heavily slatted panels. On some cars these were removable to facilitate a quick change to blanked panels when required. The re-styled nose gave a longer and leaner look but still kept within the permitted maximum overall length. Along the sides, large NACA ducts featured in the side panels, the forward ends slightly indented into the monocoque. Cars specially prepared for Le Mans in 1990 ran with a double wing set-up but still retained the short nose profile splitter. One feature first seen at the previous Le Mans race was vanes or deflector panels fixed inside the nose radiator wells.

Positioned just over the radiator, their purpose was to ensure the latter could not be seen when viewed from above. Rather belatedly, radiators became classified as mechanical, and to comply with existing rules should not be visible when looking down on the car from directly overhead.

An important change in wheels and tyres occurred in 1990, when BBS three-piece wheels with alloy rims and gold-finished magnesium centres replaced the one-piece Dymags. The new wheels wore Goodyear Eagle tyres and were fitted to Group C and GTP Jaguars, their use requiring alterations to the bodywork due to differences in tyre profiles.

While the XJR-12s appeared in just a handful of races from 1990 onwards, they underwent an interesting series of livery changes, keeping them in line with the paintwork of the regular sprint racers. For 1990 only, the Silk Cut cars sported a simplified two-tone scheme, in which the engine bulge and monocoque roof down to the base of the door windows was now finished in unbroken one-piece mauve. The lower sides and nose front were similarly finished up to the bottom of the door openings. The remaining bodywork stayed white. Thin yellow lines separated the two colours, having a noticeable effect on the white which now, to coin a phrase, really did look whiter than white. The wings remained mauve and, as before, the endplates white. All sponsorship decals on white paintwork were mauve (and vice versa), the race numbers were black, and the Jaguar logo on the endplates was green and black. At Le Mans, the JAGUAR name on the sunvisor was white on car 1 (990), red on 2 (290), yellow on 3 (1090), and green on 4 (190). The latter sported a large red dot on the engine cover, making it easy to identify it as the camera car from a helicopter flying overhead.

The IMSA GTP Jaguars retained their Castrol colours to the end of 1990. The Daytona winning XJR-12s still used double-louvre left-hand side panels and modified engine covers. The IMSA XJR-12 wing endplates were similar to those of the XJR-8 in style, and another feature on cars racing in the States (but not on WSPC Group C cars) was petrol filler caps and vents each side of the engine bulge.

New Bud Light sponsorship for 1991 and 1992 brought a number of changes to the larger 6.5-litre engined XJR-12D chassis, the D standing for Daytona. Generally the cars' physical appearance was more or less identical to their Silk Cut cousins with large NACA duct side panels, but now they were seen with 'camel' tails. The wing endplates still had angled rear edges, but for the first time IMSA V12s were fitted with stalk-mounted wing mirrors. The Bud Light livery of the IMSA Jaguars was most attractive. Although mostly white, contrasting light blue and red corporate colouring gave the cars a very smart appearance. There would be no radical changes to this livery or to the main sponsorship decals for the remainder of Jaguar's involvement in GTP racing.

The majority of 1991 IMSA GTP races included two-car entries from the Bud Light team, even at Daytona and Sebring, where in the earlier years three cars were fielded, while 1992 saw a reduction to a single car entry for most events. When two cars ran, they raced as numbers 2 and 3. Davy Jones, as the team's leading driver, always raced car number 2 regardless of chassis type. During 1991 and 1992 this number was transferred from XJR-12Ds to XJR-10s, then seen on the superb XJR-16s and

finally on XJR-14s, with a one-off return to XJR-12D at Daytona in 1993, Jaguar's last ever IMSA appearance.

The final 1993 outing featured an additional chassis unlike any other previous XJR-12. TWR's last throw of the dice combined the main body and nose of the current XJR-12s with an XJR-14 style engine cover and two-tier wing configuration. First tested at Silverstone shortly before being shipped to Daytona, it was not intended as a serious contender, more to evaluate its future Le Mans potential. Entered in the Le Mans category as car 32, this newly built chassis 193 completed 92 laps before handling problems forced its withdrawal. Unlike the regular XJR-12s, there were no rear wheel covers and it ran on XJR-14 style Speedline wheels. Ardent Jaguar race fans must have regretted the demise of Group C sportscar racing, which denied further development of this potential Championship winner.

Returning to Group C, the 1991 Le Mans 24-hour endurance race marked the final appearance of Silk Cut XJR-12s. The new drastically changed livery was designed by Ian Hutchinson to complement current sponsorship advertising, introduced at the commencement of the season on the new XJR-14s. This two-tone mauve and magenta colour scheme represented light and dark folds of draped curtains, as seen in Silk Cut's subtle magazine adverts. Although appearing quite random in nature, every car carried the same precise patterning. Lacking any white surfaces, all sponsorship decals were white, apart from small Silk Cut logos on the front wings set inside white squares. Larger white panels were used to display black race numbers. New for 1991 were NCR sponsorship decals on wing endplates.

The striking and attractive livery on the 1991 Suntec-sponsored XJR-12 LM. (Ken Wells)

TWR's last Jaguar prototype XJR-12 chassis 193 was briefly tested at Silverstone in January 1993 before shipment to the US to take part in the Daytona 24 Hours. (LAT Photographic)

The 1991 XJR-12 LM appeared more like a regular sprint car. The front nose panel was higher with a more noticeable flip-up, and for the first time it was run at Le Mans with a long sprint-style splitter. Now running the largest V12 engine so far, at 7.4 litres, three Silk Cut cars were entered. Car 33 (891) carried white sunvisor JAGUAR lettering, on car 34 (991) it was red, and on car 35 (990) green. Chassis 891 was built around a new monocoque. In a former life, 991 had been the early XJR-6 chassis 386 which had been converted to a show car. Many have expressed doubts about this seemingly improbable metamorphosis from an early XJR-6 chassis into what became one of the highly successful trio of top four finishing Silk Cut XJR-12s, but it is a fact.

A most unexpected surprise at Le Mans in 1991 was the appearance of a fourth XJR-12 LM, chassis 190, racing in the striking Japanese-sponsored Suntec livery. Completely different from anything seen to date, except in Japan where a lone Suntec sponsored XJR-11 was racing in the All Japan Sportscar-Prototype Championship, its eye-catching colour scheme was a real head turner: half green, half white, with touches of red and yellow. Sadly the car was dogged by bad luck throughout the night which finally put it out for the count with a broken transmission at 9.30 on Sunday morning. So ended an amazing series of races powered by a 20-year-old engine that many would have written off years before.

XJR-10 V6 Turbos – the next generation
Chassis numbers 389, 489, 589, 390 and 690

Raced for the first time at Lime Rock in Connecticut on 29 May 1989, the new Jaguar 3-litre V6 twin-turbocharged XJR-10 (chassis 389) raised expectations that here at last was a car to end Nissan's domination of the IMSA racing scene. As it qualified and then finished second, it sent waves of euphoria throughout TWR and Jaguar team members and personnel, after a string of disappointing results so far in 1989.

First sight of the XJR-10 gave the distorted impression that it was smaller than the V12 racers, when in fact it was built to the same overall dimensions. JaguarSport's compact 90-degree 24-valve JV6 engine, half the length of the V12 unit, enabled Tony Southgate to design chassis-hugging bodywork with much improved aerodynamics. At the front end, the high-downforce nose appeared similar in style to the XJR-9 but now rose up at a steeper angle. The nose centre panel was considerably higher, and instead of wheel arch louvres, large cut-outs featured in the inner wing surfaces. Cockpit cooling was fed through a round tubular duct halfway up the nose panel. The front-mounted radiator was cooled by a sizeable nose intake, flanked by XJR-9-style brake ducts.

Further back the XJR-10s were quite different from the V12 models. The monocoque and side panels curved inwards along the bottom to meet running board-style horizontal 'skirts', referred to as 'ankle cutters'. Both doors were fitted with deep recessed NACA ducts to feed cold air to the turbocharger intercoolers, then out through large openings each side of the engine cover. Early turbo cars featured additional ducts in the monocoque horizontal surfaces either side of the windscreen to boost this airflow. Track testing indicated that the door ducting was more than adequate, so the monocoque ducts were dispensed with. NACA ducts in the doors are one of the most important identification features of the turbo cars.

The rear bodywork differed greatly from anything seen to date, with prominent rear wheel arches, and the engine bulge sloping sharply to a point near the tail. A small round opening halfway

Valparaiso-managed XJR-10 turbo cars achieved a few good wins in IMSA racing, but chassis 489, seen here at Portland in 1989, was soon to be destroyed by fire after only one outing. (Paul Skilleter)

down the bulge allowed access to the oil filler, and further back a single NACA duct served to cool the transmission oil radiator mounted under the tail. Rear wheel covers with centre NACA style cut-outs and straight back edges were fitted as standard. At the rear, the tail panels featured upward-facing ventilation louvres. Developed principally for sprint racing only, these turbo cars were fitted with double wings and well-rounded endplates. As on the V12s, rear brake cooling was via periscope ducts fixed to the hollow uprights. These periscopes were taller but not so wide as their V12 counterparts. Another distinctive feature unique to turbo cars were large periscope turbo air intakes attached to the engine covers directly above the Garrett turbo units. With their introduction, the monocoque ducts at the sides of the windscreen were removed.

Alterations were made to the turbo cars' bodywork in 1990, which included changing the front brake ducts to NACA style

openings, inboard of the headlamps. On IMSA XJR-10s the old brake ducts were left open through the 1990 season, and not sealed over as on Silk Cut XJR-11s. Further bodywork changes were made to the XJR-10 for the 1991 season, the cars now appearing in Bud Light livery. Rectangular headlamps mounted just above splitter level eventually replaced the recessed round lamps. Now running with a wider front track, the nose bulged outwards at the top behind the wheel arches. There was also a prominent bulge in the monocoque roof for which two explanations have been given, the first being that were added to increase the driver's headroom. A more plausible reason was due to IMSA rules stipulating that rear wings were not to be higher than the monocoque roof, so the humps were added to allow more leeway for wing settings.

Turbo cars ran on 17in front wheels and 18in rears. In parallel with the V12s, Dymags with Dunlop tyres were standard up to

New sponsors and new livery for IMSA Jaguars in 1991. Davy Jones driving XJR-10 chassis 589 competed in the first two races of the season before he and race number 2 transferred to the new XJR-16. (Jaguar)

When first shown to the media at Jarama in 1989 the XJR-11 lacked periscope turbo ducts. Note the short-lived monocoque ducts just behind the stalk-mounted wing mirrors. These fed air into the turbo units via box ducting in the doors. (LAT Photographic)

1990, then the switch was made to BBS rims and Goodyears. XJR-10 livery was identical to whatever appeared on the larger V12 chassis, namely Castrol to the close of the 1990 season and Bud Light in 1991.

XJR-11 – great cars, too little time to perfect
Chassis numbers 189, 289, 490, 590, 1190, 1290 and 1390

Seven XJR-11 chassis numbers were listed from the time when 189 and 289 first raced at Brands Hatch on 23 July 1989 to their last appearance in Mexico in October 1990. However, the last four chassis numbers represent re-numbering of the first three chassis at different times during 1990.

Externally, the XJR-10 GTP and XJR-11 Group C cars were

Periscope engine cover intake ducts and NACA ducts in the doors make turbo car identification relatively simple. For example this 1989 XJR-11 clearly differs from its first-generation V12 predecessors. (Colin Taylor)

Now privately owned and running in Group C revival racing, XJR-11 chassis 590 is fitted with an endurance-style twin-headlamp nose. Was this part of a proposal to enter turbo cars at Le Mans in 1990? (Ian Jones)

more or less identical. They went through the same sequence of modification and upgrading, but these were often applied to Group C cars long before they appeared on Valparaiso-managed chassis. One good example of this was the wide front track version tried for the first time at Silverstone on 20 May 1990, where the two XJR-11s entered came first and second, Silk Cut Jaguar's first Group C win for 18 months. The new wide-track noses also featured rectangular headlamps, which were not to be seen on IMSA XJR-10s for another year.

The XJR-11 Silk Cut livery was roughly identical to that seen on the V12 models, changing in 1990 to the simplified design. One small item only seen on turbo cars was the corporate Jaguar leaper and JAGUAR SPORT name on the turbo intake periscopes. Silk Cut in yellow lettering would often be seen on the tail louvres, while it appeared in white on the underside of the rear

JaguarSport's 3.5-litre Group C JV6 turbocharged engine in its earliest form with carbon fibre plenum chambers. The Castrol XJR-10 used a 3-litre version. (Jaguar)

Problems with carbon fibre plenum chambers collapsing under pressure was overcome by conversion to cast alloy units, seen here on a 1990 XJR-11. (Bruce Malcolm)

The much-improved XJR-16 turbo car made a decisive win in its debut race at Road Atlanta in April 1991. (Author)

wing. The latter was for the benefit of pursuing drivers, making it quite clear the car in front was a Silk Cut Jaguar.

Amongst changes made in 1990 were the turbo intake periscope ducts, originally attached to the engine cover. For the new season re-designed periscopes were introduced which fitted direct to the turbo units. The engine cover came with cut-outs to enable it to be lifted on and off without disturbing the periscopes. This innovation was confined to Silk Cut Group C XJR11s and was not featured on the IMSA turbo cars.

XJR-16 – the best turbo car
Chassis numbers 191 and 291

Driving the brand new XJR-16 (chassis 191), easily the most promising forced-induction car to date, Davy Jones shook the competition in the car's debut race at Road Atlanta on 28 April 1991 by taking pole position, leading for most of the race and winning decisively. Team-mate Raul Boesel followed Davy into third place driving one of the XJR-10s, just to prove they were still worthy adversaries.

In general appearance, the handsome XJR-16 could be said to be an XJR-10 with a two-tier wing configuration. Very true on the face of it, but below the engine cover lay a completely different picture from anything seen so far. The rear suspension system that had served all previous models now changed to gearbox-mounted dampers operated by pushrods and bellcranks. There was also a multitude of engine, mechanical and electronic improvements.

The engine cover now had a modified tail section and smaller rear panels. Unlike previous XJR models there were no rear brake periscope ducts. Instead, additional NACA ducts in the side panels fed air to the uprights via flexible hoses on either side of the engine bay. The two-tier wing assembly differed somewhat from the system used on the Silk Cut XJR-14s. While the endplates were similar in shape, the lower wings were set higher in relation to the upper wings. The whole assembly was carried on support plates bolted to the gearbox end casing. Raced in Bud Light livery only between 28 April and 13 October 1991, the XJR-16s were phenomenally successful, making quite a dent in the longstanding Japanese domination of IMSA GTP racing.

Chassis 191 was brought over to the UK in 2000 and prepared for Group C revival racing by Stoke-on-Trent-based Don Law Racing.

XJR-14 – third generation World Championship winners
Chassis numbers 591, 691 791 and 192

Raced as a Group C Silk Cut chassis in 1991 and in IMSA GTP Bud Light specification during 1992 only, the XJR-14 owed nothing to its V12 and V6 turbo predecessors. TWR technical director Ross Brawn commenced design work on what was often described as a Formula 1 chassis with a fully enclosed two-seater sportscar body back in 1989, while the second-generation turbo cars were still on their learning curve. Powered by Jaguar's version of the Cosworth HB 3.5-litre normally-aspirated V8

Ross Brawn's championship-winning Jaguar XJR-14 in the new 1991 Silk Cut livery. (JDHT)

Cosworth's 3.5-litre HB engine powered the 1991 Championship winning XJR-14. (Cosworth Engineering)

XJR-14 wing assemblies remained unpainted apart from the upper surfaces of the top wings and the outer faces of endplates.(Author)

Few people ever got to see the Cosworth 3.5-litre HB engine fitted in the XJR-14. (Author)

engine, the car incorporated many ground-breaking features to make it one of the most formidable Group C contenders in the 1991 Sportscar World Championship.

There were no conventional doors as such, only removable window panels through which drivers had to prove their agility when getting inside. When seated, their first task was to become accustomed to the new central gear lever position, requiring left-hand gear changing. At the front, the low-swept high-downforce nose featured an adjustable aerofoil above a fixed wing, reminiscent of the extra wings experimented with on early XJR-6s in 1985. The wheel arches were vented by large louvred panels, some of which could be unscrewed and replaced with blank panels when required. Beneath the engine cover, the rear suspension and dampers were mounted Formula 1-style on the top of the gearbox. Breaking with tradition, the gearbox now housed the differential behind the gears.

Engine cooling changed from a single nose-mounted radiator to a pair of radiators situated in the engine bay and recessed behind two deep rectangular ducts either side of the monocoque. One of the XJR-14's most distinguishing features was the prominent roof-mounted engine air intake. Another was the rather large two-tier four-element wing configuration, with biplane-style diagonal wire bracing. Two types of engine cover were used, the

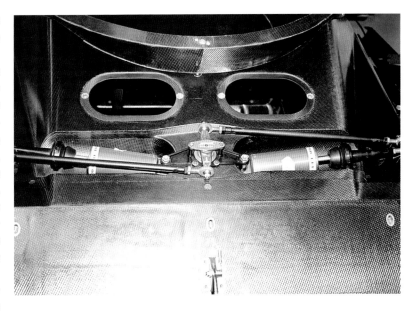

first designed to fit over a pair of prominent flat-sided rear brake periscope ducts. The other was smoother in profile, with flush-fitting NACA ducts for the same purpose.

Apart from medium-size NACA ducts and exhaust pipe outlets in the side panels, the flanks were very clean. One interesting

The new XJR-14 front dampers and torsion bar assembly. (Author)

Under the XJR-14's skin is a superbly crafted carbon fibre chassis. (Author)

detail not seen on previous TWR prototypes was the way in which the front wheel arches were chamfered at the rear to encourage smoother airflow around the wheels. There were no rear wheel covers. XJR-14s ran on 17in front and 18in rear one-piece Speedline magnesium wheels fitted with Goodyear Eagle tyres.

For Group C, all three chassis raced in the 1991 Silk Cut two-tone 'curtain folds' livery with all sponsorship details in white. After the termination of Silk Cut sponsorship at the end of 1991, and the team's withdrawal from Group C racing, the XJR-14s were dispatched to Valparaiso to compete another season of GTP racing in Bud Light livery.

During 1991, chassis 591 raced as Silk Cut Jaguar number 3 in the first half of the season. In June it was taken to Le Mans for qualifying only, but was not used. A second XJR-14, chassis 691, driven by Andy Wallace lapped at 3min 31.912sec in practice, but took no part in the race. Chassis 691 always raced as car 4 in the SWC Championship season and gained more points than the other XJR-14s. Chassis 791 raced as car 3 in the last four races of the 1991 season.

In the 1991 All Japanese Sportscar-Prototype Champion-ships, the lone Suntec sponsored XJR-11 was having a difficult time to say the least. The final SWC race of the season happened to be in Japan at Autopolis on 27 October. In order to get a result, Walkinshaw delayed returning to the UK to allow 691 and 791 to be entered in the last AJS-PC race, at Sugo a week later on 3 November, in place of the previously unsuccessful turbo car. This might have been using a sledgehammer to crack a nut and of course they won! Chassis 691 came home first with flying colours, driven by SWC World Champion Teo Fabi and David Brabham. The regular AJS-PC drivers in 791 were not so fortunate, taking

ninth place. For this last-minute appearance both cars raced in the 1991 Silk Cut colouring with all the tobacco sponsorship logos removed and replaced by Suntec decals. Chassis 691 raced as car 17 while 791 was car 18.

The XJR-14s' appearance in the 1992 IMSA GT races helped to keep Davy Jones well up in the Drivers' Championship tables, but Juan Fangio II's Toyota Eagle proved more reliable in the end. All three XJR-14s were present in the US, but only on one occasion did two race together.

All other races were single car entries in which all three chassis were driven by Davy Jones at one time or another. Chassis 691 was re-numbered 192 and took part in seven races. It later went to Germany and formed the basis for Reinhold Joest's Porsche-engined car, which took two successive Le Mans wins. In the USA, IMSA rules required the window panels to be hinged, not removable as in Group C.

However, the XJR-14 story did not quite end with Jaguar. While the three ex-Silk Cut XJR-14s were competing as Bud Light Jaguars in the 1992 IMSA Camel GT championship, a near-identical car was developed by TWR for Mazda as the MXR-01 and competed in the much-depleted 1992 Sportscar World Championship series. The nose of this car featured twin-headlamp units, and the rear body was re-styled to accommodate Mazda's own-labelled Judd V10 engine, which had replaced the Cosworth V8. This car did not enjoy the same level of success as the Jaguars had.

XJR-17 – the last prototype Jaguar

Reported to have been XJR-16 chassis 291 converted from turbocharged to normal aspiration, this one-off has no known

chassis number. According to a TWR press release, the intention was to produce two XJR-17 versions: one with a 3.5-litre engine for the FISA-sanctioned FIA Cup, the other with a smaller 3-litre unit as a possible contender in the IMSA Camel Lights series. It was listed as having the XJ220B engine but it is not certain that this was ever fitted. Today, this car is in private ownership, still fitted with a 3.5-litre JV6 race engine.

The press handout included an artist's impression of the finished car with XJR-16 style two-tier wing configuration, which it

probably never had. The nose was copied from the XJR-14 but lacks the shallow brake duct openings. Also following XJR-14 layout, engine cooling relied on two separate radiators in the engine bay cooled by large NACA ducts in the doors. The engine cover was as on the XJR-16 without turbo periscopes, but was re-modelled at the top to fit over the intake scoop. As far as is known, the car was never fitted with rear wheel covers or painted other than plain white. One or two early photos show a light blue sunvisor panel with JAGUAR in white.

Artist's impression of TWR Jaguar XJR-17 with XJR-14 style nose and XJR-16 rear end. (TWR)

While the one and only XJR-17, seen here at Donington, never raced for Jaguar it has been active in present-day Group C revival racing. (Author)

Chapter 3

1985 World Endurance Championship

Jaguar's promising entry

As 1984 drew to a close, Jaguar as a company was on a roll. John Egan, who had joined as chief executive in 1980 at the age of 40, was young and charismatic. He had taken the individuality of Jaguar's products and workforce and created an operation that was ready and able to stand on its own feet. In August, Jaguar had literally begun to stand alone when it was privatised through a share issue on the London stock exchange. The initial offering was greatly over-subscribed, and the newly-independent Jaguar was seen as the jewel in Margaret Thatcher's privatisation crown.

Just days before the shares went on sale, Tom Walkinshaw, Hans Heyer and Win Percy had driven an XJ-S to victory in Europe's greatest touring car race, the Spa 24-Hours. Walkinshaw and his TWR team had been racing the XJ-S since 1982, and racing success had been a strong card in the PR campaign that led up to privatisation. The Spa win, and Walkinshaw's subsequent victory in the European Touring Car Championship, all added to the growing reputation the company was enjoying.

The appreciation of what racing could do for the Jaguar image had taken a quantum leap forward when two of the US-based Group 44 sportscar prototypes had come over to compete at Le Mans. The public and the media did not distinguish between American and European teams, and the cars were seen simply as Jaguars. The return of the marque to its racing roots, coupled with increasing sales and improving quality of the road cars, brought the media spotlight down hard on Le Mans. General euphoria greeted Jaguar's challenge to perennial top dogs Porsche in the most glamorous race in the world, and the fact that the cars did not finish was almost overlooked. The PR payback from Le Mans was enormous, and the Jaguar board was happy to approve a budget for a return in 1985.

Having achieved the Touring Car Championship win, it was natural that TWR should move on to fresh challenges, and a move into sportscar racing was agreed. Originally, it was thought that in 1985 TWR would race a version of the Group 44 car in Europe and that both teams would contest Le Mans. Walkinshaw thought otherwise, and although the team tested the American XJR-5, it was never a realistic possibility that TWR would race anything but a car it had developed itself.

During the early months of 1985 work was progressing on both sides of the Atlantic to create Jaguar racing cars that could take on the world, and the mood was optimistic. Only one event darkened this period – on 8 February Sir William Lyons died in his 84th year. He had seen the company he founded come back to commercial health but did not live to see it regain its earlier racing glory. As the year came to an end, and before committing itself completely to sportscar racing, TWR crowned the racing career of the XJ-S by taking first and third in the classic Australian touring car race, the James Hardie 1000 at Bathurst.

Early testing of the XJR-6 at Snetterton and elsewhere showed great promise. (LAT Photographic)

Mosport, Canada was the race chosen for the debut of the new Jaguar Group C prototype, if only for the reason that the new cars could not be finished early enough to enter previous races in the 1985 WEC calendar. Of the two cars shipped over from Kidlington, chassis 185 (car 51) had been subject to a short series of track tests at Donington Park and Silverstone after initial shakedown only five weeks earlier. Much needed to be learnt and understood, and the best proving ground of all was in active

competition. Chassis 285 (car 52) arrived in Canada without having turned a wheel in anger, and is probably the only Jaguar Group C prototype to have undergone its initial shakedown in pre-race practice and qualifying.

While the cars may have been brand new, the team was highly experienced, with several years of European Touring Car Championship racing behind them. It was business as usual for all but the newest recruits. Any doubts in the minds of team

Martin Brundle's leap into the lead in 185 at the start of the XJR-6's debut race at Mosport ahead of the two Rothmans Porsches delighted onlookers while giving the opposition much to ponder. (JDHT)

Hans Heyer, Martin Brundle, Mike Thackwell and Jean-Louis Schlesser all set to launch Jaguar into Group C racing at Mosport, Canada. (JDHT)

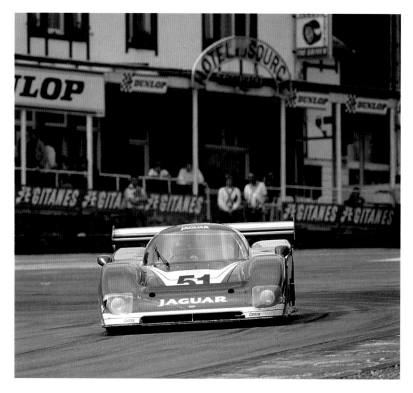

The Hotel Source hairpin bend at Spa Francorchamps is one of the photographer's favourite vantage points. Jaguar's second race was rewarded with fifth place for the Martin Brundle car number 51, chassis 185. (JDHT)

members and competitors alike as to the potential of the XJR-6 quickly evaporated during qualifying. Martin Brundle's lap time of 1min 12.6sec, a fraction behind first-placed Hans-Joachim Stuck, earned him third place on the grid, with Jean-Louis Schlesser in car 52 only two places back in fifth.

If this was not enough to impress delighted expatriate onlookers, Brundle rocketed past the two Rothmans Porsche favourites at the start to take the lead at the first corner, which to everyone's amazement he maintained for the first nine laps. Hans-Joachim Stuck then managed to gain the lead, followed shortly by Jacky Ickx in the second Rothmans Porsche. Four laps later Brundle's epic adventure was brought to an untimely end by a failed wheel bearing.

Brundle and team-mate Mike Thackwell switched to the second, as yet new car (285), on its first pit stop when running third and much to everyone's delight and great satisfaction, finished third behind the two Rothmans Porsches. No one expected a first time outright win but such an excellent start to Jaguar's new racing venture clearly pointed the way ahead.

Venue: Mosport, Canada
Round 6, 3 August 1985
Race title: The Budweiser GT 1000

Chassis type	Chassis no.	Race no.	Drivers	Grid pos.	Finish position	Laps
XJR-6	185	51	Martin Brundle, Mike Thackwell	3	DNF; wheel bearing	12
XJR-6	285	52	Martin Brundle, Mike Thackwell, Jean-Louis Schlesser	5	3	234

Race winner: Rothmans Porsche 962C, drivers Derek Bell and Hans Joachim Stuck, 253 laps

The next race at **Spa-Francorchamps** was on very familiar ground for the team. Tom Walkinshaw, Hans Heyer and Win Percy had achieved an epic win a year earlier in the gruelling 1984 24 Heures de Francorchamps driving a Group A XJ-S. This was significant as the first major 24-hour victory for a Jaguar since the C- and D-type successes at Le Mans in the 1950s. Martin Brundle and Mike Thackwell in Jaguar number 51 completed the 1000km race in a very creditable fifth place. Schlesser and Heyer in car 52 experienced insurmountable handling problems which rendered the car undrivable after only 14 laps.

The race will be remembered as the second in succession in which a top driver died as a result of a serious accident. At Mosport it had been German Formula 1 driver Manfred Winklhock. Now Stefan Belof, another German Formula 1 driver, suffered a fatal crash while attempting to gain the lead from Jacky Ickx. Winklhock, Belof and Ickx were all Porsche drivers. As a mark of respect, the race was terminated early with the 3-litre Lancia LC2-84 taking the first win of the season for the Italian team.

Two races into Group C competition, the British Racing Green Jaguars were already rated on an equal footing with the Rothmans Porsche and Martini Lancia works teams. In the few short weeks since Mosport, both Jaguars had been subject to a series of improvements in the light of problems noted during the first outing. These included subtle alterations to the nose, together with measures to prevent recurrence of wheel bearing failure.

Venue: Spa-Francorchamps, Belgium
Round 7, 1 September 1985
Race title: 1000 Km De Spa

Chassis type	Chassis no.	Race no.	Drivers	Grid pos.	Finish position	Laps
XJR-6	185	51	Martin Brundle, Mike Thackwell	8	5	120
XJR-6	285	52	Jean-Louis Schlesser, Hans Heyer	11	DNF, handling problems	14

Race winner: Lancia LC12, drivers Bob Wollek, Mauro Baldi, Andrea de-Cesaris, 122 laps

British race fans' first glimpse of the exciting new Racing Green Jaguars on home ground at **Brands Hatch** was rather disappointing in that both cars failed to finish. Alan Jones qualified fifth in car 51, alongside sixth-placed Jan Lammers in 52, both high enough up the grid to raise expectations of a good result. Jones suffered throttle problems with consequent damage to the engine. Lammers fared better and was running in fifth place after nearly two hours when a dropped valve put Jaguar 52 out of contention.

Like the animals going two by two into Noah's Ark, the start saw two Porsches, two Lancias and two Jaguars on the first three rows of the grid. The first few laps witnessed both Jaguars making gallant efforts to keep up with the leaders, Jones gaining a place over Jochen Mass in Rothmans Porsche number 1 only to lose it again shortly afterwards. By lap 15 the Australian's XJR-6 was in serious trouble, as the left rear tyre started rotating on its rim, forcing a brief pit stop to have the wheel replaced. Jones rejoined the race, now in eighth place, but a few laps later the throttle slide jammed in the fully open position, over-revving the engine to breaking point. Car 51 was the first Jaguar retirement.

Jan Lammers and Hans Heyer maintained a steady pace around sixth position behind the quartet of duelling Porsche and Lancia, until their number 52 Jaguar also fell victim to engine failure. The Rothmans Porsches and Martini Lancias finished as they had started, two by two in that order.

Venue: Brands Hatch, UK
Round 8, 22 September 1985
Race title: Shell Gemini 1000 Km

Chassis type	Chassis no.	Race no.	Drivers	Grid pos.	Finish position	Laps
XJR-6	185	51	Alan Jones, Jean-Louis Schlesser	5	DNF, engine	20
XJR-6	285	52	Hans Heyer, Jan Lammers	6	DNF, engine	77

Race winner: Rothmans Porsche 962C, drivers Derek Bell and Hans Joachim Stuck, 238 laps

Qualifying in the fourth race at **Fuji** was not without engine problems, and there was strong opposition from a considerable showing of Japanese and German turbo power. Potential Le Mans winner Jan Lammers was missing from the driver line-up, but the team now included another future endurance Champion, the Dane John ('Big John') Nielsen. For all their efforts in qualifying, the team were placed well down the grid in 19th and 20th places - all to no avail as the European teams withdrew

shortly after the race started because of a torrential downpour.

Not all of the European drivers were happy to abandon the race. In the end, it was up to the home teams to make a showing in front of a substantial 83,500-strong rain-lashed crowd, seeking whatever shelter they could find from which to watch the 18 runners who did compete. With just a handful of non-Japanese drivers in the running, it was inevitable that the top places in the much-shortened 62-lap race would go to the home teams. That they achieved this, despite the weather conditions deteriorating yet further, understandably made them the objects of much hero worship. The general consensus of opinion was that even if the Porsches and Jaguars had raced they would not have been a match for the Nissan, Toyota and Mazda brigade. Even so, all agreed that it would have been better if everybody had raced.

Venue: Fuji, Japan
Round 9, 6 October 1985
Race title: Mount Fuji 1000km

Chassis type	Chassis no.	Race no.	Drivers	Grid pos.	Finish position	Laps
XJR-6	185	51	Mike Thackwell, John Nielsen	19	Withdrawn, heavy rain	0
XJR-6	285	52	Steve Soper, Hans Heyer	20	Withdrawn, heavy rain	0

Race winner: March-Nissan 85G, drivers Kazuyoshi Hoshino, Akira Hagiura and Keiji Matsumoto, 62 laps

The final WEC race of 1985 at **Shah Alam** in Malaysia was much more encouraging, on a circuit favouring the larger normally-aspirated V12s. By now, the two Jaguars were further improved through continued trial and error. Still without a spare car, which

Alan Jones replaced Mike Thackwell at Brands Hatch but in spite of improvements to the front end neither Jaguar finished. In this picture both cars have the newly introduced brake ducts taped over. (LAT Photographic)

The Martini Lancia
LC2s led the start at
Brands Hatch. If Jaguar
were to achieve
Championship status
they, and the works
Porsches, would have
to be conquered. (LAT
Photographic)

fortunately was not required, Mike Thackwell qualified in fourth place on the grid only 1.5 seconds slower than the first Porsche and a fraction faster than Lammers, who put 52 in fifth place. Lammers was quick to move up to second place behind Jacky Ickx's Rothmans Porsche before a puncture caused him to spin out of the race on lap 19. Car 51 maintained a steady pace, keeping up with the leaders. Now boosted by Jan Lammers after 52 was put out of action, car 51's second-place finish with only one of the works Porsches ahead was all the team needed to set them on course for greater things next season.

Racing in the sticky humid conditions at Shah Alam put a heavy strain on the drivers, while to make matters worse attendance figures on this occasion were a lowly 3000. Despite

the personal patronage and trackside attendance of the Sultan of the State of Selangor, who was keen to meet the drivers, this would be the last time a Group C Sportscar Championship race took place at this venue.

Venue: Shah-Alam, Malaysia
Round 10, 9 December 1985
Race title: Selangor 800 Km

Chassis type	Chassis no.	Race no.	Drivers	Grid pos.	Finish position	Laps
XJR-6	185	51	Mike Thackwell, John Nielsen, Jan Lammers	4	2	217
XJR-6	285	52	Jan Lammers, Gianfranco Brancatelli	5	DNF, puncture	19

Race winner: Rothmans Porsche 962C, drivers Jochen Mass and Jacky Ickx, 217 laps

Chapter 4

1986 World Sportscar Prototype Championship

Jaguar's first full season

The performance of the new XJR-6 in the latter part of the 1985 season had encouraged TWR and Jaguar to believe that a realistic challenge could be mounted in the team's first full season of the World Sportscar Championship, the governing body's new name for what had been the World Endurance Championship. The Silk Cut Jaguar team was not the only newcomer to challenge Porsche. Peter Sauber of Switzerland had a promising new Mercedes-powered car, sponsored by the Yves St Laurent range of men's toiletries, Kouros. Porsche's factory team retained Rothmans sponsorship and was backed up by a number of private entries. Lancia, however, which had carried Italy's colours in endurance racing in 1985, scaled back its involvement considerably for 1986.

The format of the races changed somewhat, with a number being run as shorter 'sprint' events rather than longer endurance events of 500km or more. It was for this reason that the word 'endurance' had gone from the series title. The fuel allowance was restricted, so fuel-efficiency from the engines and careful driving on the part of the drivers were both important. There were

Championships for teams and individual drivers, but only five of the races scored team points while drivers' points could be won in all nine Championship rounds. Alongside the premier Group C cars was a Championship for the smaller-engined C2 class cars.

Commercially, Jaguar was continuing to thrive. Some 42,000 cars had been sold in 1985, an all-time record, and the mood was bullish in the lead-up to the launch of the all-new saloon, code-named XJ40, in the late summer of 1986. This much-anticipated new model was well received, and the combination of a successful new road car and a steadily improving performance by the race team kept spirits high.

The new sponsorship deal with Gallaher International for 1986, in which the upgraded Jaguars would now appear in Silk Cut corporate colours and insignia, came with all the trappings of a top international sportscar racing organisation. In addition to the vehicle livery, designed by the Ian Hutchinson Studio, all team members and associated Jaguar personnel were now seen in very smart teamwear, and were carried to the circuits in matching

New season, new cars: XJR-6s 51 and 52 (chassis 186 and 286) ready for action at Monza. Wheel trims were tried on occasions but never saw general use. (Malcolm Bryan)

identifiable transporters, with increasing support from the rapidly enlarged facilities at Kidlington and from the Jaguar factory. Foremost amongst the army of enthusiastic supporters, Jaguar chairman and chief executive John Egan regarded entry into international sportscar racing as an important and integral part of Jaguar's heritage.

A Championship of 11 races was proposed in early pre-season press releases but Mugello, scheduled for early April, and the penultimate Selangor meeting in Malaysia, together with a final round at Surfers Paradise in Australia, were deleted. The Spanish Jarama venue for August was changed to Jerez, and the Norisring in Germany was chosen to host an alternative sprint race which was to be included in the revised Championship standings.

Regular drivers for 1986 were to be Derek Warwick (UK), Eddie Cheever (USA), Jean-Louis Schlesser (France) and Gianfranco Brancatelli (Italy). Two new XJR-6s, chassis 186 and 286, were ready to take part in the first round at Monza. The last 1985 chassis, 385 completed in January 1986, was also ready to attend the meetings, mainly as a spare car.

As part of winter testing, the two 1985 cars, 185 and 285, were taken to Estoril in Portugal in early February. Chassis 185 remained in the 1985 green livery while 285 appeared for the first time in the Silk Cut colours. Representatives from Gallaher International were present to assess the new livery, and the potential of the cars.

Round one at **Monza** was not quite the start the new Silk Cut Jaguar team had hoped would set them on course for the top of the Championship tables. The much revised, lighter weight cars pushed hard to match the reigning Porsches' turbo power. While their performance set firm foundations for eventual success, this was not achieved in the first instance.

A crowd of around 25,000 eager Latin supporters came to watch fellow countrymen Andrea de Cesaris and Sandro Nannini start the race from pole position in the distinctive Lancia Martini. de Cesaris was soon overwhelmed by Klaus Ludwig in the Taka-Q Porsche 962. Cheever in Jaguar 51 was well up with the front runners, moving into second place after having got the better of Hans Stuck in the Rothmans Porsche. Warwick took the car over after it made its first pit stop - rather early, some thought - only to suffer a broken driveshaft a little later on lap 47.

Brancatelli took over 52 during the same round of pit stops, exiting in fourth place. Following Warwick's abrupt departure, the Italian soon found himself running up in second, tailed by Sandro Nannini's Martini Lancia and a trio of Brun Porsches. The Lancia soon slipped by, relegating the Jaguar to third once again, while Rothmans Porsche number 1 took over the lead position.

Tension mounted in the pits at Silverstone when the team seemed on course to take the first Group C win. (Malcolm Bryan)

The Warwick/Cheever Jaguar XJR-6 (chassis 286) on its way to take an historic first Group C race win at Silverstone. (Malcolm Bryan)

Bell and Stuck remained in front to take the flag while the Lancia, being the only other car on the same lap, came home to a satisfying second place in front of thousands of ecstatic Italian supporters. As for the remaining Jaguar, the slightly premature pit stop took its toll, and it ran out of fuel on the penultimate lap. Believing the tank to be empty, the crew were understandably peeved to discover that eight litres remained, and it was all down to a faulty fuel pick up. Third place was in the bag... then it was not. Disappointed as the Silk Cut Jaguar team members were, they remained confident that the cars had the potential to come up trumps, given a little more time.

A worried Tom Walkinshaw, here on the wall at Silverstone with Roger Silman, broke into a broad smile as Eddie Cheever took the flag. (Malcolm Bryan)

Venue: Monza, Italy
Round 1, 20 April 1986
Race title: Kouros Cup 20 Trofeo Filippo Caracciola

Chassis type	Chassis no.	Race no.	Drivers	Grid pos.	Finish position	Laps
XJR-6	186	52	Jean-Louis Schlesser, Gianfranco Brancatelli	9	DNF, fuel	61
XJR-6	286	51	Eddie Cheever, Derek Warwick	6	DNF, driveshaft output flange	47
XJR-6	385	53T	T car used only in practice			

Race winner: Rothmans Porsche 962C, drivers Derek Bell and Hans Stuck, 63 laps

Home ground **Silverstone** was the venue for round two, dubbed the 'battle of the Dereks', with Porsche works team ace Derek Bell pitted against Jaguar's Derek Warwick. In contrast to the shorter 360km Monza Sprint, this was a full-blown 1000km endurance race, sponsored by perfume manufacturer Yves St Laurent. In addition to the usual bevy of Rothmans and privateer Porsches, one of the favourites to win the race was the works Martini Lancia of Sandro Nannini and Andrea de Cesaris.

Warwick and Cheever got the Silk Cut Jaguars off to a good start, qualifying number 51 third, while Schlesser and Brancatelli, only a fraction slower, managed fifth place on the grid for number 52. The first three hours settled into a hotly contested duel between the Jaguars and the lone Lancia. On lap 49 the Warwick/Cheever XJR-6 took the lead, while the Schlesser/Brancatelli car dropped back a little, following pit stops to sort out gear lever damage. The lever bracket had pulled out of its fixings, not an easy problem to remedy in the pits. Up to lap 134, few would have predicted who might be the eventual winner. The Warwick/Cheever XJR-6 traded the lead with the Italian entry a number of times, until falling fuel pressure dealt a cruel blow to the Lancia, forcing a 70-minute pit stop during which the problem could not be satisfactorily rectified.

While all this was taking place, the works Porsche of Bell and Stuck was running two to three laps behind the lead cars, unable to make better headway. After four hours and four minutes, Cheever crossed the finishing line to a glorious first ever Group C win for the Silk Cut Jaguars. Now for Le Mans.

Venue: Silverstone, UK
Round 2, 5 May 1986
Race title: Kouros 1000 Km Yves Saint Laurent

Chassis type	Chassis no.	Race no.	Drivers	Grid pos.	Finish position	Laps
XJR-6	186	52	Jean-Louis Schlesser, Gianfranco Brancatelli	5	7	204
XJR-6	286	51	Derek Warwick, Eddie Cheever	3	1	212
XJR-6	385	51T	T car used only in practice			

The strong nine-man driver line-up for round three at **Le Mans** included the four '86 regulars and five names from Jaguar's earlier races. The original intention was to run the two regular 1986 chassis, 186 and 286, with the same driver pairings as at Monza and Silverstone, and no third driver. In the end, Cheever and Warwick were joined by Jean-Louis Schlesser in the Silverstone winning car (286), collectively being the strongest team and the most likely winning combination. Brancatelli shared the re-worked chassis (385) with Win Percy and Armin Hahne for this particular

Chassis 286 in Tony Southgate's full 1986 Le Mans trim with extended tail and twin headlamps. (Ken Wells)

car's one and only race. The other '86 car was manned by Hurley Haywood, Brian Redman and Hans Heyer.

Tony Southgate's XJR-6LM specials, with their sleek extended aerodynamic tails and single-element wings, certainly looked promising. Still heady with the wonderful Silverstone victory, everyone felt Jaguar was in with a chance. Such sentiments were reinforced when two cars achieved first and second fastest times during the pre-race test session at Le Mans on 9 May. Schlesser clocked the fastest time down the Mulsanne at 221mph, while Cheever managed fastest lap overall at 3min 28.29sec.

Qualifying fifth, seventh and 14th, all three XJR-6s were amongst the first six runners during the initial three hours' racing before Hans Heyer, in 52 (186) retired with fuel problems. In the early hours of Sunday morning, a broken driveshaft ended the endeavours of Brancatelli, Hahne and Percy in Jaguar 53 (385). For Win Percy, stuck out on the circuit with no hope of getting the stricken car back to the pits, this was a bitter blow. He had expected better things on this occasion, his first time at Le Mans. The car was running fourth at the time.

The remaining Jaguar number 51 was running strongly in sixth place, the drivers fully aware that they were now the centre of attention, not only in the pits, but also to the many thousands of loyal Brits anxious to see Tom's white and mauve cats topple Porsche's supremacy. A further eight hours passed by while Warwick, Cheever and Schlesser picked their way up to second, when a right rear puncture just after the Hunaudières kink caused terminal damage to the suspension and gear box. Schlesser

The Haywood/ Redman/Heyer XJR-6 (186) turns into Mulsanne corner with two Porsches behind a sister Jaguar. (Malcolm Bryan)

would like to see it performing once again.

At this point in the Championship table, the Silk Cut team was second with 20 points to Rothmans Porsche's 35 points. Eddie Cheever and Derek Warwick shared fifth place in the Drivers' Championship alongside Al Holbert with 20 points, compared to Bell and Stuck who shared first place with 55 points.

Venue: Le Mans, France
Round 3, 31 May/1 June 1986
Race title: 54eme Edition Des 24 Heures Du Mans

Chassis type	Chassis no.	Race no.	Drivers	Grid pos.	Finish position	Laps
XJR-6 LM	186	52	Hurley Haywood, Brian Redman, Hans Heyer	7	DNF, fuel pump	53
XJR-6 LM	286	51	Eddie Cheever, Derek Warwick, Jean-Louis Schlesser	5	DNF, puncture, suspension	239
XJR-6 LM	385	53	Gianfranco Brancatelli, Win Percy, Armin Hahne	14	DNF, driveshaft	154

Race winner: Rothmans Porsche 962C, drivers Derek Bell, Hans Stuck and Al Holbert, 367 laps

Gianfranco Brancatelli, Armin Hahne and Win Percy teamed up to drive chassis 385 as car 53 at Le Mans, but a broken driveshaft put an end to their race hopes on lap 154. (Malcolm Bryan)

nursed the car back to the pits, but retirement was unavoidable.

Of the first ten finishers, only one car was not wearing a Porsche badge. Hans-Joachim Stuck, Derek Bell and Al Holbert took the flag in the number 1 Rothmans works 962, completing 367 laps in total. From the outset, Tom Walkinshaw had indicated three years would be necessary before Le Mans could be conquered by Jaguar prototypes. Nevertheless, many valuable lessons had been taken on board and there was always next year. As for the 1986 XJR-6 Le Mans specials, their like would never be seen again. Chassis 385 is now in private ownership and remains in full 1986 Le Mans trim. At the time of writing, it has not been involved in Group C revival racing. No doubt there are many who

The parkland circuit of **Norisring** in what was still in 1986 West Germany, was the setting for round four of the WSPC Championship. Considered one of the country's biggest sporting events, this one driver 180km sprint race was the natural home for abundant Porsche 962C and 956C team entrants.

Hans-Joachim Stuck started the race from pole position in the

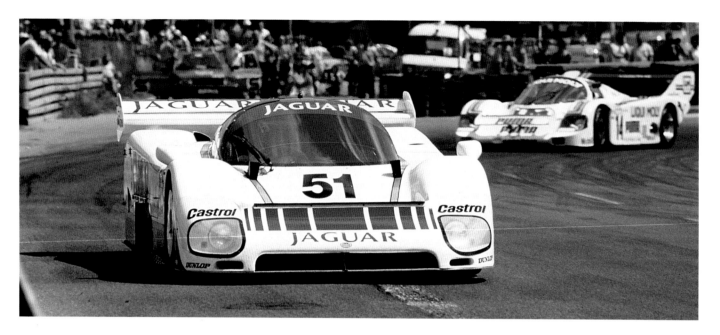

One litre of fuel remained in the tank as Eddie Cheever swept past the flag in 286 to take second place at Norisring. This venue being in Germany, the team raced unbranded. (Malcolm Bryan)

works Blaupunkt Porsche 962, but fellow countryman and local hero Klaus Ludwig in a Joest Porsche 956 took control on lap 25 for the remainder of the race. Two of the three Jaguars entered fought off one and then another challenger to stay up with the leader. With no fuel stops allowed, the main concern for many drivers was keeping a watchful eye on the gauge, easing back when the needle went into the red.

Eddie Cheever in Jaguar 51 and Derek Warwick at the wheel of 52 made a tremendous impression on the 70,000 crowd by coming home in magnificent second and third places respectively behind Klaus Ludwig and ahead of the remaining eleven Porsches. Cheever was now third in the Drivers' Championship with 35 points, while Warwick was fourth with 32.

Venue: Norisring, Germany
Round 4, 29 June 1986
Race title: 200 Meilen von Nürnberg

Chassis type	Chassis no.	Race no.	Drivers	Grid pos.	Finish position	Laps
XJR-6	186	52	Derek Warwick	6	3	79
XJR-6	286	51	Eddie Cheever	4	2	79
XJR-6	386	53	Jean-Louis Schlesser	8	17	67

Race winner: Joest Blaupunkt Porsche 956/117, driver Klaus Ludwig, 79 laps

A promising 36-car entry for round five at the **Brands Hatch** 1000km included 14 Group 1 cars and no less than 21 Group C2 cars. After their excellent showing at Norisring, the Silk Cut Jaguars were now believed to pose the biggest threat to the Championship-leading Porsches. The regular Rothmans works cars had not been included in the entry list for this particular race. Following Silk Cut Jaguar's magnificent victory at Silverstone in May, the XJR-6s were highly tipped to clinch another good win in front of a large and enthusiastic home crowd.

Derek Bell and co-driver Stuck had arranged to drive one of the Joest Porsches, on to which the Rothmans sponsorship livery

had been transferred as part of a one-off deal. The car in question was the 956B chassis, number 117, twice winner of the Le Mans 24-hour race, and the car which had taken the win ahead of Cheever and Warwick in the previous race at Norisring. After two relatively uneventful practice and qualifying days, the Jaguars took second and third places on the grid, leading to high expectations. For the race, Warwick and Schlesser transferred to chassis 186 following fuel tank problems with 386. The official time sheets still had the pair listed as having raced in this chassis as car number 53. Cheever and Brancatelli raced 286 as car 51.

The race itself was a catalogue of disasters, with collisions and consequent fires from lap one. Hardly did one pace car stint end, when further mishaps brought it out again. Warwick and Schlesser did well to finish in fourth place, well up with the victorious Porsches. The Cheever and Brancatelli Jaguar was no more than one lap down from them, finishing sixth. Still, the result was not to be considered bad at the halfway point of their first full season.

Venue: Brands Hatch, UK
Round 5, 20 July 1986
Race title: Shell Gemini 1000 Kms

Chassis type	Chassis no.	Race no.	Drivers	Grid pos.	Finish position	Laps
XJR-6	186	52	Derek Warwick, Jean-Louis Schlesser	3	4	231
XJR-6	286	51	Eddie Cheever, Gianfranco Brancatelli	2	6	230
XJR-6	386	53	Derek Warwick, Jean-Louis Schlesser	Did not race, switched to T car number 186		

Race winner: Liqui Moly Porsche 956 GTI, drivers Bob Wollek and Mauro Baldi, 236 laps

Round six, the 360km sprint at **Jerez**, saw the three Silk Cut XJR-6s as numbers two, three and four on the grid. For the race, Tom Walkinshaw enlisted two of the sport's most competitive drivers - Martin Brundle and Jan Lammers - to bolster the team's chances of taking a win. With three cars entered and the continued absence of the works and Joest Porsche teams, this 360km sprint race should have been a Jaguar walkover. Derek Warwick even went as far as saying, 'without the usual strong opposition from the Porsche teams, the race could be rather boring.' The locals must have felt similar sentiments as only about 4,500 came along to watch.

Being Spain in the first week of August, a midday start was planned to avoid rising afternoon temperatures. It was already 100° Fahrenheit, and few were keen to delay any longer than was necessary. What happened at the first corner, after the trio quickly overwhelmed the pole Brun Porsche, left everyone smarting with egg on their faces. Derek Warwick in car 52 turned across the front of Gianfranco Brancatelli in 53 and both were struck by Eddie Cheever in the third Jaguar. Warwick spun into the gravel and lost two laps digging out, then managed to rejoin the race and finished third. The two remaining cars suffered driveshaft failures which put them out on laps 12 and 40 respectively. This unfortunate mishap prevented what might have been certain victory for the Warwick/Lammers car.

Venue: Jerez, Spain
Round 6, 3 August 1986
Race title: Sprint WSE 360kms Jerez Trofeo Silk Cut

Chassis type	Chassis no.	Race no.	Drivers	Grid pos.	Finish position	Laps
XJR-6	186	53	Jean-Louis Schlesser, Gianfranco Brancatelli	2	DNF, driveshaft	12
XJR-6	286	51	Eddie Cheever, Martin Brundle	3	DNF, driveshaft	40
XJR-6	386	52	Derek Warwick, Jan Lammers	4	3	84

Race winner: Brun Porsche 962, drivers Oscar Larrauri, and Jesus Pareja, 86 laps

Heavy rain and high winds were the dominant factors which turned round seven at **Nürburgring** into a dismal calamity. The Silk Cut Jaguars had been snapping at the heels of the Championship-leading Porsches all season. Qualifying was a battle between the Rothmans and Brun Porsches and the three-car Jaguar entry. Derek Warwick crashed car 52 (386) into the barriers, leaving Eddie Cheever in 51 (286) to take position number three on the grid, while car 53 (186) was further back in ninth. Repairs to 52 in order for it to compete in the race were not possible, so only two Jaguars made the grid.

As the race started, drizzle turned into rain. The Silk Cut drivers were not altogether happy to run three men to a car as a result of losing one car, but in the end Brancatelli and Heyer stood

Tom Walkinshaw was always on hand, ready to pitch in if needed. Here he keeps watch as the Warwick/Schlesser chassis 386 makes a pit stop at Brands Hatch, where on this occasion the cars raced branded. (Malcolm Bryan)

The three Jaguars seconds before calamity at Jerez. Car 52 (386) made it to the finish in third place while the other two retired with broken driveshafts. (Malcolm Bryan)

down after the Italian caught 'flu. On lap four Cheever experienced temporary engine failure, dropping back 13 places before getting started again, but three laps later transmission problems forced retirement. Conditions grew worse and a number of top runners smashed into each other as they raced up to the back of the queue behind the pace car, unaware that it had been brought out. The ensuing chaos was every racing driver's nightmare.

The remainder of the race, still in appalling conditions, saw the track littered with crashed cars, while red flags were waved and teams bickered with marshals. Following a three-hour stoppage the factory Porsches withdrew, declaring conditions too dangerous to continue. Warwick, now with Lammers running the one remaining Jaguar, kept going until a burst oil pipe ended what might have been a win to make up for the Jerez debacle.

Venue: Nürburgring, Germany
Round 7, 24 August 1986
Race title: ADAC-Kouros 1000km

Chassis type	Chassis no.	Race no.	Drivers	Grid pos.	Finish position	Laps
XJR-6	186	53	Derek Warwick, Jan Lammers, Gianfranco Brancatelli	9	DNF, engine	92
XJR-6	286	51	Eddie Cheever, Jean-Louis Schlesser, Hans Heyer	3	DNF, driveshaft	6
XJR-6	386	52	Derek Warwick, Jan Lammers		Crashed during qualifying, did not race. Switched to 186 T car.	

Race winner: Sauber Mercedes C8, drivers Mike Thackwell and Henri Pescarolo, 121 laps

Podium places might not have been as numerous as all that so far in the 1986 WSPC season, but round eight at the beautiful **Spa-Francorchamps** circuit could still put Derek Warwick ahead in the Drivers' Championship. All he had to do was to win, and hope that the Championship leaders Bell and Stuck could not make it to the flag. It didn't quite finish that way, but a brilliant hard-fought second place put him well into the running with 69 points against Bell's and Stuck's 82.

To many, practice and qualifying were expected to be as exciting as the race itself, especially in the knowledge that some drivers could do much better in wet weather than others. Most eyes were on the year-long duel between the Silk Cut Jaguars and the Porsches of the works and Brun teams. For this race, a works Sauber Mercedes was also deemed to be in with a chance, particularly if it rained on race day. The Jaguars were expected to perform well on a dry circuit, which at Spa would suit the powerful V12s.

Fears grew in the pre-race days that too much heavy rain might cause a repeat of the Nürburgring washout. This did not happen, and both Jaguars ran well. The Cheever/Schlesser car lost time because of punctures but, like the Warwick/Lammers car, harried the Porsches to the bitter end. The last half hour or so saw Cheever as the fastest man on the circuit. All three top finishers crossed the line coughing and spluttering on their last drops of fuel. How much closer could anyone have forecast the

race would end? The two Jaguars and the lone Sauber Mercedes were the only non-Porsches in the top ten, and the race has been described as the best in the five-year history of Group C racing.

Venue: Spa-Francorchamps, Belgium
Round 8, 14 September 1986
Race title: 1000km Spa Kouros Yves Saint Laurent

Chassis type	Chassis no.	Race no.	Drivers	Grid pos.	Finish position	Laps
XJR-6	186	51T	T car used in practice by all drivers			
XJR-6	286	51	Eddie Cheever, Jean Louis-Schlesser	4	5	143
XJR-6	386	52	Derek Warwick, Jan Lammers	5	2	145

Race winner: Brun Porsche 962, drivers Thierry Boutsen and Frank Jelinski, 145 laps

Although the race was not part of the World Championship, the lone Jaguar XJR-6 entry in the final round of the German Supercup Championship at **Norisring**, piloted by Eddie Cheever, gave Jaguar its second Group C win. Pitted against the cream of German drivers on home ground, car 51 (186) passed the chequered flag less than one second ahead of Hans Stuck's Rothmans Porsche 962C, making up for the earlier season's defeat at the same circuit.

As was normal in the short German Supercup races, much of the field was made up of home teams running Porsche 962s and 956s. Everything about the event seemed to be Porsche-orientated, programmes and posters all displaying them as if it were a one-make race. That it attracted so much popularity with the locals was down to extensive TV coverage, not only for the race itself but also for the two seven-lap qualifying heats on the Saturday.

After a one-minute time penalty was awarded against the original pole man Hans Stuck during Saturday, Cheever inherited pole position, sitting alongside Oscar Larrauri in one of the Brun Porsches. Larrauri led to the first corner, but was soon overtaken by Cheever and two other Porsches. Stuck's Blaupunkt Porsche eventually took the lead, chased hard by the Jaguar. For 20 laps Cheever kept up the pressure all the way to the last corner, when Stuck's engine faltered just enough to allow the determined American to dash by and make his long-awaited run to the flag.

Venue: Norisring, Germany
Round n/a, 21 September 1986
Race title: XIII Int ADAC Bilstein-Super-Sprint (Non-Championship Race)

Chassis type	Chassis no.	Race no.	Drivers	Grid pos.	Finish position	Laps
XJR-6	186	51	Eddie Cheever	3	1	39

The 1986 WSPC final race, round nine at **Fuji** in Japan, ended in drama when Derek Warwick was proclaimed Drivers' Champion after erroneously being placed second in front of the Frank Jelinski/Stanley Dickens Brun Porsche 956C. The race organisers checked again, realised their mistake, and dropped the Jaguar down to third with Warwick at 81 points, just one point behind

rightful champion Derek Bell. Hans Stuck also scored 82, but some time after the race Bell was declared sole champion after taking into account early race results. Oddly enough Rothmans did not take the Team Championship or second place, these going to Brun Motorsport and Joest Racing, both Porsche teams. Rothmans did in fact share third place with the Silk Cut Jaguar team. Had Warwick been rightful second place finisher the Drivers' and Team Championships would have been Jaguar's.

In the previous year the Japanese race had been a washout for the European teams, so when it rained on Wednesday fears grew that the same might happen again. Wet-weather tyres were not needed though, as the weather remained dry for the rest of the week. Qualifying the normally-aspirated Jaguars on this circuit was fraught with difficulties, made worse for Warwick by traffic impeding him on what he felt was going to be his best run. Cheever could only manage 13th on the grid, while Warwick, desperate to do well, started even further back in 17th place after colliding with Kris Nissen's Porsche 956.

Both Jaguars ran a cautious first stint, gradually easing up the field after the first round of pit stops. Warwick's main championship rivals Bell and Stuck seemed on course to take the win, but a broken driveshaft on lap 106 put an end to their chances. Some time later, Jaguar 52 of Lammers, Brancatelli and

Schlesser was blighted by gearbox problems. Lammers managed to get it back to the pits, but the time lost relegated the car back to a 17th-place finish. The Warwick/Cheever Jaguar 51 also had problems but these were overcome, allowing Warwick to get close up behind the lead Porsche. Unfortunately, a loose wire in the injection system caused serious misfiring, forcing a brief pit stop to have it corrected and dropping the Jaguar back into third place. During the final laps the timekeepers had him second, causing much confusion in the pits, where the computer was out of action.

Venue: Fuji, Japan
Round 9, 5 October 1986
Race title: Fuji Speed Race 1000kms

Chassis type	Chassis no.	Race no.	Drivers	Grid pos.	Finish position	Laps
XJR-6	286	51	Eddie Cheever, Derek Warwick	13	3	225
XJR-6	386	52	Jan Lammers, Gianfranco Brancatelli, Jean-Louis Schlesser	17	17	211

Race winner: Rothmans Porsche 956, drivers Paulo Barilla and Piercarlo Ghinzani, 226 laps

To sum up the season, Jaguar clearly demonstrated that they had come to stay, while the Porsches' supremacy had suffered a few setbacks. Would Jaguar let them they stay at the top in 1987?

A fabulous line-up of Group C cars in the 1986 final race at Fuji. The two Jaguars entered started well back but Cheever and Warwick in car 51 (286) impressed all by coming home third. (Malcolm Bryan)

Chapter 5

1987 World Sportscar Prototype Championship

The year it all came together (almost)

With the new XJ40, sold under the familar 'XJ6' label, hailed a success in both home and export markets, Jaguar was continuing to make good progress. There was a substantial investment programme in place, and more personnel were being recruited for the Browns Lane plant in Coventry. Production was on the increase and the target for 1987 was 48,000 cars, more than three times the total produced five years previously.

Sportscar racing was gaining in public awareness thanks in no small measure to the presence of Jaguar, but other than at Le Mans that awareness was not yet translating into crowds of spectators. Another problem was that of the 10 races in the Championship, nine took place in Europe. The fact that races planned for Japan and Australia were cancelled did nothing to give credibility to a 'world' Championship. The situation was not improved by Porsche's decision half way through the year to withdraw from the Championship with effect from the beginning of 1988. Although Porsche had a number of customer teams that would continue to campaign the 962, the pull-out, after years in which it had dominated over token opposition, did not reflect well on the Porsche company. Some saw it as a capitulation in the face of the TWR Jaguar Silk Cut operation.

The early months of 1987 were full of announcements from Jaguar and the Silk Cut team, foremost of which was the granting of a prestigious design award for Tony Southgate's XJR-6. The

Podium places were plentiful in 1987 for the four regular drivers, seen here at the Jarama season opener. Jan Lammers and John Watson shared top place, with Raul Boesel and Eddie Cheever third. (Malcolm Bryan)

Design Council recognised the car's combination of advanced features and materials with state-of-the-art production techniques. Throughout the season, stickers proudly proclaiming this very special achievement would adorn the engine covers wherever the XJR-6's successors, the upgraded XJR-8s, took to the track.

Two new faces appeared in the regular driver line-up. Eddie Cheever was joined by a brilliant ex-Formula 1 and Indy Car driver, Raul Boesel from Brazil. They would man car 4, chassis 287. Jan Lammers was now to be partnered by British Formula 1 ace John Watson racing in car 5, chassis 187. The former XJR-6 chassis 386 became the spare car, still wearing much of its telltale XJR-6 panelwork but re-painted in 1987 livery. Eventually its place would be taken by the last XJR-8 chassis 387.

As in the previous year, more races (13 in total) were listed in the pre-season calendar, but the final tally would be reduced to 10. The Le Mans 24-hour race would be included in the Championship.

Round one at **Jarama** was the first of two successive races in Spain in which the much-improved Jaguar prototypes made their mark straight away. The factory Rothmans Porsches, together with those of the Brun and Joest teams, had been just that much ahead of the Silk Cut XJR-6s during most races in 1986, denying Jaguar the Championship, but now things seemed destined to improve.

Qualifying saw Jaguar number 4 (287) on pole position with the number 5 (187) car alongside, making this the first all-Jaguar front row so far. The cars were about to put on an impressive display in front of a huge crowd who had come to see Spanish drivers including Jesus Pareja swelling the ranks of Porsche drivers who were bidding to outrun the Jaguars.

Both Silk Cut cars got away to a clean start, leaving Hans Stuck on the grid struggling to coax life into his reluctant Porsche. By the time his Rothmans 962 pulled away, the field had already completed the first lap. Cheever and Lammers kept the Jaguars out front throughout the first 40 laps or so, with Stuck, now having made up the deficit, trailing behind. A small oil leak prompted Cheever to pit on lap 45 for a top-up and driver changeover. Lammers handed over to John Watson 10 laps later, and now it was number 5 Jaguar leading the pack.

The rest of the race saw some determined dicing between John Watson, Derek Bell and Raul Boesel. The brilliant win of Jaguar number 5 was no real surprise for Lammers, who felt it

was firmly in the bag from lap one. Less than two seconds separated the Jaguar from the Rothmans Porsche. With one exception, Bell and Stuck would never come home this close behind the Silk Cut Jaguars during the rest of the 1987 season.

Venue: Jarama, Spain
Round 1, 22 March 1987
Race title: 360 Km Del Jarama De Sport-Prototipos

Chassis type	Chassis no.	Race no.	Drivers	Grid pos.	Finish position	Laps
XJR-8	187	5	John Watson, Jan Lammers	2	1	109
XJR-8	287	4	Eddie Cheever, Raul Boesel	1	3	109
XJR-8	386	4T	T car			

Still in Spain, round two at **Jerez** was to be another of many Jaguar versus Porsche contests in which the Silk Cut drivers came away heading for Championship honours. The Bell/Stuck Rothmans Porsche captured pole position with a lap time of 1min 29.19sec, only 0.75sec quicker than Jan Lammers in Jaguar

number 5, which stood alongside in second place on the grid. A broken gearbox casing in this car, discovered early on race day, cast doubts on whether it would start the race, but repairs were carried out just in time.

Tom Walkinshaw had voiced concerns about this supposedly 1000km race being flagged after six hours. All teams were allocated fuel for the full distance but, in the certainty it would run considerably less, the turbo cars knew they had a huge advantage, being able to turn up the boost at will. As it turned out, the Jaguar team's fears were unfounded.

The initial laps were as predicted, a Rothmans/Silk Cut group travelling as one until lap 17, when a wheel bearing failed on Lammers's number 5 Jaguar and it lost a wheel. Lammers three-wheeled to the pits, losing four laps while replacement parts were fitted. Later, with Watson at the wheel, a driveshaft broke on lap 66. This time there was no getting back to the pits.

Cheever and Boesel in Jaguar number 4 were to spend some time behind the lead Rothmans Porsches, eventually taking the

Re-worked XJR-6 chassis 386 acted as T car in the first four 1987 races. Although clad in 1987 livery it retained full 1986 bodywork.
(Malcolm Bryan)

In round three at **Monza** Jaguar maintained its winning streak, but some measure of Porsche's opposition was indicated by the fact that behind the Lammers/Watson Jaguar the next five places fell to the 962C turbos. Stuck and Bell in the Rothmans Porsche were now seemingly established as the best of the rest. Once again, Derek Bell earned pole position for Rothmans Porsche number 17 with a lap time of 1min 32.17sec. In terms of average speed this was 7mph faster than Jaguar number 5 of Lammers and Watson back in fourth place.

Bell's team-mate Hans Stuck nearly lost it at the start, unable to surge forward quickly enough to beat the pack to the first turn. Raul Boesel was amongst those putting on the most pressure, breathing right down the German's neck, and it was not long before for the Brazilian gained the lead. An over-eager Lammers tried to move up to second place on lap six but luck turned against him, and his Jaguar went into a spin which lost him several places. In a race where the Porsches suffered one mishap after another, the two Jaguars took control during the latter half. Lammers pulled into the pits to change tyres when heavy rain descended on the closing stages of the race. Regarded as the master of wet-weather racing, he took a comfortable win. Boesel in number 4 risked another lap on slicks but paid the price by spinning off the track and out of the race.

*Both Jaguars took spins at Monza, Boesel in Number 4 (287) being left stranded in the sandtrap. Bell and Stuck's second place in the number 17 Rothmans Porsche gave them a brief lead in the Driver's Championship ahead of Lammers and Watson.
(Malcolm Bryan)*

lead, albeit very briefly, when Derek Bell's boost control sensor played up. From then on, one by one, the lead cars suffered an assortment of mishaps and the number 4 Jaguar finished first, after improvised repairs had been carried out to keep its nose section in place.

Venue: Jerez, Spain
Round 2, 29 March 1987
Race title: 1000 Km De Jerez

Chassis type	Chassis no.	Race no.	Drivers	Grid pos.	Finish position	Laps
XJR-8	187	5	John Watson, Jan Lammers	2	DNF, driveshaft	65
XJR-8	287	4	Eddie Cheever, Raul Boesel	4	1	211
XJR-8	386	4T	T car			

Venue: Monza, Italy
Round 3, 12 April 1987
Race title: 23rd 1000km Di Monza 21st Trofeo Filippo Caracciola

Chassis type	Chassis no.	Race no.	Drivers	Grid pos.	Finish position	Laps
XJR-8	187	5	John Watson, Jan Lammers	4	1	173
XJR-8	287	4	Raul Boesel, John Nielsen	5	DNF, spin	167
XJR-8	386	4T	T car			

*The new Thackwell/Pescarolo Sauber Mercedes, on its debut at Silverstone, started second on the grid behind poleman Hans Stuck's Autoglass-sponsored Porsche 962 but soon took the lead. Here Eddie Cheever chases both en route to a second consecutive victory at Jaguar's declared home circuit.
(Malcolm Bryan)*

Silverstone, always regarded as Jaguar's home circuit, was the venue for round four. In addition to the two regular sprint cars, a third former 1986 XJR-6 upgraded to XJR-8LM specification was also entered. Manned by two future Le Mans winners, Martin Brundle and John Nielsen, and running as car number 6 (chassis 186), it was not expected to keep pace with the sprint cars. However, it managed 10th on the grid and put on a good show while driven by Nielsen, before engine damage finished what was basically a Le Mans test session. One item of interest is that on the official timesheets the number 6 Le Mans test Jaguar was listed as an XJR-9. The two regular cars dominated the race and finished one-two with only six seconds between them.

Practice and qualifying were dominated by the number 17 Porsche works car of Hans Stuck/Derek Bell and its number 18 sister car driven by Jochen Mass/Bob Wollek. Splitting them up at the front of the grid was the dark blue liveried 5-litre turbocharged Sauber Mercedes C9-01. Driven by Mike Thackwell and Henri Pescarolo on its debut outing, it raised many eyebrows by springing into the lead as the race started. Thackwell's moment of glory lasted 10 laps before Cheever got the better of him in Jaguar number 4. The Mercedes gradually slipped back down the field and the race settled into the usual Jaguar-Porsche contest.

Eddie Cheever completed a fastest lap time of 1min 18.65sec during the race, setting a new record. In this 210-lap race, lasting five hours and three minutes, the six Jaguar drivers between them

led an astonishing 180 laps in total. John Watson and Jan Lammers finished top of the Drivers' Championship table with 55 points each, whilst Silk Cut Jaguar were well ahead in the Team Championship with 80 points, against the works Porsches' 54 points.

Venue: Silverstone, UK
Round 4, 10 May 1987
Race title: Autoglass 1000kms

Chassis type	Chassis no.	Race no.	Drivers	Grid pos.	Finish position	Laps
XJR-8	186	6	Martin Brundle, John Nielsen	10	DNF, valve spring	165
XJR-8	187	5	John Watson, Jan Lammers	5	2	210
XJR-8	287	4	Eddie Cheever, Raul Boesel	4	1	210
XJR-8	386	4T	T car			

Round five at **Le Mans** was to be the big test, run in front of an estimated 40,000-strong army of British fans who travelled to see what they referred to as the 'British race held in France'. Some measure of who might be the most likely Le Mans winner could be gauged by observing the official programme front cover. For 1987, Jaguar XJR-8 chassis 187 was featured, and after four Championship wins in a row this choice was not surprising. British fans were looking forward to a win of one kind or another – if not Jaguar, then Englishman Derek Bell in the Rothmans Porsche.

Silk Cut Jaguar's three-car entry for Silverstone included the ex-XJR-6 chassis 186, upgraded to XJR-8LM specification, in what was basically a Le Mans test session. Here it runs alongside the Lammers/Watson XJR-8 (187) before retiring on lap 165 with a broken valve spring. (Malcolm Bryan)

One of the 1985 XJR-6s (285?) during an early test day at Le Mans, now seen in the full 1987 livery. The old pits look rather primitive without masses of people milling around as they do on race day. (Jaguar)

Tom Walkinshaw with the driver line-up at Le Mans. After the team's brilliant start to the season, a good result seemed almost inevitable. They stand behind chassis 186, still racing as car number 6. (JDHT)

There is a tradition at Le Mans that the pole car never wins, but it was hardly likely that the Silk Cut drivers allowed the Rothmans Porsches to claim the grid front row as a safeguard against maintaining it. As it turned out, Jochen Mass, Bob Wollek and Vern Schuppan in the number 18 works Porsche started from

pole position, only to suffer engine problems which put them out after a mere 16 laps. The Silk Cut team were more than well satisfied with their third, fourth and fifth grid places, and apart from the two Sauber Mercedes in seventh and eighth positions they were the only non-Porsche 962s in the first twelve qualifiers.

Tom Walkinshaw's prediction that three years would be required before there was any chance of Jaguar winning Le Mans must have echoed through the minds of everyone present as car number 5 (286) exited the race in spectacular fashion. In the early hours of the morning with Win Percy in the driving seat, a left side rear tyre blow-out, just past the Mulsanne kink, sent the car soaring upwards and then crashing back down onto the track, where it skidded upside down and slid to a halt in an eerie silence. Percy's helmet was holed where his head had scraped along the road surface; another few yards and his skull might have suffered the same fate. Extracting himself from the shattered wreck, he was amazed and delighted to find no broken bones - in fact he was remarkably unscathed. Like some great hero returning from outer space, he was urged by Tom Walkinshaw to stand on the pit wall opposite the Jaguar grandstand to prove to the anxious fans that he really was unhurt. They responded with an overwhelming

The third 1987 XJR-8LM, chassis 387, on its debut outing at Le Mans, was the only Jaguar finisher there, coming home in fifth place. (Malcolm Bryan)

As evening wears on at Le Mans, Jaguar number 5 (286) leaves the pits. A few hours later it would race no more. (Malcolm Bryan)

A further identification aid for timekeepers as the cars streaked by took the form of coloured strips on the windscreens to identify particular drivers, in this case 1987 Championship winner Raul Boesel. (Malcolm Bryan)

bout of clapping and cheering such as is rarely seen or heard in the middle of events like this.

After 15 hours 47 minutes John Nielsen brought Jaguar number 6 into the pits with terminal engine damage. Now all hopes rested with the last 1987 chassis (387), driven by Cheever, Boesel and Lammers. The last hours were not without drama when this car too became affected by a series of problems, the most serious requiring a full gearbox strip and rebuild. The pit crew performed miracles, keeping the car going until it finished in fifth place and thus earning a special trophy for team effort. Certainly a win would have been to everyone's satisfaction but the general feeling, amongst TWR personnel and fans alike, was that they were on the right track.

Derek Bell's superb win earned much praise from the Jaguar fans despite their disappointment. All the pre-race banter meted out to him 24 hours earlier changed as the finish approached to chants of 'We want Tom', and 'Egan, Egan, Egan'. Nothing could alter the fact that it was a great day for Britain – a fifth win by an Englishman in the greatest race of all was a truly remarkable achievement.

Venue: Le Mans, France
Round 5, 13-14 June 1987
Race title: 55eme Edition Des 24 Heures Du Mans

Chassis type	Chassis no.	Race no.	Drivers	Grid pos.	Finish position	Laps
XJR-8 LM	387	4	Raul Boesel, Eddie Cheever, Jan Lammers	3	5	325
XJR-8 LM	186	6	Martin Brundle, John Nielsen, Armin Hahne	4	DNF, engine	231
XJR-8 LM	286	5	Jan Lammers, John Watson, Win Percy	5	DNF, accident	158

Race winner: Rothmans Porsche 962, drivers Derek Bell, Hans Stuck and Al Holbert, 354 laps

For round six at **Norisring** one might have been forgiven for thinking the tide was turning against Jaguar. The Rothmans works Porsches were now out of Championship racing for the rest of the season but there would be no Jaguar walkover.

Silk Cut Jaguar's chief rivals, Hans Stuck and Derek Bell, were now entered in the colourful yellow and red Dunlop Shell Porsche 962, and hoped to repeat their Le Mans success. Qualifying on pole position on the short twisty street circuit was easier for a turbo car than for the high-downforce normally-aspirated Jaguars. The V12 cars had been tipped as most likely winners, but Stuck and Bell must have thought otherwise.

Lack of permanent pit facilities on this circuit called for two 77-lap races, separated by a 45-minute break. The first race soon had Mike Thackwell in the Sauber Mercedes leading, seemingly untouchable until lap 40 when he ground to a halt, not through mechanical problems but through severe driver fatigue. Jan Lammers gained a brief two-lap lead before loss of drive ended the number 5 Jaguar's race on lap 42, and John Watson was therefore denied any involvement.

Eddie Cheever in number 4 became delayed in the first race due to fuel pressure problems, finishing the heat in 13th place.

Raul Boesel took the flag in the second heat, earning the car fourth place overall. Had not the second place Jelinski/Ludwig Joest Blaupunkt Porsche 962 been disqualified for having an oversized fuel tank, the pair would have been fifth. Hans Stuck had come second in heat one, but in heat two his Shell Porsche retired with engine failure on lap 130.

Derek Bell and Hans Stuck still led the Drivers' Championship by 4 points, with Cheever and Boesel joint third. Silk Cut Jaguar remained the clear leader in the Teams' Championship, 22 points ahead of the Porsche works team, which was now at a standstill with 74 points.

Venue: Norisring, Germany
Round 6, 28 June 1987
Race title: 200 Meilen von Nürnberg

Chassis type	Chassis no.	Race no.	Drivers	Grid pos.	Finish position	Laps
XJR-8	187	5	John Watson, Jan Lammers	7	DNF, transmission	42
XJR-8	287	4	Eddie Cheever, Raul Boesel	4	4	147

Race winner: Liqui Moly Porsche 962, drivers Mauro Baldi and Jonathan Palmer, 154 laps

Raul Boesel was chosen to drive the lone XJR-8 (387) Jaguar in the non-Championship Wurth Supercup race at **Hockenheim** in July. Eddie Cheever had won the previously entered Supercup race in 1986 but there would be no repeat performance this time. Of the first 10 finishers, nine were Porsche 962Cs. The only non-Porsche was the gallant Boesel in third place.

Venue: Hockenheim, Germany
Round n/a, 5 July 1987
Race title: Wurth Supercup '87 (Non Championship)

Chassis type	Chassis no.	Race no.	Drivers	Grid pos.	Finish position	Laps
XJR-8	387	4	Raul Boesel	7	3	27

Race Winner: Porsche AG Porsche 962C, driver Hans-Joachim Stuck, 27 laps

Back on home ground for round seven at **Brands Hatch**, the Silk Cut Jaguars were on winning form again. Jan Lammers thrilled the crowds with the circuit's fastest-ever Group C qualifying lap. Both Silk Cut Jaguars occupied the front row of the grid, determined that this time they would win after disappointing results at this circuit in the two previous years. Bell and Stuck, now racing in the Joest Porsche, seemed just as determined to stop the Jaguars.

The race was notable for a record C2 entry list but only eight C1 cars attended, one of which never made it to the start. The Del Bello/Hecher ex-works 5-litre turbo Mercedes crashed during qualifying, so the 1978 Le Mans winner Jean Pierre Jaussaud was denied a race. Cheever was absent, running in the German Grand Prix, and in the Brands Hatch race Boesel was partnered by John Nielsen. After 1000 kilometres and five and a half hours of battling with one Porsche after another, Jaguar number 4 took the chequered flag, 73 seconds ahead of the Liqui Moly Porsche of Mauro Baldi and Johnny Dumfries. John Nielsen remains very

Raul Boesel and John Nielsen's win at Brands Hatch was cause for great satisfaction for Tom Walkinshaw and Jaguar PR man Ian Norris. Perhaps a shower and a well-earned rest were all that filled the minds of the drivers. (Malcolm Bryan)

proud of the fact that this was the first win by a Dane in an international Championship motor race.

At one point it seemed Boesel might not make it to the finish after he attempted to overtake Baldi at the Paddock Bend. The Jaguar made contact with the Porsche before spinning into the barriers, damaging the rear end. The Brazilian lost time in the pits while a new tail was fitted. Watson and Lammers in Jaguar number 5 lost nine laps while a faulty rear wheel bearing was replaced. They still managed third place and increased Jaguar's Team Championship lead over the second-placed Porsche team by 42 points.

Venue: Brands Hatch, UK
Round 7, 26 July 1987
Race title: Shell Gemini 1000 Km

Chassis type	Chassis no.	Race no.	Drivers	Grid pos.	Finish position	Laps
XJR-8	187	5	John Watson, Jan Lammers	1	3	229
XJR-8	287	4	Raul Boesel, John Nielsen	2	1	238
XJR-8	387	4T	T car			

Cheever and Boesel's victory in round eight at **Nürburgring** clinched the team title for Jaguar but still left the Drivers' Championship in the balance. Eddie Cheever was back in harness, ready to help Raul Boesel to increase his Drivers' Championship lead and hoping to put it beyond the reach of Derek Bell and Hans Stuck in joint second place.

The Mercedes entry was regarded as a formidable - even the most formidable - challenger to the Silk Cut team. With no works Porsche team participating, the most prominent 962 contender, the BLR/Liqui Moly Porsche of Mauro Baldi and Jonathan Palmer, was fastest of the 11 entered, capturing pole position ahead of the Cheever/Boesel Jaguar number 4 in second place. The Sauber Mercedes C9 was third, and then came the Watson/Lammers Jaguar.

In one of the hardest fought races of the season, the Jaguars duelled for the lead in the early stages with the Mercedes C9 of Thackwell, Dumfries and Pescarolo, along with the usual Porsche contingent. Jan Lammers pushed harder than ever before in XJR-

8 number 5 but was eliminated by a broken valve after only 28 laps, which left the Cheever/Boesel Jaguar to maintain the challenge. Under the strain, the Mercedes retired with a broken gearbox, and 22 laps later the Ludwig/Wollek Joest Porsche suffered similar problems. Bell and Stuck in the remaining Brun Porsche came second, maintaining the threat to Raul Boesel's lead in the Drivers' Championship.

Venue: Nürburgring, Germany
Round 8, 30 August 1987
Race title: ADAC-1000km

Chassis type	Chassis no.	Race no.	Drivers	Grid pos.	Finish position	Laps
XJR-8	187	5	John Watson, Jan Lammers	4	DNF, engine	28
XJR-8	287	4	Eddie Cheever, Raul Boesel	2	1	221
XJR-8	387	4T	T car			

Three Silk Cut Jaguar XJR-8s were in the line-up for the penultimate round nine at **Spa-Francorchamps**. Within the rules, Raul Boesel had been nominated as third driver in all three Jaguars in order to guarantee him top points in the Drivers' Championship, regardless of which car might take first place.

In spite of only winning one race against Jaguar's six so far this season, Derek Bell and Hans Stuck were still contenders if blessed with good fortune. Boesel would have to lose though, but Tom Walkinshaw's strategy had already stacked the odds in his favour. Jaguar number 6, Boesel's ultimate winning car, looked set not to take part in the race after Brundle suffered a heavy crash in it on Friday, and Johnny Dumfries followed suit on Saturday. That it took the flag on Sunday was all down to a fantastic repair job by the mechanics, who made the car whole again for the start.

Qualifying saw the dark blue Sauber Mercedes C9 rattle the opposition by capturing pole position, this time driven by two former Jaguar stalwarts, Jean-Louis Schlesser and Mike Thackwell. Second place went to another of the season's top challengers, the Baldi/Palmer Liqui Moly Porsche. Then came two Jaguars and a Brun Porsche, with Jaguar number 6 the last of the Silk Cut cars on the sixth spot. This car was in the care of Tony Dowe and Ian Reed, brought over from Valparaiso on a getting-to-know-you exercise before launching the 1988 IMSA challenge for TWR Jaguar.

Jaguar number 6 took an emphatic win after Boesel joined Brundle and Dumfries halfway through the race when theirs was the best-placed team car in the race. Rain in the later stages posed a threat but all TWR cars performed well. The Lammers/Watson number 5 Jaguar finished one lap behind number 6 and many believed it could have been a Jaguar one-two-three if the race had gone on for a further two or three laps. Boesel's regular car 4 managed fourth place behind the Mass/Larrauri Brun Porsche. Of the top six finishers, three were Jaguars and three Porsche 962s. Boesel was now World Championship driver, denying Bell a third consecutive title.

Venue: Spa-Francorchamps, Belgium
Round 9, 13 September 1987
Race title: 1000 Km De Spa Kouros

Chassis type	Chassis no.	Race no.	Drivers	Grid pos.	Finish position	Laps
XJR-8	187	5	John Watson, Jan Lammers	3	2	141
XJR-8	287	4	Eddie Cheever, John Nielsen	4	4	140
XJR-8	387	6	Raul Boesel, Martin Brundle, Johnny Dumfries	6	1	142

Round ten at **Fuji** in Japan was a Silk Cut one-two in the face of tough opposition from 12 Porsches, three Nissans and a couple of Toyotas. Only the Jaguars had normally-aspirated engines in this C1 grouping. With its out-of-date facilities and cramped pits Fuji was not a circuit which drivers looked forward to racing on. All concerned wondered what they were doing there. This far-away venue is notoriously wet on occasions and in such conditions anything could and usually did happen to upset the apple cart. Having greatly assisted Raul Boesel to win the 1987 Drivers' Championship, Eddie Cheever was busy in Spain, and his place in the Fuji race was taken by Johnny Dumfries.

Qualifying commenced in wet weather, resulting in mixed fortunes for the European entries. The final session, in drier conditions, still resulted in the top three places being taken by Japanese cars. Lammers snatched pole position provisionally in the earlier session with a number of good times, but eventually finished up starting from fifth spot. Not that this bothered him, as he leapt into the lead shortly after the start and held it for a few laps. During the first hour the lead changed six times between Jaguar, Nissan and Toyota.

A little later, the two Jaguars were led by the Minolta Toyota for a full two hours before electrical problems put it out of the race for good. Three pace-car intervals then worked in Jaguar's favour, allowing them to gain a lead which they maintained all the way to the flag as one by one the strongest contenders dropped out. The number 4 Jaguar's second place pushed Boesel's final Championship score up to 127, while Watson and Lammers shared second place with 102 each. As one of the regular Silk Cut drivers, Eddie Cheever with 100 points made it a top four score for Jaguar drivers. He beat Bell and Stuck on 99 each by just one point.

Venue: Fuji, Japan
Round 10, 27 September 1987
Race title: WSPC In Japan, Fuji 1000 Km

Chassis type	Chassis no.	Race no.	Drivers	Grid pos.	Finish position	Laps
XJR-8	187	5	John Watson, Jan Lammers	5	1	224
XJR-8	287	4	Raul Boesel, Johnny Dumfries	10	2	224

After Fuji the Championship was due to compete an 11th round at Sendai, but following an inspection by FISA officials the circuit was deemed to lack adequate safety standards and the race was abandoned. Having taken eight wins in 10 races the Silk Cut team returned to the UK, fully aware that they had set a new benchmark for other teams to aspire to.

Jan Lammers in the number 5 XJR-8 (187) went into an early lead at Fuji, soon losing it to a Toyota, but the race ended well for Jaguar with a hard-earned 1-2. (Malcolm Bryan)

Chapter 6

1988 World Sportscar Prototype Championship

Le Mans in the bag at last

As 1988 opened, Jaguar was coming to terms with the stockmarket crash in its biggest market, the USA. There were fears that sales of luxury cars would collapse, but the XJ6 saloons continued to sell well, although the dollar's loss of strength against the pound cut into Jaguar's profits. There were also problems connected with the new car. John Egan said that, with the benefit of hindsight, he would never allow the company to introduce another new model that combined a new engine design with an all-new body. This had been the case with the XJ40, and the warranty costs of the car were weighing heavily on the company's balance sheet.

Profitability was helped, however, by the introduction of the first true Convertible version of the XJ-S. This replaced the targa-topped Cabriolet version, introduced in 1984 to provide production experience with the new AJ6 engine that was to power the XJ40. The smooth and elegant XJ-S Convertible was a natural for Jaguar dealers in the wealthy and sun-drenched states of California, Florida, Texas and Arizona, and on France's Côte d'Azur. Building on the racing link between their two companies, Jaguar and TWR announced the creation of a joint venture, JaguarSport, which would produce high-performance versions of Jaguar road cars in limited numbers.

Jaguar dominated the Birmingham Motor Show in October with a dazzling new concept car, the XJ220. A true supercar, it used the V12 engine as the keystone of an exciting engineering exercise, and it was clothed in styling that encapsulated every aspect of Jaguar's design heritage. The company was unsure about putting it into production, but customers who turned up on the show stand waving blank cheques made a limited edition look like a tempting proposition.

On the racing front, things looked very bright. The Team and individual Drivers' Championships had put Jaguar at the forefront of the sports racing hierarchy, and the success of TWR persuaded Jaguar that its racing activities should be extended to cover the US as well. In the World Championship, the highly professional Silk Cut Jaguar Team was now the one to beat, and although the Porsche factory was no longer competing, customer teams such as Joest and Brun provided tough opposition. However, the strongest challenge came from the Swiss-based Sauber team, which was receiving increasing support from the Mercedes factory. For TWR, one target was paramount. When Tom Walkinshaw had made his proposal to Jaguar for a racing team, he had stipulated that the target was to win Le Mans within three years. 1988 was the third year...

Team manager Roger Silman and designer Tony Southgate stand between the new Silk Cut Jaguar XJR-9 chassis 588 (car number 1) and 488 (number 2), with a full complement of drivers, engineers and pit crew at Jerez at the commencement of the 1988 WSPC season. (Malcolm Bryan)

Now the defending World Championship team, Silk Cut Jaguar embarked on the busiest year so far. Raul Boesel was absent from the regular WSPC driver line up, having already made his mark with Nielsen, Lammers and Brundle in the Daytona opening round of the IMSA Camel GT Championship, taking Jaguar's first win in Castrol colours. There would be much to-ing and fro-ing for some Silk Cut and Castrol team drivers during the next year or so. TWR's Valparaiso workshops would operate largely as a separate entity much of the time, exchanging drivers when required, and dispatching cars complete with crew members to increase the odds for Jaguar at Le Mans.

In the WSPC series, Porsche-supported privateers and the Sauber Mercedes cars would make certain that Jaguar could not afford to rest on its laurels. While the upgraded XJR-9 was considered to be even better than last year's XJR-8, there would be no walkovers this time. The season commenced with two early spring rounds in Spain and ended at Sandown Park in Australia, also in the spring, of the southern hemisphere kind.

The first round at **Jerez** on 6 March was a triumph for the single new 5-litre turbocharged Sauber AEG Mercedes C9-88, which spearheaded Daimler-Benz's return to the international sportscar racing scene. Silk Cut Jaguars had successfully seen off the proliferation of Porsche works entries and privateers during the 1987 season, but Mercedes, the old rivals from 30 years before, might be a tougher nut for Jaguar to crack.

However, many doubted the new Mercedes C9's reliability when it had to battle around Jerez's twisty circuit. This was noted for wrecking transmissions, a feature the Silk Cut Jaguars would be sharply reminded of. Jean-Louis Schlesser took pole with a record fastest time in the Mercedes. He was followed by the Jaguar trio with the next three fastest times, putting the two new

XJR-9 chassis, 488 and 588, and last year's ex-XJR-8 chassis 187, second, third and fourth on the grid in that order.

Schlesser kept Mercedes 61 out front for the first half hour before Brundle snatched the lead in Jaguar number 2. After the first round of pit stops Cheever took over, still maintaining the lead position and soon joined by Dumfries and Watson, making it a Jaguar one-two-three. Sadly the Jerez bug began to take its toll: both the new 1988 XJR-9 chassis 488 (car 2) and 588 (car 1) suffered transmission problems and were out, but not before putting up a good scrap. Although the Silk Cut challenge was now reduced just to Jaguar number 3, chassis 187, this maintained pressure on Schlesser to the bitter end. Andy Wallace's debut with the team in 187 was rewarded with a second-place podium finish, shared with team-mates John Nielsen and John Watson.

Venue: Jerez, Spain
Round 1, 6 March 1988
Race title: 800 Km De Jerez

Chassis type	Chassis no.	Race no.	Drivers	Grid pos.	Finish position	Laps
XJR-9	187	3	John Nielsen, John Watson, Andy Wallace	4	2	190
XJR-9	488	2	Jan Lammers, Johnny Dumfries	2	DNF, transmission	132
XJR-9	588	1	Eddie Cheever, Martin Brundle	3	DNF, transmission	139

Race winner: Sauber Mercedes C9-88, drivers Jean Louis Schlesser, Mauro Baldi, and Jochen Mass, 190 laps

Round two at Spain's other circuit, **Jarama**, one week later saw Jaguar turn the tables on the Schlesser/Baldi Mercedes. The lone Sauber Mercedes entry qualified in first place as it had done at Jerez, with Jaguar number 1 occupying the third spot. Practice and qualifying were marred by one or two mishaps, one in

Eddie Cheever and Martin Brundle took Silk Cut Jaguar's first win of the season at Jarama, but staying ahead of the AEG Sauber Mercedes was not an easy task. For the second race in a row, chassis 488 failed to finish.
(Malcolm Bryan)

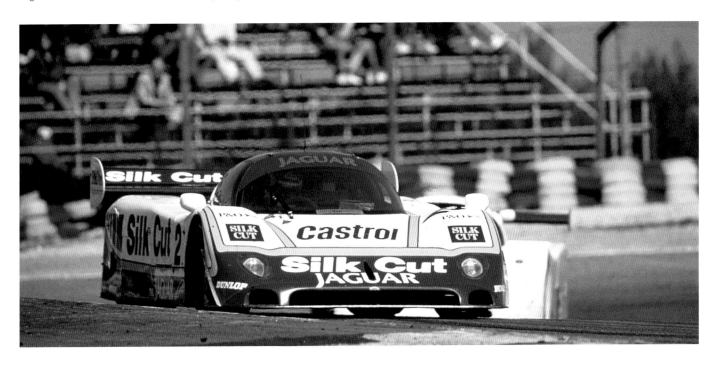

particular when Nielsen spun off the track and collided with an illegally parked marshal's car, causing serious damage to both vehicles.

The team had experienced problems at Jerez with the cars' set-up. Anxious to get it right for Jarama, urgent improvements were made to a number of components at the Kidlington workshops, all parts being flown out for fitting in the hours leading up to the race. Jan Lammers's qualifying time was the best of the three Jaguars entered. John Nielsen did well to take fourth place on the grid after running into the rear of Gordon Spice's C2 car. A new nose was fitted, and he completed a superb qualifying lap before the marshal's car incident.

On a circuit reputed to be hard on tyres, Jaguar's choice had the edge on the Sauber Mercedes which was leading at one point but was forced to drop back when its tyres went off. Chased hard by Schlesser, Dumfries's number 2 Jaguar spun out of the race 12 laps from the end. The Mercedes was then kept at bay by Brundle to the finish - he crossed the line 20 seconds ahead, exactly the same time margin as at Jerez but in reverse order.

Venue: Jarama, Spain
Round 2, 13 March 1988
Race title: 360 Km De Jarama

Chassis type	Chassis no.	Race no.	Drivers	Grid pos.	Finish position	Laps
XJR-9	187	3	John Nielsen, John Watson	4	3	107
XJR-9	488	2	Jan Lammers, Johnny Dumfries	2	DNF, spin	96
XJR-9	588	1	Eddie Cheever, Martin Brundle	3	1	109

Second win of the season went to Jaguar in round three at **Monza**, where they beat the principal adversary Sauber Mercedes into second place once again. Eddie Cheever and Martin Brundle still had problems attempting to out-qualify the turbo power of Schlesser and co, but were more than one lap ahead of them at the finish. For the third time in a row, Jaguar number 2 (488) failed to finish.

So far this season, Mercedes and Jaguar had monopolised the limelight, but the Porsche entries were not yet ready to be ruled out of the equation. Hardly had Jean-Louis Schlesser taken off on a race of his own, or so he thought, than Klaus Ludwig in the Blaupunkt Porsche was hard on his heels. The Jaguars had been left standing, or at least Jan Lammers was when his engine refused to fire up at the start. He got number 2 going with the aid of marshals who reluctantly pushed his car into action, but for the third time in a row 488 never made it to the flag.

Having earlier ploughed into the side of the Mercedes, Dumfries was running number 2 back to the pits for repairs when the car spun into the sandtrap on the Parabolica corner and he was forced to abandon it.

The race was past the halfway point before Martin Brundle in Jaguar number 1 gained control. Cheever took over for the final stint on lap 112, easily outrunning the duelling turbo Mercedes and Porsche rivals as their fuel reserves became critical. Ludwig's

Porsche was one of a quartet of 962s taking the next four places behind the winning Jaguar and the Mercedes runner-up. The Kidlington boys had toppled the Porsches from their perch in 1987, and now Mercedes were helping to relegate them further down the field.

Venue: Monza, Italy
Round 3, 10 April 1988
Race title: 1000 Km Di Monza Trofeo F Caracciola

Chassis type	Chassis no.	Race no.	Drivers	Grid pos.	Finish position	Laps
XJR-9	187	1T	T car			
XJR-9	488	2	Jan Lammers, Johnny Dumfries	5	DNF, spin	114
XJR-9	588	1	Eddie Cheever, Martin Brundle	4	1	173

Back home again for round four at **Silverstone**, the two Silk Cut Jaguars faced a pair of Sauber Mercedes in the *Autosport* 1000km. Those racegoers who were fortunate enough to be present at Jaguar's home circuit on this glorious day for British racing witnessed a thrilling duel between the reigning Champions and their equally dynamic would-be successors.

Cheever once more led the hotly-contested battle between Jaguar number 1 and the two Mercedes. Team-mate Martin Brundle took second stint after the first round of re-fuelling pit stops and pushed the Jaguar ahead of the Mercedes, thereby placing a strain on the fuel consumption of the German cars which helped to keep them at bay in the later stages. Eddie Cheever and Martin Brundle in Jaguar number 1 kept the Schlesser/Mass Mercedes 61 behind them for almost the entire race, only allowing it brief turns at the front during the earlier laps.

While these two slogged it out, the number 2 Jaguar of

Lammers and Dumfries fought a similar duel for third and fourth places, keeping up a Jaguar-Mercedes-Jaguar-Mercedes formation lap after lap, hour after hour. Only for brief moments did any other car manage to join this quartet on the lead lap, the most prominent being Derek Bell and Tiff Needell in the re-styled Richard Lloyd Racing Porsche 962.

The Cheever/Brundle Jaguar remained strong to the very end, crossing the line well ahead of the two Mercedes and taking one of the most exciting wins in Group C racing. Once again the other regular chassis (488) of Lammers and Dumfries had been affected by gremlins, this time before the race. Instead, the pair used the T car, last year's 187 chassis, in which they seemed set to take third place or possibly even second. A computer error left them without fuel six laps from the end. Disappointment and frustration had been their companions during every race so far this season, and little did they imagine that the very next race would bring them a success which only a select band of drivers would ever experience.

After Silverstone, Jean-Louis Schlesser topped the Drivers' Championship table with 115 points. Cheever and Brundle shared third place with 100 points each.

Venue: Silverstone, UK
Round 4, 8 May 1988
Race title: Autosport 1000km

Chassis type	Chassis no.	Race no.	Drivers	Grid pos.	Finish position	Laps
XJR-9	187	2	Jan Lammers, Johnny Dumfries	6	DNF, fuel	204
XJR-9	488	2	Jan Lammers, Johnny Dumfries		Developed faults, 187 T car used in race	
XJR-9	588	1	Eddie Cheever, Martin Brundle	2	1	210

Jaguar's memorable win at **Le Mans**, still a Championship race as round five, was the goal which hundreds of devoted team members, backroom boys and unsung heroes had striven for years to obtain, and now it was Jaguar's once more. For Tom Walkinshaw the name of the game was strength in numbers to combat the very best from Porsche, which included three distinctive bright yellow and red Shell-sponsored works 962Cs, one of them manned by 1987 winners Bell and Stuck with Klaus Ludwig as third driver. Three members of the popular Andretti family from America shared another of the yellow perils.

Three of the Swiss Sauber Mercedes were entered, only to be withdrawn from the race after one suffered an unexplained tyre burst during the Wednesday practice session. Their exit was a universal disappointment to spectators and competitors alike. Of the five Le Mans Jaguars present, three were managed by

Four of the five XJR-9LMs. The victorious number 2 was the only Kidlington finisher. Jaguar race manager Ron Elkins is standing extreme left next to John Nielsen. (Jaguar)

The number 2 Jaguar XJR-9LM stayed at the sharp end hour after hour. (Colin Taylor/JDHT)

Jan Lammers in the winning XJR-9LM (488) leads the two American finishers 186 and 188 home to a tumultuous reception. (Jaguar)

The victorious Jaguars were swamped by a sea of exuberant fans. (Jaguar)

Kidlington. Of the other two, number 21 (188) was a regular IMSA car managed by TWR Inc personnel. They also ran chassis 186, similarly upgraded in 1988 as an XJR-9LM.

The factory Porsches startled everybody in qualifying, hacking seconds off Bob Wollek's pole-winning time of the previous year, and placing themselves one, two and three on the grid. Martin Brundle's best lap pipped the old time by a whisker and earned fourth place for Jaguar number 1 (588) - the car in which he and Eddie Cheever had already taken three memorable wins this season. The eventual number 2 Jaguar was two seconds down on Brundle, starting from sixth, while the three remaining Silk Cut cars were grouped together a few rows further back.

Porsche fans were treated to a tantalising early-race spectacle, with all three yellow and red works cars travelling nose

Jan Lammers, Johnny Dumfries and Andy Wallace's brilliant win in the number 2 Jaguar prevented Derek Bell and Hans Stuck, sharing the number 17 works Porsche, from taking what would have been a sixth Le Mans win for Bell. (David Cundy)

to tail at the head of the field until they eventually came up on slower backmarkers. Jan Lammers in Jaguar number 2 was soon to break up the Porsche formation, and for the next 24 hours he and his co-drivers remained either in second place or, as the race progressed, out in front. For the first 11 hours or so their main challenger was the number 18 works Porsche of Wollek, Schuppan and Van der Merwe. After that car's retirement with engine failure, the previous year's winners, Bell and Stuck, with co-driver Klaus Ludwig, took over, keeping up the pressure hour after hour. They were still on the same lap at the end of yet another truly historic Jaguar-Porsche duel.

It is a strange irony that the victorious Jaguar number 2, chassis 488, was the only Kidlington car to finish. As the winner, it was withdrawn from racing to become a major attraction in the Jaguar Daimler Heritage Trust collection. Le Mans was the one and only time this historic car ever finished in any race. Both of the American-run cars finished, number 22 (186) coming fourth while 21 (188) finished in 16th place. Chassis 186 is now owned by Jaguar Nederland and remains exactly as it raced at Le Mans.

Venue: Le Mans, France
Round 5, 11-12 June 1988
Race title: 56eme Edition Des 24 Heures Du Mans

Chassis type	Chassis no.	Race no.	Drivers	Grid pos.	Finish position	Laps
XJR-9 LM	588	1	John Nielsen, Martin Brundle	4	DNF, head gasket	306
XJR-9 LM	488	2	Jan Lammers, Johnny Dumfries, Andy Wallace	6	1	394
XJR-9 LM	287	3	John Watson, Raul Boesel, Henri Pescarolo	12	DNF, transmission	129
XJR-9 LM	188	21	Danny Sullivan, Davy Jones, Price Cobb	9	16	331
XJR-9 LM	186	22	Derek Daly, Kevin Cogan, Larry Perkins	11	4	383

For round six, the teams travelled behind the iron curtain to **Brno** in Czechoslovakia, scene of three memorable Group A victories for Tom Walkinshaw. To the locals he is a racing legend. Driving TWR-prepared Motul- and Jaguar-sponsored XJ-S cars he became affectionately referred to as 'Major Tom', a name still used by fans and journalists to this day.

Winning Le Mans drivers Jan Lammers, Andy Wallace and Johnny Dumfries, seen here parading the XJR-9s through the streets of Coventry, embarked on a long series of public and corporate appearances. (JDHT)

Deeper wing endplates on the Silk Cut XJR-9s, first seen at Brno in Czechoslovakia, seem to have lost favour after the following race at Brands Hatch. (Malcolm Bryan)

The third Silk Cut Jaguar, chassis 187, racing as car number 3 at Brands Hatch, was fitted with the experimental 48-valve engine. Its race was cut short on lap 39. The Klaus Ludwig/Bob Wollek Blaupunkt Porsche 962 finished second behind the number 1 winning Jaguar, chassis 588. (David Cundy)

The two XJR-9s entered now sported deeper wing endplates, and were again in competition with two Sauber Mercedes, back after their disappointing withdrawal from Le Mans.

With Eddie Cheever engaged in Formula 1 duties in the British Grand Prix, John Nielsen partnered Martin Brundle in Jaguar number 1, as one of only 17 cars entered. While many regular teams failed to support this first running of a Group C FIA World Sportscar race in a socialist bloc country, the locals turned out in their thousands - 78,000 in fact - brimming with enthusiasm and anxious to see Major Tom's cats repeat their Le Mans success.

Jaguar number 2 was the third 1988 XJR-9 chassis 688, which was brought into use for the first time in place of the Le Mans-winning 488. Martin Brundle's provisional pole position in qualifying seemed set to stand but, towards the end, the two Mercedes threw caution to the wind and eventually claimed the front row. Both Jaguars were bugged by understeer throughout the race and, try as they did, could not reel in the Mass/Schlesser

Mercedes, eventually settling for second and third places. Mauro Baldi and James Weaver followed with a close fourth. The season seemed set to remain a Jaguar-Mercedes duel.

Venue: Brno, Czechoslovakia
Round 6, 10 July 1988
Race title: Grand Prix CSSR-Brno

Chassis type	Chassis no.	Race no.	Drivers	Grid pos.	Finish position	Laps
XJR-9	187	1T	T car			
XJR-9	588	1	Martin Brundle, John Nielsen	3	2	67
XJR-9	688	2	Jan Lammers, Johnny Dumfries	5	3	67

Race winner: Sauber Mercedes C9-88, drivers Jochen Mass and Jean-Louis Schlesser, 67 laps

Qualifying for Jaguar in round seven at **Brands Hatch** was a series of disasters due to spells of rain and drizzle coupled with time lost after a C2 accident. In addition, just when things seemed

to be going right, an emergency practice session for the safety crew was called for by the race organisers. The closest a Jaguar could get to the front row of the grid was fourth, the other two cars starting further back in sixth and eighth positions.

Once again the two Sauber-entered cars made a good start, but the Schlesser/Mass car lasted only seven laps before it was sent into the barrier after being struck by one of the C2 cars. Jaguar number 3 (187) was acting as a test bed, fitted with an experimental 48-valve engine. At one time it was running second when a deflated tyre necessitated a pit stop. John Watson managed to regain fifth place before handing over to Davy Jones. Shortly afterwards, ominous vibrations in the test engine forced retirement.

Brundle and Nielsen in Jaguar number 1 eventually took control of the race after a good stint by Andy Wallace, with the Lammers/Dumfries number 2 a short distance behind. With less than 40 laps to go Dumfries grew alarmed when the cockpit began to fill with smoke. On reaching the pits a fire in the cockpit wiring was quickly extinguished, but now all hopes rested on car number 1.

Brundle's superb finish left him only four points behind Schlesser in the Drivers' Championship with 155 against 159. With another four races to go the outcome was far from predictable. No such doubts with the Team Championship though, as Silk Cut Jaguar's 245 points were 86 ahead of the Sauber Mercedes.

Venue: Brands Hatch, UK
Round 7, 24 July 1988
Race title: Brands Hatch 1000kms

Chassis type	Chassis no.	Race no.	Drivers	Grid pos.	Finish position	Laps
XJR-9	187, with four valve engine	3	John Watson, Davy Jones	8	DNF, engine timing	39
XJR-9	588	1	Martin Brundle, John Nielsen, Andy Wallace	6	1	240
XJR-9	688	2	Jan Lammers, Johnny Dumfries	4	DNF, electrics	212

Sauber Mercedes were to get their revenge in round eight at **Nürburgring**, perhaps the most controversial race so far. This 1000km event was split into 500km heats, the first taking place

Jan Lammers soon took the lead in the number 2 Jaguar (688) during the rain-lashed first heat at Nürburgring, but his two pit stops, as against the Mercedes team's one-stop strategy, worked against the Silk Cut cars.
(Colin Taylor/JDHT)

on Saturday evening and finishing in darkness. The second heat was held as normal, if it could be called that, on Sunday afternoon. The two Mercedes were fastest in qualifying and started the first heat in ghastly conditions, being instantly passed by Lammers in Jaguar number 2. Both Lammers and Cheever stayed at the forward end, having planned a couple of pit stops each. The Saubers gambled on one pit stop and this strategy paid off for Schlesser and Mass, who finished first. Lammers and Dumfries were second, in front of team-mates Brundle and Cheever, who came third.

The second heat on Sunday started in better weather conditions, though not quite dry enough to rely on slicks. Each team chose the tyres which they hoped would see them through. Dumfries spun Jaguar number 2 off the track, causing damage to the rear wing supports which resulted in a long pit stop. Once more, the main battle was between the Cheever/Brundle number 1 car and the first heat winning Mercedes. Cheever was firmly in the lead on lap 90, with Schlesser resigned not to catching him, but with not many laps to go the Jaguar's engine started grumbling. Cheever felt compelled to ease up, preferring to finish second rather than lose altogether by pushing the machine to breaking point.

Of the 11 Championship wins in 1988, Jaguar took six, the other five going to the dark blue Mercedes C9-88. (JDHT)

Venue: Nürburgring, Germany
Round 8, 3-4 September 1988
Race title: Int-34 ADAC 1000 Km

Chassis type	Chassis no.	Race no.	Drivers	Grid pos.	Finish position	Laps
XJR-9	287	1T	T car			
XJR-9	588	1	Eddie Cheever, Martin Brundle	5	2	199
XJR-9	688	2	Jan Lammers, Johnny Dumfries	4	8	186

Race winner: Sauber Mercedes C9-88, drivers Jochen Mass and Jean-Louis Schlesser, 200 laps

Round nine at **Spa-Francorchamps** confirmed the Team Championship for Silk Cut Jaguar for the second year running, but still left the Schlesser v. Brundle Drivers' Championship contest running close. Mauro Baldi was also in the running, but whatever the result the Championship was going to go to a Jaguar or Mercedes driver as the nearest Porsche contender Bob Wollek was well down, 110 points behind the leader. Spa was yet another rain-soaked affair in which Jan Lammers won praise for his outstanding performance. Friday's practice, acted out in persistent wet weather, saw the Dutchman bombing around in front of nervous marshals, performing antics which were to stand him in good stead for another rain-lashed day on Sunday.

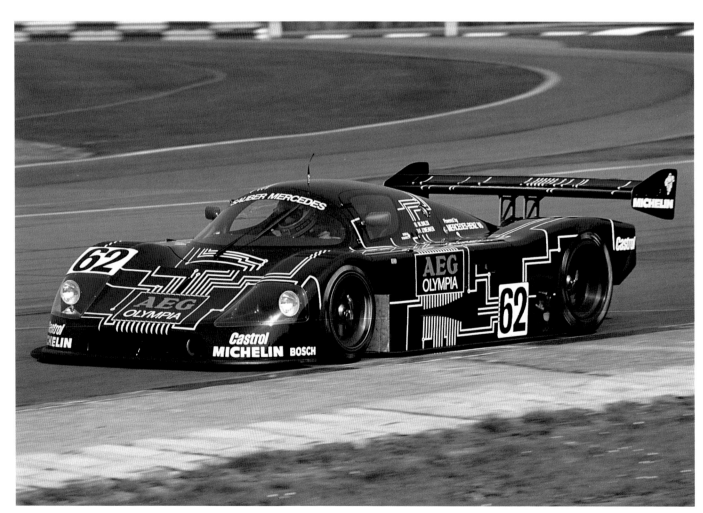

Qualifying on Saturday was blessed with dry weather conditions after overnight rain dried out. All eyes were on the two main protagonists for the Championship title. One of the Mercedes took pole position - this time not Schlesser and Mass but the sister car of Mauro Baldi and Stefan Johansson. Jan Lammers qualified Jaguar number 2 second, then came Mass and Schlesser.

Drizzle had already set in for the start of the race, and in these conditions Lammers soon took the lead from Baldi, increasing the gap over the first five laps to 13 seconds. A puncture in his left rear tyre sent him back to the pits for a wheel change, knocking him back to seventh place on his return. Much of the race was then dominated by the two Sauber Mercedes. Alarmingly for the Jaguar team, Cheever ran out of fuel on lap 50, leaving the stranded vehicle far from the safety of the pits. Brundle now transferred to Jaguar number 2 and brought it home to an excellent second place, only 23 seconds behind the pole Mercedes of Baldi and Johansson. The points he earned put him ahead in the Drivers' Championship.

Venue: Spa-Francorchamps, Belgium
Round 9, 18 September 1988
Race title: 1000 Km De Spa 1988

Chassis type	Chassis no.	Race no.	Drivers	Grid pos.	Finish position	Laps
XJR-9	287	1T	T car			
XJR-9	588	1	Eddie Cheever, Martin Brundle	4	DNF, fuel pick-up	49
XJR-9	688	2	Jan Lammers, Johnny Dumfries, Martin Brundle	2	2	142

Race winner: Sauber Mercedes C9-88, drivers Mauro Baldi and Stefan Johansson, 142 laps

Relax, relax, we've got the double! So echoed great sighs of relief around the Jaguar encampment at **Fuji** during the penultimate round 10. For Silk Cut Jaguar this was a triumph to savour, particularly as they were pitted against one of the strongest fields ever seen at the circuit. Eddie Cheever had contributed much to Raul Boesel's Championship the year before, and now he stood alongside Martin Brundle on the podium for the same reason. The pair had taken an emphatic win, ahead of the AG Omron Porsche 962 of Klaus Ludwig and Price Cobb.

Wet and unsettled weather bedevilled qualifying, in which nobody tried harder than the local teams. Pole position was taken by a Fuji-based team running one of the seven Porsche 962s which, with one Jaguar, one Sauber Mercedes and a Nissan, made up the top 10 finishers. The lone Japanese car in this list was surprising in view of the number of Toyotas, Mazdas and March-Nissans entered on their home soil. Martin Brundle was not intimidated by their presence or by the other visiting European teams he was up against.

Regrettably Jan Lammers went out of the race after only 35 laps due to a burst tyre which sent him spinning into the barriers. One of the Mercedes suffered a similar fate later, although this still left the surviving Schlesser/Mass/Acheson car as the main rival to

Jaguar number 1. Then a broken electronic sensor took the Mercedes back to the pits, resulting in four laps lost. From then on, any attempt to catch up with Brundle, now on the final stint, was doomed. Jean-Louis Schlesser's hopes of taking the Drivers' Championship were at an end.

Venue: Fuji, Japan
Round 10, 9 October 1988
Race title: 1988 World Sports-Prototype Championship WEC In Japan

Chassis type	Chassis no.	Race no.	Drivers	Grid pos.	Finish position	Laps
XJR-9	588	1	Eddie Cheever, Martin Brundle	7	1	224
XJR-9	688	2	Jan Lammers, Johnny Dumfries	6	DNF, accident	35

The final round 11 at **Sandown Park** in Australia was a splendid one-two for the Saubers, with the two Jaguars taking third and fourth places. Sandown's slow turns were bad news for the high-downforce XJR-9s. The turbo cars were able to boost away from these turns but the Jaguars took more time to build up speed again, a sequence repeated at each turn. No matter which setting the Jaguars tried, nothing could match the torque available to the Mercedes. Fortunately the outcome did not affect Silk Cut's Championship status.

Throughout the weekend the team tried one set-up after another, to no avail. While Jean-Louis Schlesser's pole-winning qualifying lap easily chopped into the previous record time, the Jaguars' carbon front brakes produced one or two setbacks. Wheel bearings began to cook, and the brake fluid boiled when the cars were left at a standstill for a minute or two. On a circuit where braking features so much, excessive overheating could spell disaster. Johnny Dumfries had one nasty moment during qualifying when loss of brakes at the end of the main straight sent him spinning into the gravel trap. Lammers managed one superb lap fast enough to start from the number three spot. Cheever and Brundle could not quite match his performance but still bettered the rest of the field by gaining fourth place.

From lap one the race was a Sauber Mercedes monopoly. On occasion Mauro Baldi and Stefan Johansson in the number 62 car attempted to take the honours from Schlesser and Mass but failed. After lap 55, Martin Brundle in Jaguar number 1 leapfrogged the number 2 sister car to take third, this being the only time any of the top four runners changed positions from start to finish.

Venue: Sandown Park, Australia
Round 11, 20 November 1988
Race title: Sensational Sandown Lucas Supersprint 360

Chassis type	Chassis no.	Race no.	Drivers	Grid pos.	Finish position	Laps
XJR-9	588	1	Eddie Cheever, Martin Brundle	4	3	93
XJR-9	688	2	Jan Lammers, Johnny Dumfries	3	4	92

Race winner: Sauber Mercedes C9-88, drivers Jean-Louis Schlesser and Jochen Mass, 93 laps

Chapter 7

1989 World Sportscar Prototype Championship

Jaguar's turbo era begins

Success at Le Mans had dominated 1988, when the normally-aspirated V12 of the XJR-9 had proved fast, fuel-efficient and reliable. In the World Championship, however, turbocharged cars were gaining the upper hand and TWR had plans to catch up, even if it meant abandoning the V12's link to production road cars.

The investment in sportscar racing by manufacturers like Jaguar, Mercedes and Nissan had attracted increasing interest from FISA, the governing body of world motor sport. The interest manifested itself in shorter races and in plans to introduce normally-aspirated 3.5-litre engines from 1991. The fact that engines designed to fulfil that requirement would be closer to those used for Formula 1, and that the manufacturers might prefer to do their racing on that stage rather than with sportscars, did not go unnoticed by the conspiracy theorists. The fields were bigger and the organisation more professional, but sceptics wondered what the future would bring. Le Mans was no longer a part of the World Championship but, secure in its position as a major world-class event, the race did not suffer. In fact, its exclusion encouraged its organisers to greater independence.

But the politics of racing were of little concern at Jaguar's headquarters in Coventry. The company's profitability was slipping, although sales were holding up with the introduction of enlarged engines for the XJ series. Millions had been invested in a new technical centre but there was a shortage of capital for future model development. On its own, Jaguar would never be able to

fund new models in an environment where such activities were becoming ever more expensive and labour-intensive.

The company needed a partner, and in 1989 the management under John Egan set out to find one. After courtship rituals with General Motors and Ford, the partnership Jaguar sought turned into a takeover by Ford at a cost of £1.6 billion. As a subsidiary of the American giant, Jaguar had entered an entirely new phase of its life.

Silk Cut Jaguar's Team Championship of 1988 was hardly the overwhelming achievement of the previous year. Rather, it was a reward for the tremendous team effort and skills of a select band of the sport's finest drivers, brought together to handle cars which were deemed to be no longer competitive against an overwhelming preponderance of turbocharged rivals. An XJR turbo car was under development at Kidlington and meanwhile the question was whether the ageing V12s could continue to hold their own until the new era dawned. New WSPC rules for 1989 slashed race lengths by half: gone forever were the lengthy five- to six-hour epics in favour of more spectator and television friendly events. Notably, the Le Mans 24-hour race was excluded from this year's Championship.

Round one at **Suzuka** in Japan was a foretaste of what lay ahead. New to the Silk Cut Jaguar line-up was Frenchman Patrick Tambay, who would partner Jan Lammers for most of the season. As in previous years, the entry list abounded with Porsche teams,

The last appearance of XJR-9s still fitted with roof engine intakes was in Round 1 at Suzuka in 1989. Visible on the side of Jaguar number 2 (688) in Japanese is the name of Jaguar Japan, the host sponsors. (Colin Taylor)

The same car at Dijon a few weeks later with revised side intake engine covers and Jaguar France host sponsorship. (Colin Taylor)

but there was a strong contingent of Japanese works entries from Nissan, Toyota and Mazda. Of particular concern to Jaguar were the Sauber Mercedes C9-89s, improved during the winter off-season and now seen in the traditional Mercedes silver livery - the 'Silver Arrows' were back. Spurred on by their 1988 successes and with even greater commitment from Daimler-Benz AG, they were undoubtedly one of the strongest teams in the Championship.

In qualifying, Britain's Geoff Lees and ex-Silk Cut Le Mans winner Johnny Dumfries were fastest in one of the Toms Toyotas, and second place also went to a Toms Toyota. Jan Lammers and Patrick Tambay took grid position three, no doubt hoping to remain ahead of Sauber Mercedes number 61 parked alongside in fourth place. John Nielsen and Andy Wallace's Jaguar started the race well back from 12th position.

Almost from the start the two Silver Arrows took control of the race, finishing an easy one-two while the Jaguars, mindful of fuel limitations, could do nothing to pull a reasonable result out of the bag. Lammers spluttered out of fuel barely one lap from the finish. The Nielsen/Wallace Jaguar fared better by coming home fifth. Not a happy situation for the Silk Cut team, and much midnight oil was burned in the following weeks.

Venue: Suzuka, Japan
Round 1, 9 April 1989
Race title: 89 WSPC In Japan, Suzuka 300 Miles

Chassis type	Chassis no.	Race no.	Drivers	Grid pos.	Finish position	Laps
XJR-9	588	1	Jan Lammers, Patrick Tambay	3	DNF, fuel	80
XJR-9	688	2	John Nielsen, Andy Wallace	12	5	81

Race winner: Sauber Mercedes C9-89, drivers Mauro Baldi and Jean-Louis Schlesser, 82 laps

Jaguar Motorsports Manager, the late Ron Elkins, seen here at Dijon with racecar designer Tony Southgate, was a popular member of the Silk Cut team. (Colin Taylor)

Suzuka had seen a particularly large entry list, including 30 C1 cars, a clear indication of the popularity sportscar racing enjoys in that country. Round two at **Dijon** couldn't quite match that but 25 C1s, together with 14 C2s, still constituted all the necessary ingredients for a great race. All expected that the two Sauber Mercedes would fill the grid front row, but Johnny Dumfries and Geoff Lees in the yellow Toms Toyota had other ideas, muscling into second place. The Joest Blaupunkt Porsche of Bob Wollek (ironically a Jaguar dealer from Strasbourg) and Frank Jelinski, as well as the Porsche of Derek Bell/Tiff Needell and another Japanese entry, all bettered the Jaguar times, leaving the two Jaguars to start from seventh and ninth places.

From quite early on the Sauber Mercedes took control, only to experience tyre problems which severely affected grip. Wollek and Jelinski in the Joest Blaupunkt Porsche traded the lead with the Schlesser/Mass Mercedes each time they pitted to change tyres, and finally crossed the finishing line 40 seconds ahead. Lammers racing in Jaguar number 1 (588) was poised to take fourth place but ran out of fuel yet again two laps from the finish. Wallace in car number 2 spun out much earlier following a tyre burst. As he walked back to the pits he heaped praise on whoever had designed the runoff area of the track. So the race finished with a surprise win for a Jaguar dealer driving a Porsche 962C. Both Silk Cut Jaguars failed to finish, something which had not happened since 1986.

Dijon was significant in being the debut race for the new Group C Aston Martin. New also was a works-entered Nissan, cousin of the highly successful GTP ZX turbos already dominating the IMSA Championships in America. It remained to be seen what impact they would have on World Sportscar Championship racing.

Venue: Dijon, France
Round: 2, 21 May 1989
Race title: Coupe de Dijon

Chassis type	Chassis no.	Race no.	Drivers	Grid pos.	Finish position	Laps
XJR-9	588	1	Jan Lammers, Patrick Tambay	7	DNF, fuel	125
XJR-9	688	2	John Nielsen, Andy Wallace	9	DNF, tyre	79

Race winner: Joest Porsche 962C, drivers Bob Wollek and Frank Jelinski, 127 laps.

The third 1989 outing for the Silk Cut team was to the big one at **Le Mans**, not included in the Championship this year. Pictures of Silk Cut Jaguars had adorned the front cover of the 1987 and 1988 official programmes, indicating the bookies' favourites to capture the most coveted racing trophy of all. For 1989 a pair of Sauber Mercedes Silver Arrows graced the cover, the natural

choice after they had scored several good wins in the latter races of 1988 and had begun this year so well.

Of the four Jaguars entered, two were the season's regulars, chassis 588 (car 1) and 688 (car 2). The upgraded 287 from the previous year competed once again, still as car number 4. The lone American-managed car was the Castrol 1988 Daytona winner chassis 288, racing here as car 3. The only change to the XJR-9s in general appearance from 1988 was the revised engine covers with the NACA duct side air intakes. A mixture of modified and Camel engine covers were used. Seven nationalities were represented in the 12-man driver line-up, which included for the first time the brothers Alain and Michel Ferte from France.

Heavy rain shortened the first qualifying session but conditions improved next day, allowing Silk Cut drivers to take four of the first eight grid positions. In spite of his best time in Jaguar number 1, Lammers remained cautious in the knowledge that two Silver Arrows had claimed the front row of the grid.

After one hour Jaguar number 3 was in the lead, and it stayed out front for two more hours. During the fourth hour things started to go wrong for the Silk Cut cars. A broken exhaust on the third-placed number 1 car sent it back to the pits for repairs. Worse was in store for the lead car when Derek Daly came to a halt on the Mulsanne straight with an inoperative gear selector. Acting on instructions over the pit radio, he finally managed to cobble the gears together well enough to crawl back to the pits. Much time was lost, ending any hope of a good finish for the American car. Seven laps later a dropped valve heralded the first Jaguar retirement.

The nearest that the Jaguar number 4 of the Ferte brothers

The American-managed IMSA XJR-9 (288), seen here in full Silk Cut livery as car number 3 at Le Mans, won the Daytona 24 hour race in 1988 but only completed 85 laps in the French classic before engine problems forced retirement. (David Cundy)

and Eliseo Salazar got to the lead was during the fourth hour, when they reached second place behind the Stuck/Wollek Porsche. From then on they began dropping back, maintaining a halfway position through the early hours but later gaining slightly to finish in eighth place overall.

The Nielsen/Wallace/Cobb Jaguar number 2 started well, running behind race leader Lammers in second place, but on the fifth lap it was hit by one of the Nissans. The Nissan did not survive but much time was lost in the pits repairing the Jaguar, and it dropped well down the field over the next few hours. Just before dawn, number 2 suffered a blown head gasket, which reduced the number of Jaguars running to two.

Jaguar number 1 of Lammers, Tambay and Gilbert-Scott was running consistently, although not without niggling hiccups in the early stages. Ripples of excitement began to run through late night and early morning spectators and pit crews alike as Lammers took number 1 into the lead around 1.30am, maintaining this position for a good five hours while hotly pursued by two of the Sauber Mercedes. Just when it seemed Jaguars were in the running to achieve another historic win, Lammers, having taken over from Tambay, drove into the pits with gearbox problems. Nearly an hour was lost while the pit crew remedied the fault but now the car was back in eighth place. The near-exhausted drivers clawed it back through the field to finish a heroic fourth.

With first and second places going to the immensely reliable turbocharged Mercedes, it seemed that TWR could not expect to compete on equal terms until they had their own forced-induction engine to take up the challenge.

Venue: Le Mans, France
Round n/a, 10/11 June 1989
Race title: 57eme Edition Des 24 Heures Du Mans (Non-Championship Race)

Chassis type	Chassis no.	Race no.	Drivers	Grid pos.	Finish position	Laps
XJR-9 LM	588	1	Jan Lammers, Patrick Tambay, Andrew Gilbert-Scott	3	4	380
XJR-9 LM	688	2	John Nielsen, Andy Wallace, Price Cobb	8	DNF, head gasket	215
XJR-9 LM	288	3	Davy Jones, Derek Daly, Jeff Kline	4	DNF, engine	85
XJR-9 LM	287	4	Alain Ferte, Michel Ferte, Eliseo Salazar	6	8	368

Race winner: Sauber Mercedes C9, drivers Jochen Mass, Manuel Reuter and Stanley Dickens, 389 laps

Jan Lammers, Andrew Gilbert Scott and Patrick Tambay finished fourth in the number 1 Le Mans Jaguar, chassis 588. (Colin Taylor)

The two Ferte brothers and team-mate Eliseo Salazar ran a steady race, bringing the number 4 Jaguar home in eighth place. (David Cundy)

To help reduce cockpit temperature levels whilst stationary at circuits like Jarama, heat-reflecting blankets were placed over the windscreen. Note also the kettle spout-like device fitted to the driver's cooling duct in the nose to boost the level of air intake. (Colin Taylor)

praise for their mastery in bringing the car home in second place. The other Jaguar was hampered by a troublesome seatbelt buckle and made a cautious finish in sixth place, the drivers not wanting to run out of fuel as had happened in early races.

With 20 points for a win and 15 for second place, the Sauber Mercedes Team Championship score, following two wins and one second place in the first three Championship races, stood at 55 points. Joest Porsche were second with 32, and Jaguar, with 23 - less than half the top score - third. Had Le Mans been included, the differential would have been much greater due to the double value of points awarded in such races. Jaguar's score had been boosted by winning at the Sarthe a year earlier, but now they were probably pleased that Le Mans had been excluded from the Championship this year as Mercedes were the victors.

Venue: Jarama, Spain
Round 3, 25 June 1989
Race title: Il Trofeo Repsol, Jarama

Chassis type	Chassis no.	Race no.	Drivers	Grid pos.	Finish position	Laps
XJR-9	588	1	Jan Lammers, Patrick Tambay	3	2	144
XJR-9	688	2	John Nielsen, Andy Wallace	4	6	142

Race winner: Sauber Mercedes C9, drivers Jochen Mass and Jean-Louis Schlesser, 145 laps

Putting aside their disappointment of two weeks earlier, the teams resumed their Championship effort in round three at **Jarama** in sweltering conditions. The Mercedes Silver Arrows had experienced persistent problems with tyre deterioration caused by overheating, and many thought that here at least the Jaguars might have the edge. Unfortunately this was not to be, as both Sauber Mercedes qualified on row one, from where one or the other led the race from start to finish, first Baldi and Acheson, then from lap 33 Schlesser and Mass.

The heat was to take its toll on the Jaguars and caused just the sorts of problems expected for the Mercedes - slower lap times as tyres softened, and adversely affected instrument readouts. Jan Lammers and Patrick Tambay in Jaguar number 1 won

Now for something completely different - so the team must have thought when Jan Lammers put one of the new turbocharged V6-engined XJR-11s on pole position in round four at **Brands Hatch** on its first time out. The XJR-11 had only been revealed to the press during the previous race at Jarama, and two were entered, together with one of the regular XJR-9s, chassis 688, still racing as car 2.

The debut race for the two 1989 XJR-11 turbo cars was at Brands Hatch, where they were joined by one of the XJR-9 V12s (688). Of the three, only the Lammers/Tambay number 1 turbo car (189) finished. (Colin Taylor)

The rolling start saw Lammers targeted by just about everyone: the Mercedes, Nissans and Porsches were all at it, and three actually jumped the line ahead of the pole car. A long tussle for the lead ensued, the game being to beat Mercedes, while the Jaguar turbos did what they could to stay in contention. Jaguar number 3 (289) of Jones and Ferte reached second place before a loose distributor cap called for a pit stop with the loss of several laps. Davy Jones took the car out again only to return shortly afterwards as he suspected more serious engine damage would result if he continued to race.

Lammers in Jaguar number 1 (189) was struck by the Toyota of Johnny Dumfries. The collision damaged the exhaust and turbo wastegate pipes, which slowed him down through loss of boost. All the same, his fifth-place finish was not bad for the XJR-11's debut race. Nielsen driving the single V12 Jaguar entered was involved in what he described as the most serious accident he had had in a Jaguar so far, when loss of brakes sent him careering into the tyre wall at Hawthorns, the impact causing severe damage to the front end. Chassis 688 did not race again here or anywhere else.

Venue: Brands Hatch, UK
Round 4, 23 July 1989
Race title: Brands Hatch Trophy

Chassis type	Chassis no.	Race no.	Drivers	Grid pos.	Finish position	Laps
XJR-11	189	1	Jan Lammers, Patrick Tambay	1	5	111
XJR-9	688	2	John Nielsen, Andy Wallace	11	DNF, accident	101
XJR-11	289	3	Alain Ferte, Davy Jones	5	DNF, ignition	80
XJR-9	287	1T	T car			

Race winner: Sauber Mercedes C9, drivers Mauro Baldi and Kenny Acheson, 115 laps

From now on, the Sauber Mercedes were going to have it much their own way in the remaining 1989 races. At **Nürburgring** in round five Jaguar's hopes had been boosted by a good Castrol-sponsored win at Portland in the IMSA series. This was the first success for the XJR-11's 3-litre cousin, the Castrol XJR-10, driven by Jan Lammers and Price Cobb.

In qualifying, the two Sauber Mercedes commandeered the front row, this time Baldi making the fastest time of 1min 23.125sec in car 62. Lammers, back in Europe again, managed

John Nielsen's heavy crash at Brands Hatch in the XJR-9 (688) put it out of racing for good. (David Cundy)

third spot on the grid in Jaguar number 1, while John Nielsen and Andy Wallace could only manage ninth. Their car had suffered a disastrous fire on the Friday and required a complete engine and rear end replacement, carried out during the night by a dedicated pit crew. The damage might not have been quite so severe if the marshals at the point where Wallace halted the car had been equipped with adequate fire fighting equipment.

Loss of grip and a multitude of problems affecting the new cars made for a disappointing race. Car number 2's fifth place at least kept Silk Cut Jaguar up in the points tables. In only the second race for the new V6 turbos, so much needed doing on what was the first part of a steep learning curve. Reaching a satisfactory level of confidence and reliability with the V12s had taken a year and a half through 1985-86. By the same measure, the new cars might just be right when the predicted 1991 turbo ban came into force. Allan Scott in the engine department faced an enormous task.

Venue: Nürburgring, Germany
Round 5, 20 August 1989
Race title: ADAC Trophy, Nürburgring

At Donington the silver Mercedes continued their winning streak while both Jaguars failed to finish. (Colin Taylor)

Chassis type	Chassis no.	Race no.	Drivers	Grid pos.	Finish position	Laps
XJR-11	189	1	Jan Lammers, Patrick Tambay	3	10	103
XJR-11	289	2	John Nielsen, Andy Wallace	9	5	104
XJR-9	588	1T	T car, John Nielsen			

Race winner: Sauber Mercedes C9, drivers Jochen Mass and Jean-Louis Schlesser, 106 laps

Before round six at **Donington Park**, both XJR-11s had been subject to extensive rebuilds since Nürburgring but niggling problems persisted from day one. An electrical fault caused Jaguar number 2 to keep cutting out during the first practice session. It was traced to a short circuit and damaged starter motor. At the same time, a missing cam belt on number 1 necessitated a full engine change. Saturday's qualifying sessions were less troublesome for the XJR-11s and Jan Lammers's time of 1min 21.44sec earned fifth place on the grid. Alain Ferte came next in number 2 with a time only 0.013sec slower.

The race saw both XJR-11s out before the finish, but not without a thrilling and crowd-pleasing start by Lammers, who gave the Sauber Mercedes a good run for their money. He swapped the lead with Jean-Louis Schlesser several times before the first driver change, when Tambay took over. Shortly afterwards, Tambay returned with an engine misfire which was eventually traced to a bent distributor driveshaft. Jaguar number 2 was slowed down by an overheated starter motor. Later still, its endeavours ended a few laps from the finish because of fuel problems. Lammers expressed confidence that the cars were making good progress although, as the result showed, there was much to do before any of them would grace the podium again.

Venue: Donington Park, UK
Round 6, 3 September 1989
Race title: Wheatcroft Gold Cup Race

Chassis type	Chassis no.	Race no.	Drivers	Grid pos.	Finish position	Laps
XJR-11	189	1	Jan Lammers, Patrick Tambay	5	DNF, electrics	45
XJR-11	289	2	Andy Wallace, Alain Ferte	6	DNF, fuel	115
XJR-9	588	1T	T Car			

Race winner: Sauber Mercedes C9-88, drivers Jochen Mass and Jean-Louis Schlesser, 120 laps

Threats of rain are not uncommon at **Spa-Francorchamps**, the venue for round seven. In between spells of heavy rain during qualifying both the turbo Jaguars made good times, resulting in second and third places on the grid. Electrical problems were still to bug the cars, but Tom Walkinshaw expressed the opinion that things were on the up.

Strict fuel monitoring was to be the main consideration this time, rather than all-out battling with the Sauber Mercedes. This was how the race started, but Lammers was determined to get ahead of the pole Mercedes driven by Mauro Baldi, and to everyone's amazement he lunged between it and the barrier with millimetres to spare. Alas, a faulty turbo unit stopped his bid on lap 16. Jaguar number 2 of Nielsen and Wallace lost power and returned to the pits, where the car failed to re-start, all down to a short between the battery and starter motor.

In the early part of the season, races had developed into battles royal between the trusty V12 Jaguars and the all-powerful Sauber Mercedes with their sizeable 5-litre turbo engines. This rather unequal contest saw Jaguars giving the Mercedes a good run for their money, and still retaining title hopes.

Disappointing results from the XJR-11s kept the Silk Cut team and driver points tally to an all-time low. The Sauber team had already clinched Championship honours after their win at Donington Park, which left the drivers' title to be fought for amongst their own. Had Schlesser not run out of fuel on lap 69, the title would have been his there and then. Baldi's win put him five points behind the Frenchman, and everyone now looked forward to Mexico to see who would come out on top.

Venue: Spa-Francorchamps, Belgium
Round 7, 17 September 1989
Race title: WSPC Coupes De Spa

Chassis type	Chassis no.	Race no.	Drivers	Grid pos.	Finish position	Laps
XJR-11	189	1	Jan Lammers, Patrick Tambay	2	DNF, engine	16
XJR-11	289	2	John Nielsen, Andy Wallace	3	DNF, electrics	25
XJR-9	588	2T	John Nielsen, Andy Wallace			

Race winner: Sauber Mercedes C9, drivers Mauro Baldi and Kenny Acheson, 70 laps

So far but not so good - the question was what to do next. For round eight, the final race in **Mexico**, something more forceful was required. Tom Walkinshaw's recourse was to leave the turbos at home, and instead he sent two of the highest-scoring XJR-9s from his stable. Car number 1 (588) had many good wins to its credit, as did car 2 (287), which in 1987 was the chariot Raul Boesel used to gain his World Championship title. The Silk Cut

The old and the new at Spa Francorchamps. The view over the XJR-9's (588) camel engine cover at the two XJR-11s during a rather wet qualifying session. (Colin Taylor)

The Spa race was disappointing in that both Jaguars failed to finish, victory again being taken by Mercedes. (Colin Taylor)

In Mexico XJR-9s 287 and 588 (the latter seen here in the pits) ran as sprint cars for the last time. (Colin Taylor)

team were well pleased with their practice times, but the altitude of the circuit was detrimental to the non-turbo cars. Baldi completed a splendid qualifying lap which put him on pole position, while Schlesser was alongside in second spot. For the race, Jan Lammers was affected by altitude sickness, so it was left to Patrick Tambay to take the lion's share of driving in Jaguar number 1. Due to the altitude no car was allowed to be manned by one driver only. Andy Wallace drove two stints in Jaguar number 2.

Soon after the start, Schlesser passed his Mercedes team-mate rival and led for much of the first half. At no time did either of the two Jaguars pose any real threat to the front runners. Baldi and Kenny Acheson led one or two laps and were at the front on lap 47 when, without warning, the car spun hard into the barriers and out of the race. They could have won, and had they done so they would have been one-two in the drivers' Championship if Schlesser and Mass had taken the dive instead. As it was, Jean-Louis Schlesser was a worthy winner of the Drivers' Championship, with Mauri Baldi runner-up.

In view of the fact that the prevailing conditions favoured the turbo cars over the normally-aspirated V12s, the Jaguar team did well to finish fifth and sixth, only one lap down on the winning Mercedes, and although they did not win the team felt a certain satisfaction, which had understandably been lacking in some of the earlier events.

Venue: Mexico City, Mexico
Round 8, 29 October 1989
Race title: Trofeo Hermanos Rodriguez

Chassis type	Chassis no.	Race no.	Drivers	Grid pos.	Finish position	Laps
XJR-9	588	1	Jan Lammers, Patrick Tambay	5	6	108
XJR-9	287	2	Andy Wallace, Alain Ferte	10	5	108

Race winner: Sauber Mercedes C9-88, drivers Jochen Mass and Jean-Louis Schlesser, 109 laps

So ended a most disappointing year for the Jaguar team. They had not won a single race, their best place was the second for Lammers and Tambay at Jarama in June, and in three of eight Championship races they had not finished at all. Could they turn their fortunes around in 1990, the final season for the turbo cars?

Chapter 8

1990 World Sportscar Prototype Championship

Le Mans once more

The effects of the Ford take-over were making themselves felt at Jaguar during 1990. Sir John Egan had negotiated an excellent deal for his shareholders when Jaguar was sold, but he personally had been more attracted towards a link with General Motors than Ford during the bidding battle of 1989. It was therefore no surprise when he left the company to be replaced by William Hayden. Bill Hayden was a man who had made his career with Ford and he joined Jaguar to apply Ford standards of quality and efficiency. His initial comments about the company's production facilities were harsh and hurt many Jaguar people, but he had not been brought in to make friends. His arrival was the signal for the beginning of a period of radical change.

In terms of products the XJ40 was still the mainstay of the Jaguar range, but the XJ-S was to be given a new lease of life with a fairly extensive make-over which arrived in 1991. Reacting to the success the XJ220 had achieved when it was shown at Birmingham in late 1988, Jaguar announced that it would bow to customer demand and build the car for sale. A new company, Project XJ220, was formed as an offshoot to JaguarSport to productionise the 1988 concept car and build a limited run of 350 cars, originally at a price of £400,000 each.

The sport of endurance racing was again overshadowed by politics as the end of the Group C era loomed. It was the last year of the classic engines of the category, the turbocharged Mercedes and Porsches and the normally-aspirated V12 Jaguars, so power unit development for the current year was not a top priority. Some teams, like Peugeot, were already looking to the cars they would race next year.

Le Mans was once again not part of the World Championship but that did not deter the spectators, who were drawn by the battles between Jaguar, Porsche, Mercedes, Toyota and Nissan in numbers the circuit had not seen since the 1950s. However, agreement was reached between the French organisers and the international federation for Le Mans to regain its championship status in 1991. The conditions imposed were that chicanes should be inserted to break up the Mulsanne straight, and new pits should be built to replace the cramped and antiquated facilities that had served for far too long. But the changes gave the race organisers stability on which to build.

The significance of 1990 was that, apart from 24-hour endurance racing and the Sebring 12-hour, the old reliable V12s, so long the mainstay of Jaguar sportscar racing, were now relegated to the

history books. It was also the last year in which turbo-powered cars were to take part in World Sportscar Prototype Championship events. Motor racing publications were full of speculation concerning the changes for 1991, and about how long sportscar racing could survive in its present form under threats and pressures from all directions.

Round one of the 1990 WSPC season at **Suzuka** in Japan started well for the Jaguars in untimed practice sessions, where Jan Lammers in car number 4 (289) finished with second fastest time. The much-improved XJR-11s had shown great promise during pre-season testing, and the team felt more confident that this year would bring results to make up for last year's disappointments. Qualifying was hampered by niggling problems made worse by delays clearing crash debris from the track, and then rain in the final stages. The two Jaguars occupied the fourth row on the grid.

The Championship holder, Mercedes, was the favourite to win, but all did not go well for Schlesser in the completely new C11 prototype. Winter testing had promised much for this beautifully-designed potential Championship winner, seen publicly for the first time here. Schlesser crashed it in qualifying and thus denied everyone a chance to watch it in action. The team raced last

Martin Brundle, seen here with Tom Walkinshaw, drove in every race during the 1990 season, taking wins at Silverstone and Le Mans. (Jaguar)

Chassis 189 (car 3) and 289 (car 4), with revised livery, in preparation for the 1990 season opener at Suzuka. New features included a restyled nose with NACA brake ducts, front wheel arch louvres, fixed turbo periscope ducts and twin alloy plenum chambers.
(Zoom Photographics)

year's C9s to good effect but, to the delight of Japanese onlookers, the two Toms Toyotas took pole and third place on the grid.

Shortly after the start, Brundle took Jaguar number 3 (189) into the lead, with Lammers in number 4 not far behind. Following the first pit stops and driver changeovers, they were running third and fourth, when Wallace pulled into the pits with a failed turbo unit. Back out again after a long stop, it was not long before further engine problems brought the car to a halt on the circuit. Meanwhile, Alain Ferte began losing ground to the Mercedes and was called into the pits to allow Brundle to take over. Brundle soon gained on the leading Sauber, but cruel fate intervened, ending his run when an oil pump-related engine failure sent him back to the pits. The Schlesser/Baldi Mercedes now enjoyed a trouble-free run to the finish.

Venue: Suzuka, Japan
Round 1, 8 April 1990
Race title: WSPC Fuji Film Cup

Chassis type	Chassis no.	Race no.	Drivers	Grid pos.	Finish position	Laps
XJR-11	189	3	Martin Brundle, Alain Ferte	8	DNF, engine	77
XJR-11	289	4	Jan Lammers, Andy Wallace	7	DNF, turbo	44

Race winner: Sauber Mercedes C9, drivers Mauro Baldi and Jean-Louis Schlesser, 82 laps

A second convincing win for Sauber Mercedes in round two at **Monza** must have caused a feeling of *déjà vu* in the Silk Cut camp. The XJR-11s had shown promise, and their good qualifying times in both first and second sessions were extremely encouraging, but breaking the Mercedes dominance was a difficult task. The Sauber team were now equipped with the new-season C11s, which made easy meat of capturing the grid front row. Jaguar number 3 driven by Martin Brundle and Alain Ferte was a brand-new chassis, 490.

A first lap mishap occurred when Mercedes number 2 of Jochen Mass came into contact with Lammers's number 4 Jaguar while both were attempting to occupy the same piece of track simultaneously. They were sent spinning in different directions. In the resultant chaos, both cars ended at the back of the pack, while Mauro Baldi in the other Mercedes took a comfortable lead, followed close behind by Martin Brundle in Jaguar number 3.

The remainder of the race saw the two delayed cars gradually climbing back up through the field, catching up with the leaders towards the end. Baldi remained in front and crossed the finishing line 17 seconds ahead of Mass in the other Mercedes. Brundle in the new Jaguar coasted home nine seconds behind. If the Jaguars had not suffered persistent brake problems the result might have gone their way. Tom Walkinshaw continued to express confidence that the Jaguar situation was improving with each race: 'Monza is a speed circuit and doesn't allow us to exploit the superior handling of the XJR-11.' He promised that the niggling problems would soon be sorted out.

Venue: Monza, Italy
Round 2, 29 April 1990
Race title: 23 Trofeo Filippo Caracciola

Chassis type	Chassis no.	Race no.	Drivers	Grid pos.	Finish position	Laps
XJR-11	490	3	Martin Brundle, Alain Ferte	4	3	83
XJR-11	289	4	Jan Lammers, Andy Wallace	3	4	82
XJR-11	189	T car				

Race winner: Sauber Mercedes C11, drivers Mauro Baldi and Jean-Louis Schlesser, 83 laps

Round three at **Silverstone** saw the introduction of the much-vaunted wide front track XJR-11s, now running as chassis numbers 490 and 590. The new chassis 490 had appeared for the first time at Monza but without the wide nose, although it had the 1990-style NACA front brake ducts. Jaguar was always the favourite to win on home ground. The XJR-11s had shown considerable improvement in the earlier rounds, and now they were to make good at last with a magnificent one-two victory.

Free practice and qualifying saw predictable battles between Mercedes and Jaguar for top placing, with Schlesser and Baldi securing pole position in Mercedes number 1. Mercedes number 2 had been excluded by the stewards after a rule infringement by

Jochen Mass's novice co-driver, a young man by the name of Michael Schumacher – which however in the long run did not greatly damage his career. (There may be those who wish that it had!)

The race commenced with Schlesser in the lead keeping Brundle at bay, while the gap between them and the rest of the field extended lap by lap. After the first round of pit stops the position changed quite unexpectedly when the Mercedes came to a halt with a broken engine. Ferte was now in the lead, cheered on by thousands of exuberant Jaguar fans. Earlier, Lammers bought car number 4 into the pits only to have it dropped off the jacks onto his foot. Andy Wallace had the honour of bringing that car home second behind Brundle. A most satisfactory result, especially in front of home crowds.

Venue: Silverstone, UK
Round 3, 20 May 1990
Race title: Shell BRDC Empire Trophy

Chassis type	Chassis no.	Race no.	Drivers	Grid pos.	Finish position	Laps
XJR-11	490	3	Martin Brundle, Alain Ferte	2	1	101
XJR-11	590	4	Jan Lammers, Andy Wallace	3	2	100
XJR-11	189	3T	T car			

Mercedes were back on form again during round four at **Spa-Francorchamps**, a venue renowned for wet weather which can upset the best-laid plans. However, good fortune might not have

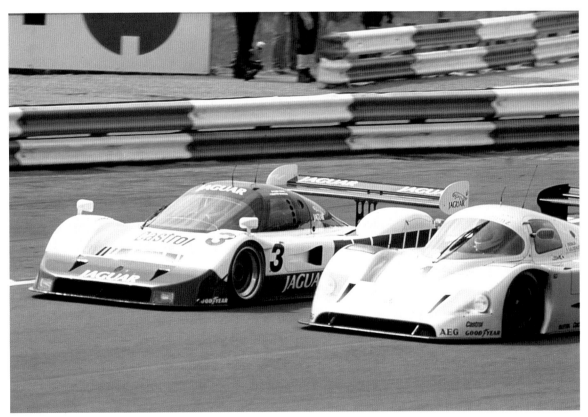

The wide-track XJR-11's first race, at Silverstone, was rewarded with a splendid 1-2 finish for Jaguar number 3 (490), seen here dicing with one of the Sauber Mercedes C11s, and number 4, chassis 590. (JDHT)

Le Mans Jaguars had come a long way since the C-type and D-type successes of the 1950s. (Ken Wells)

The Lammers/ Wallace/Conrad XJR-12LM Jaguar number 2 (290), at Le Mans in 1990. Livery was part sponsored by Jaguar Holland. One can only speculate what Jaguar's racing manager Ron Elkins had on his mind as he gazed down on it. (Ken Wells)

smiled on Mercedes if Martin Brundle's Jaguar had not been put out of the race on lap 45 with an engine wiring loom fire.

Qualifying was in much the same format as so often before, with two Sauber Mercedes on the front row and two Jaguars behind. Alain Ferte took part in qualifying but went down with 'flu on race day, leaving Martin Brundle as sole driver in car number 3 (490) until the fire put it out of action.

Jan Lammers took the first two stints in Jaguar number 4, harassing the Mercedes even though a fuel leak caused some concern, especially with petrol fumes seeping into the cockpit. Andy Wallace took the final stint with the car already in a strong position, and finished some 90 seconds behind the leading car. Had the fuel leak not caused both drivers to act cautiously, this was another race that could have been Jaguar's.

Venue: Spa-Francorchamps, Belgium
Round 4, 3 June 1990
Race title: 1990 Coupes De Spa

Chassis type	Chassis no.	Race no.	Drivers	Grid pos.	Finish position	Laps
XJR-11	490	3	Martin Brundle, Alain Ferte	3	DNF, wiring fire	46
XJR-11	590	4	Jan Lammers, Andy Wallace	4	2	70
XJR-11	189	T car				

Race Winner: Sauber Mercedes C11, drivers Jochen Mass and Karl Wendlinger, 70 laps

At this point in the Drivers' Championship, the top four places were held by Mercedes drivers, Jochen Mass and Karl Wendlinger leading with 21 points each. Joint fifth place was shared by Jan Lammers and Andy Wallace. Silk Cut Jaguar was second in the Team Championship, with 19 points against 27 for the Sauber Mercedes.

The 1990 season so far had seen hot rivalry between the 1989 Champions Mercedes and the 1987 and '88 Champions Jaguar, but only a significant improvement to the XJR-11 chassis would restore the latter to centre place on the podium. The Sauber Mercedes team's dominance over Silk Cut in World Sportscar racing was being echoed in America by Electramotive Nissan's mastery over the Castrol Jaguars in IMSA racing. And while the Silk Cut Jaguars chased the Mercedes more often than not, all they saw in their rear view mirrors was one or other of the up-and-coming Nissan R90C works cars. All Silk Cut team members hoped that was where they would always remain.

Victory at **Le Mans** was a welcome tonic for the Jaguar team, putting them back at the top where they so richly deserved to be. Four XJR-12LMs were entered: two new chassis and two reworked XJR-9s. Chassis 990 was the former Silk Cut chassis 588, a highly successful car in its earlier history. Chassis 1090, the winning car, was formerly IMSA Castrol chassis 288, winner at Daytona in 1988. As was fitting, this car was managed by an American team, with Dave Benbow as chief engineer. The other two cars, 190 and 290, were built for IMSA racing, although like the Silk Cut Jaguar V12s their use would be limited to a small number of races only. Attempting to gain pole position was not a priority for Jaguar as anything could happen, and usually did, to stir things up during lengthy events like this. The fastest Jaguar time of 3min 30.10sec was set by Davy Jones. As in 1989, the 12-man driver line-up was multinational, with Price Cobb as the other American driver.

All four Jaguars got off to a good start, calling into the pits for tyre changes and driver changes in the early stages with no reports of serious problems. The new Mulsanne chicanes were certainly making life harder than in previous years. By 10pm small problems were being dealt with during pit stops, but all the cars were running well and continued to do so through the early hours. Andy Wallace in car 2 was running third at 2am, only to be delayed later when Franz Konrad spun the car into the sand after braking at the first chicane, which lost him a couple of laps. Car 3, now leading, needed repairs to its nose, during which it also lost two laps.

The most seriously affected Jaguar was number 4, with a broken nose box which, even after repair, caused it to run low on the track, badly affecting handling. The matter seemed to have been resolved after more stops, and for a while the car ran quite

The ultimate Le Mans-winning car, chassis 1090, being readied for the big event. (Zoom Photographics)

*The Nielsen/Brundle/
Cobb number 3 XJR-
12LM (1090) on its way
to taking Jaguar's
seventh victory at Le
Mans. For 1990 the
cars ran with two-
element rear wings but
still retained short nose
profile splitters. (Zoom
Photographics)*

No! WRONG COLOUR
JAG on screen
& has roof light!
This is not @ Le Mans!

*The shallow diffuser
tunnels on the 1990
Le Mans-winning
XJR-12LM changed
little from the 1988
version, while in
America the Valparaiso
Jaguars continue to
use XJR-6-8 style deep
tunnels. (Author)*

smoothly. After what had been a generally good night, Jaguar
number 1 retired at 7.30am with water pump problems. Martin
Brundle then transferred to car number 3. Andy Wallace and Jan
Lammers, driving double stints, were now running Jaguar number
2 in fourth place. A long pit stop at 8.45am for number 4 involved
additional repairs to the nose and brakes. This cast doubts on the
car's ability to finish, especially after it required further pit stops to
tackle the same problems. The now ailing Jaguar managed
a further three and a half hours, at one point dropping back to
12th place, before engine sickness finally forced retirement shortly
after midday.

Car number 3 maintained a one-lap lead on the Repsol Brun
Porsche, with Jaguar number 2 running third, three laps down
from the Porsche, and this situation remained unchanged
throughout the last four hours. It seemed that Jaguar would have
to settle for first and third place when, with only fifteen minutes
left, the Porsche came to a standstill on the Mulsanne straight,
smoke pouring from its engine. The two Jaguars, now in
formation, crossed the finish line to tumultuous applause from a
vast army of fans and supporters.

This brilliant win was cause for great satisfaction for the TWR
organisation, the component suppliers, the sponsors and for
Jaguar. For one person in particular, Sir John Egan, it was also
perfectly timed. He could not have wished for a better leaving
present as he stepped down as chairman and chief executive of
Jaguar Cars.

*Davy Jones and Andy
Wallace's fourth-place
finish in Mexico was
moved up to third
when the winning
Mercedes was
disqualified for fuel
infringement. This was
the last time the Jaguar
turbo cars raced in Silk
Cut livery. (Jaguar)*

Venue: Le Mans, France
Round n/a, 16-17 June 1990
Race title: 58eme Edition Des 24 Heures Du Mans (Non-Championship Race)

Chassis type	Chassis no.	Race no.	Drivers	Grid pos.	Finish position	Laps
XJR-12 LM	990	1	Martin Brundle, Alain Ferte, David Leslie	8	DNF, water pump	220
XJR-12 LM	290	2	Jan Lammers, Andy Wallace, Franz Konrad	17	2	355
XJR-12 LM	1090	3	John Nielsen, Price Cobb, Eliseo Salazar, Martin Brundle	9	1	359
XJR-12 LM	190	4	Davy Jones, Eliseo Salazar, Michel Ferte, Luis Perez-Sala	7	DNF, engine	287

The next round of the WSPC, due to be held on 24 June at **Jarama**, was cancelled as the circuit was not up to the safety standards required by FISA. Round five at **Dijon** was very much a return to the status quo, with the Silk Cut Jaguars amongst the best of the rest, behind the seemingly ultra-reliable winning Sauber Mercedes. A flying lap during qualifying by Martin Brundle put Jaguar number 3 second on the grid, with number 4 behind in fourth place. Brundle had suffered a nasty accident practising at Dijon a week earlier - not that this affected his attempts to gain pole position. Jean-Louis Schlesser was so impressed with Brundle's recovery and superb driving that he made a point of calling into the Jaguar pit to offer congratulations.

Lack of grip, high track temperatures and difficult handling put all four drivers to the test as they attempted to match the Mercedes. Jaguar's fourth and fifth places came after what to most was a rather unenjoyable race. That they finished at all was testimony to dedicated team effort and the unflagging perseverance of the drivers, who kept the cars running in the most difficult circumstances. It seemed that at least one of the Nissans was not content to stay behind the Jaguars. For this race, Julian Bailey and Mark Blundell in the number 23 Nissan Motorsports R90C managed to slot themselves neatly into third place behind the first and second Mercedes and in front of both Silk Cut cars.

Venue: Dijon, France
Round 5, 22 July 1990
Race title: Championnat Du Monde Des Voitures De Sport-Prototypes

Chassis type	Chassis no.	Race no.	Drivers	Grid pos.	Finish position	Laps
XJR-11	490	3	Martin Brundle, Alain Ferte	2	5	125
XJR-11	590	4	Jan Lammers, Andy Wallace	4	4	125
XJR-11	189		T car			

Race winner: Sauber Mercedes C11, drivers Mauro Baldi and Jean Louis-Schlesser, 127 laps

The Silk Cut Jaguars seemed destined to stay behind the Mercedes but, although finishing third and fourth at **Nürburgring** in round six, the team's optimism remained high. Considering that

Jaguar number 3 suffered with recurring electrical problems which drastically reduced the amount of time that Martin Brundle had for qualifying, one might speculate that his third place time of 1min 22.780sec could have been improved upon, perhaps enough to gain pole position. Dijon proved he could knock on Schlesser's door, and there was always the next time. However, time with the XJR-11s was running short, and back home all thoughts were focusing on its non-turbo successor, due to take over in 1991.

Poor weather during the afternoon session prevented any improvement on the team's earlier times. Jan Lammers took Jaguar number 4 out on the Sunday morning warm-up, only to be left stranded on the circuit with oil pump failure. The pit crew worked wonders, fitting a replacement engine in time for the start at 1pm. The re-numbered XJR-11s were behaving slightly better once the race got under way, and tyres were not subject to quite the same level of problems experienced at Dijon. There were a few instances where loose bodywork required attention during pit stops. Both cars ran well and finished two laps ahead of the fifth-place Nissan driven by Mark Blundell. Fastest lap time in the race was achieved by Michael Schumacher in Mercedes number 2.

Venue: Nürburgring, Germany
Round 6, 19 August 1990
Race title: ADAC Sportwagen Weltmeisterschaft

Chassis type	Chassis no.	Race no.	Drivers	Grid pos.	Finish position	Laps
XJR-11	1190	3	Martin Brundle, Alain Ferte	3	3	105
XJR-11	1290	4	Jan Lammers, Andy Wallace	4	4	105

Race winner: Sauber Mercedes C11, drivers Mauro Baldi and Jean-Louis Schlesser, 106 laps

Throughout the Jaguar camp, hopes were high of a possible home-ground double for the Silk Cut Jaguars in round seven at **Donington Park**. Martin Brundle was indeed hero of the day after coming home third at the end of a 120-lap solo race, only to be disqualified along with Jan Lammers and Andy Wallace in Jaguar number 4 for fuel allocation errors. Martin's car was found to have been topped up with one litre of fuel over the permitted limit. Even though three litres were drained out after the race, both cars were excluded. Tom Walkinshaw blamed the error on the journalists and photographers who crowded round the cars and hampered the refuelling crew, causing a slight delay in removing the hose at the finish of one refuelling stop. Martin's car ran a troublefree race but the Lammers/Wallace car was not at all smooth running, and suffered incurable oversteer in addition to a time-consuming puncture. The two Mercedes were virtually unreachable from start to finish.

For the second year running, the result after the Donington Park race confirmed Mercedes as the winners of the Team Championship. Their total of 54 points was just over twice Silk Cut's score of 26. Nissan was next with 17, and Spice was in front of the top Porsche teams. In this race, a pair of Spice Engineering C2 cars did incredibly well, coming home in fourth and sixth

Andy Wallace, seated in the car, came fourth in the 1990 Drivers' Championship while team-mate Jan Lammers shared fifth place with the young Mercedes driver Michael Schumacher. (Jaguar)

places amongst the all-powerful Mercedes, Jaguar and Nissan C1 top finishers. Following the disqualification of the Jaguars, they were moved up to third and fifth. A whole bevy of Porsche 962Cs made up the mid-field finishers, the best of which could only finish in ninth place, or seventh after Jaguar's disqualification.

Venue: Donington Park, UK
Round 7, 2 September 1990
Race title: Shell Donington Trophy Race

Chassis type	Chassis no.	Race no.	Drivers	Grid pos.	Finish position	Laps
XJR-11	1190	3	Martin Brundle, Alain Ferte	4	3 (disqualified, over-fuelled)	119
XJR-11	1290	4	Jan Lammers, Andy Wallace	7	8 (disqualified, over-fuelled)	117

Race winner: Sauber Mercedes C11, drivers Mauro Baldi and Jean-Louis Schlesser, 120 laps

Qualifying for round eight at **Montreal** started well for Brundle, who provisionally took pole position at one point during the first qualifying session. Davy Jones joined the team and was also doing quite well, but a broken driveshaft robbed him of valuable time. The second day's qualifying was a very wet affair with no real chance of improving on lap times, leaving Jaguar number 3 (1190) third on the grid with number 4 (1290) back in sixth place. Martin Brundle started the race magnificently by gaining the lead on lap two, only to be held up behind the pace car for 11 laps. The race was marred by accidents, pace car intervals and, for the Jaguars, two more broken driveshafts, putting Andy Wallace out on lap 37 and Jan Lammers on lap 58. Jan was running third when his went, but a much rarer, freak accident was to curtail the race after only 61 laps. The tremendous suction exerted on the track surface beneath these high-downforce racers caused a manhole cover to pop out into the path of the Repsol Brun Porsche driven by Jesus Pareja, smashing through his windscreen and tearing open the fuel tank. Pareja managed to get out of the car seconds before it was enveloped by an inferno. Confusion ensued, with all drivers returning to the pits, after which the race was red-flagged - although this did not affect the Jaguar team, which was already in the process of packing up.

Venue: Montreal, Canada
Round 8, 23 September 1990
Race title: Mondial Players LTEE

Chassis type	Chassis no.	Race no.	Drivers	Grid pos.	Finish position	Laps
XJR-11	1190	3	Martin Brundle, Jan Lammers	3	DNF, driveshaft	58
XJR-11	1290	4	Davy Jones, Andy Wallace	6	DNF, driveshaft	37

Race winner: Sauber Mercedes C11, drivers Mauro Baldi and Jean-Louis Schlesser, 61 laps

The final race, round nine in **Mexico**, could and should have been rather better for the two Jaguars, especially after Martin Brundle's fastest qualifying time put him on pole position. This was the first time an XJR-11 had managed the number one spot since its debut race at Brands Hatch. This achievement came as a result of

tremendous effort by the team working through the night to get the cars' balance just right for final qualifying.

From the start Brundle was under very strong pressure first from one Mercedes, and then, having been forced to concede, he was taken on by the other. After pitting on lap 20, the Jaguar's electrics caused concern. Two battery changes did nothing to improve matters, but eventually a broken alternator was diagnosed, and retirement was inevitable.

While Brundle was delighted with the general handling of Jaguar number 3, Davy Jones and Andy Wallace were not entirely happy with number 4. They felt that track conditions and lower ambient temperatures had not helped them to improve on their sixth position on the grid. The Anglo-American duo stayed the course though, finishing the last part of the race in very wet conditions, but thankfully took fourth place. The two Mercedes took first and second, although Baldi and Schlesser in car number 1 were disqualified for the same reason - fuel infringement - as had led to the Jaguars' exclusion at Donington Park. The second Mercedes of Mass and Schumacher was now declared the winner, and Wallace and Jones moved up to third.

Venue: Mexico City, Mexico
Round 9, 21 October 1990
Race title: Trofeo Hermanos Rodriguez

Chassis type	Chassis no.	Race no.	Drivers	Grid pos.	Finish position	Laps
XJR-11	1190	3	Martin Brundle, Jan Lammers	1	DNF, electrics	46
XJR-11	1290	4	Andy Wallace, Davy Jones	6	4, moved up to 3	107

Race winner: Sauber Mercedes C11, drivers Mauro Baldi and Jean-Louis Schlesser, 109 laps, disqualified, making Jochen Mass and Michael Schumacher winners, also in Sauber Mercedes C11

Poor as the 1990 season may have seemed, with only one win in eight Championship races apart from Le Mans, Silk Cut Jaguar still finished second in the Team Championship, with 30 points against Sauber Mercedes's total of 67.5. Andy Wallace was fourth in the Drivers' Championship, while the first three places were taken by Mercedes drivers. Jan Lammers shared equal fifth place with Karl Wendlinger and Michael Schumacher. Martin Brundle was eighth and Alain Ferte 12th.

Chapter 9

1991 Sportscar World Championship

Team and Drivers' World Champions once more

Some teams, such as Jaguar, Mercedes and Peugeot, had prepared cars for the 3.5-litre non-turbo formula that started in 1991, but others had believed that the governing body would postpone the new rules and lagged behind. The result was that sportscar grids were very sparse. Only 16 cars were registered for a World Championship series that had attracted 36 entries in 1989. Of the 16, just eight complied with the new rules, for FISA had been forced to accept private entries with Group C cars in order to create viable grids.

With races shortened to less than 500 kilometres because the new smaller engines would not last over traditional endurance race lengths, with small grids and with only three factory teams, crowd figures were well down. And yet FISA demanded as much as $600,000 from race promoters as registration fees and swamped the races with officialdom, using techniques honed in the rarefied air of Formula 1. Very little of the registration money made it back to the private teams who needed it, and the factory teams, with budgets running into millions of dollars, were no better served - start money was a miserly $3000 per car. Those who felt that FISA and the powers behind it were out to destroy endurance racing and force the factories into Formula 1 had much to support their argument.

Le Mans was a different matter. The new cars were unsuitable for a 24-hour race, so Group C ruled and the entry-list was full. In addition, the rise in popularity of the race since Jaguar returned in 1984 had given it a new international standing, with thousands of British fans making the pilgrimage to 'Britain's best sportscar event.' As the World Championship waned, the future of the French race seemed set fair.

On the commercial front the recession was now hitting both the USA and Europe, Jaguar's two major markets. Sales for 1991 suffered, as all the premium car manufacturers felt the effect. (omitted) Strong measures were required. Ford processes were used to build up quality standards at the plants in Coventry and Birmingham, and this was accompanied by a major drive to improve operating efficiency.

The now renamed Sportscar World Championship for 1991 did not start as FISA had intended when back in late 1988 they had decreed that entry would be restricted to 3.5-litre non-turbo cars, to the exclusion of all others. Even before the 1990 season got under way, it became clear that only the major manufacturers such as Jaguar, Peugeot and Mercedes were in a position to comply with the new formula. So a re-think became necessary. Turbo cars would be allowed a further season's respite but would be subject to weight penalties, giving an advantage to the non-turbo cars. When it became obvious that the balance was too much in favour of normally-aspirated cars, more moderate weight

The 1991 two-tone 'curtain folds' livery on all sprint XJR-14s and Le Mans XJR-12LMs was a complete departure from earlier designs. The V12s ran the 24 hours classic with sprint-style longer front splitters. (Jaguar)

The XJR-14 third-generation TWR Jaguar prototypes kept the Silk Cut team at the sharp end during 1991, gaining both the Drivers' and Manufacturers' Championship. The number 3 car (591) took the first win at Monza, while XJR-14 number 4 (691) came second. (Jaguar)

Derek Warwick led the start from pole at Suzuka, only to be thwarted when a troublesome starter motor robbed him of what could have been victory. (JDHT)

penalties were introduced. Whatever the decision of the powers in charge, teams with cars built to the new formula, such as the Jaguar XJR-14 and Peugeot 905, were destined to dominate the Championship.

Pre-season Jaguar press releases listed four regular drivers: Martin Brundle, Derek Warwick, Teo Fabi and John Nielsen. All took turns testing the revolutionary new XJR-14s with great enthusiasm, full of confidence that Jaguar now had the means to provide podium places, just like earlier days. There was just one fly in the ointment for 'Big John' Nielsen, which was precisely that – his size. In fact he was too large in stature to get in and out of the window openings with ease, a problem as the XJR-14 lacked conventional doors. As the intended 'floating' driver it was also impossible for him to occupy the car specially tailored for the diminutive Teo Fabi. One report describes how on one occasion he managed to enter the car but needed help to get out, a much too dangerous scenario in an emergency. In consequence, Nielsen only got to drive a Jaguar at Le Mans this year, and that was one of the old XJR-12 cars. However, he also had four drives in the XJR-11 in the Japanese Championship (see Chapter 10).

For the first half of the season, the three remaining drivers would race, with Martin Brundle switching from one car to the other. When Martin returned to Formula 1 activities, the Australian

David Brabham (a son of Sir Jack) became third driver, transferring from car to car as required, allowing the main drivers a well-earned rest period.

Round one at **Suzuka** started brilliantly for Derek Warwick in Jaguar number 3 (591), qualifying in pole position, ahead of Keke Rosberg driving one of the new formula 3.5-litre Peugeot 905s. Martin Brundle's second place qualifying time in number 4 (691) became the centre of controversy when race officials measured its rear wing height at 7cm more than it should have been. Martin eventually started from sixth place on the grid, but not before strong protests to the officials from Tom Walkinshaw, who was convinced they were interpreting the rules incorrectly.

Warwick took the lead from the start and was 29 seconds ahead of Rosberg's Peugeot when he made his first pit stop but the starter motor failed in the pit and valuable time was lost while a new starter was fitted. Back on the track, number 3 was by far the fastest car in the race, setting a new sportscar lap record of 1min 49.148secs.

Brundle was less fortunate. After moving up to second place behind Warwick on lap four, he lost fuel pressure and the car came to a halt on the circuit. The cause was later found to have been fluid from the drinks bottle getting into the fuel pump relay and shorting it out. The team felt they had been robbed of a certain victory by a most trivial problem.

Venue: Suzuka, Japan
Round 1, 14 April 1991
Race title: SWC Fuji Film Cup

Chassis type	Chassis no.	Race no.	Drivers	Grid pos.	Finish position	Laps
XJR-14	591	3	Derek Warwick, Martin Brundle	1	DNF, starter	64
XJR-14	691	4	Teo Fabi, Martin Brundle	6	DNF, electrics	4

Race winner: Peugeot 905, drivers Mauro Baldi and Philippe Alliott, 74 laps

Round two at **Monza** gave the Silk Cut Jaguars a magnificent one-two victory after a dramatic last-minute engine change to Jaguar number 3, completed just in time to let Martin Brundle start the race from the pit lane.

After the first day's qualifying, both Jaguars provisionally occupied the front row of the grid. Teo Fabi set fastest time of 1min 33.672sec in Jaguar number 4, while Derek Warwick was less than a second behind with 1min 34.027sec. Heavy rain prevented any improvement on these times during official qualifying, although of those who ventured onto the track Martin Brundle managed best time of the day.

Both cars ran well, although this time it was number 4 which was affected by starter motor problems when Fabi brought it in for the first pit stop, losing three laps in the process. From then on, most delays stemmed from other sources, such as oil spray emitted from cars in front, necessitating pit stops to have windscreens cleaned. Other problems occurred, although not Jaguar related. Teo Fabi moved to car number 3 on lap 50, taking over from Martin Brundle, after which the two XJR-14s moved into the lead, which they held to the finish.

Venue: Monza, Italy
Round 2, 5 May 1991
Race title: 24 Trofeo Filippo Caracciola

Chassis type	Chassis no.	Race no.	Drivers	Grid pos.	Finish position	Laps
XJR-14	591	3	Derek Warwick, Martin Brundle, Teo Fabi	2	1	75
XJR-14	691	4	Teo Fabi, Martin Brundle	1	2	74

Back on Jaguar's favourite home ground circuit for round three at **Silverstone**, the race was completely dominated by the XJR-14s' awe-inspiring power and speed. They averaged over four seconds a lap quicker than their Mercedes and Peugeot main rivals, and claiming front row of the grid was almost routine. Martin Brundle set the quickest time of 1min 27.478sec to take pole position. Derek Warwick later expressed deep frustration, convinced he could have done even better if traffic had not hindered all his attempts to complete a faster lap.

For the race, Martin Brundle in car number 3 was forced back to the pits at the end of the first lap to have a broken throttle cable replaced. Having lost seven laps in the process, he drove the car solo for the remainder of the race, gradually working up to finish third. With Jaguar number 4 favourite to take the flag, Derek Warwick took over from Teo Fabi for the final stint, crossing the line one lap ahead of the second place Wendlinger/Schumacher Sauber Mercedes. Believing he had earned maximum points to

TWR went to great lengths to cover up certain features of the XJR-14, as seen here in the pits before the Silverstone race. (Michael Scott)

The beautiful, aerodynamic, lightweight XJR-14 (691) sharing a test day at Silverstone with an XJR-15. (Zoom Photographics)

add to his championship total, an elated Warwick celebrated with the traditional podium champagne frolics, only to learn that his epic win had been disallowed. Some 40 minutes later he was declared winner, but lost the points through not being nominated driver for Jaguar number 4. But for this, he would have shared joint third place with Fabi on 35 points, against Mass and Schlesser's joint top score of 37 points each. This was a bitter blow for Warwick and the Silk Cut team.

Venue: Silverstone, UK
Round 3, 19 May 1991
Race title: Castrol BRDC Empire Trophy

Chassis type	Chassis no.	Race no.	Drivers	Grid pos.	Finish position	Laps
XJR-14	591	3	Martin Brundle, Derek Warwick	2	3	79
XJR-14	691	4	Teo Fabi, Derek Warwick	1	1	83

Everyone loves a winner, which in the classic 24-hour race at **Le Mans** was not to be Jaguar, or the equally dominant Mercedes C11s but, rather to everybody's surprise, a Mazda 787B driven by Volker Weidler, Bertrand Gachot and future Jaguar Formula 1 driver Johnny Herbert. Silk Cut Jaguar's brilliant second, third and fourth places hardly rated headlines, but to have three cars out of three finish so well was a tremendous achievement. A fourth XJR-12LM also competed but was kept separate from the Silk Cut contingent. Raced in Japanese Suntec colours, it was manned by Mauro Martini and Jeff Krosnoff, regular drivers of the lone Suntec-sponsored XJR-11 in the 1991 All Japan Sportscar-Prototype Championship race series. For this event only, they were joined by David Leslie, formerly a driver with the short-lived Aston Martin Group C team.

This year, the official Le Mans programme featured an XJR-14 on the front cover, no doubt in response to Tom Walkinshaw having entered two of that season's regular sprint cars in addition to the V12 line-up. FISA regulations for Le Mans required that teams must enter the cars used in other SWC races during the 1991 season. Walkinshaw's intention was to use the XJR-14s to

The nine 1991 Silk Cut Le Mans drivers pose for the pre-race photo shoot in front of the V12s and XJR-14s. (Ken Wells)

The Suntec-sponsored number 36 XJR-12LM (290) looked very different. (Ken Wells)

gain pole position, possibly run them awhile, and then concentrate on winning with the 7.4-litre V12 endurance cars. The rules for 1991 reserved the first 10 grid positions for 3.5-litre non-turbo cars only, and Walkinshaw's aim was to frustrate the Peugeots who were tipped as being most likely to be the fastest qualifiers. Only one of the XJR-14s, chassis 691, took part in qualifying, driven by Andy Wallace. His fastest time in practice was eventually bettered by a Sauber Mercedes. In the meantime Walkinshaw withdrew the car, much to Wallace's disappointment. The V12s all qualified well, but were not pushed to better the Mercedes times.

The first eight hours saw the three Silk Cut cars running steadily, stopping for fuel, new tyres and driver changes, without major problems. Derek Warwick in car 33 spun into the gravel at 9.30pm, causing slight body damage but not enough to require an immediate pit stop. Around 2.30am next morning he stopped at Arnage with loss of fuel pressure due to a disconnected fuel pump plug. This was quickly remedied with the loss of only 10 minutes. Andy Wallace spun the same car into the gravel around

daybreak, losing a further 15 minutes. Kenny Acheson in Jaguar 34 hit a rabbit on the track just before 6am, making it necessary to call into the pit, where the nose panel was replaced.

At 8am, Jaguar 35 was running in second place and by midday the three Jaguars were in third, fourth and fifth places behind the leading Mercedes C11 of Schlesser, Mass and Alain Ferte, who were three laps ahead of the second-placed Mazda of

The number 35 XJR-12LM's second place at Le Mans, followed by third- and fourth-placed Jaguars 34 (991) and 33 (891), was a superb achievement. (Ken Wells)

At Le Mans, the Silk Cut and Suntec Jaguars were kept apart. Pictures like this where both cars are in the same frame are quite rare. (Sutton Photographic)

Weidler, Herbert and Gachot. From time to time the number 35 Jaguar and the Mazda swapped second and third places until disaster struck the leading Mercedes, ending its lengthy run in first place. Now it was the Mazda in front, followed by all three Silk Cut Jaguars, with little chance of them overtaking the Japanese entry unless fate intervened to put it out. What an incredible result it would have been, but the Mazda was certainly a worthy winner, especially as it was the first win at Le Mans for a Japanese car.

By complete contrast, the Suntec Jaguar was plagued by a series of breakdowns and mishaps from the end of the second hour onwards. The car was managed by a first class pit crew with Dave Benbow as chief engineer, and all three drivers felt confident of a good race. Benbow had been the engineer responsible for the previous year's winning Jaguar XJR-12, chassis 1090, so hopes were high for another good result. Two hours after the start, the fuel pump switch burned out, leaving Mauro Martini stranded at the first Mulsanne chicane. He managed to get the car started and back to the pits for repairs, only to damage the suspension shortly after getting back in the race. Two more hours were lost during the second session of repairs.

With all chances of a points finish gone, number 36 completed several hours of steady running in the hands of Krosnoff and Leslie. The next mishap occurred when Mauro Martini skidded on oil at Tertre Rouge. He hit the wall and damaged the rear wing and mounting plates. At 6.40am Jeff Krosnoff hit a barrier, losing the rear wing and inflicting more damage, which resulted in another long pit stop. Back in the race, Krosnoff finally came to a halt with a broken gearbox input shaft. The car was officially retired at 9.30am, to the great disappointment of all concerned after so much effort had been put into it.

Venue: Le Mans, France
Round 4, 22-23 June 1991
Race title: 59eme Edition 24 Heures Du Mans

Chassis type	Chassis no.	Race no.	Drivers	Grid pos.	Finish position	Laps
XJR-14	591	3	Andy Wallace		Not used	
XJR-14	691	4	Andy Wallace		Used in practice only	
XJR-12 LM	891	33	Derek Warwick, John Nielsen, Andy Wallace	24	4	357
XJR-12 LM	991	34	Teo Fabi, Bob Wollek, Kenny Acheson	27	3	359
XJR-12 LM	990	35	Davy Jones, Raul Boesel, Michel Ferte	18	2	361
XJR-12 LM	290	36	David Leslie, Mauro Martini, Jeff Krosnoff	28	DNF, gearbox	183

Race winner: Mazda 787B, drivers Volker Weidler, Johnny Herbert and Bertrand Gachot, 362 laps

After a seemingly long summer break, Le Mans aside, round five at **Nürburgring** was not without incident. For Derek Warwick, his win was tinged with sadness, for he had lost his younger racing driver brother Paul in a Formula 3000 accident at Oulton Park only four weeks earlier. New to the team at the 'Ring' was David Brabham, racing son of Sir Jack Brabham, standing in for Martin Brundle, who was absent due to F1 commitments. As Brundle

had done, Brabham now acted as second driver to Fabi in one car, and to Warwick in the other.

An incident involving Michael Schumacher running into Warwick's car during practice caused a great deal of uproar in the pits. Luckily for Schumacher, Tom Walkinshaw had not arrived at the circuit, and all ended with the young Mercedes driver receiving a warning from FISA. The two XJR-14s continued their record run of top two grid places in qualifying, Teo Fabi taking pole position with a new sportscar record time of 1min 19.519sec.

For the race, the Jaguars expected tough opposition from the two Mercedes and Peugeots, but one by one they fell by the wayside, Rosberg's Peugeot first on lap eight, then Schumacher's Mercedes with a broken engine two laps later. Schlesser's Mercedes lasted 28 laps and the Baldi/Alliot Peugeot succumbed to engine failure on lap 56. The remaining cars were not considered a threat, enabling the Jaguars to ease up during the final laps. Warwick crossed the line first in Jaguar number 3, with Brabham on the last stint in number 4 a few seconds behind.

Venue: Nürburgring, Germany
Round 5, 18 August 1991
Race title: ADAC Sportwagen Weltmeisterschaft

Chassis type	Chassis no.	Race no.	Drivers	Grid pos.	Finish position	Laps
XJR-14	591	T car				
XJR-14	691	4	Teo Fabi, David Brabham	1	2	95
XJR-14	791	3	Derek Warwick, David Brabham	2	1	95

After Nürburgring, Teo Fabi led the Drivers' Championship with 62 points. Derek Warwick was second with 50 points. Jaguar was well in the lead in the Team Championship with 75 points against 50 for Mercedes.

The Silk Cut Jaguars' winning streak ended with a fighting comeback from the Peugeot team during round six on the French home soil of **Magny Cours**. Peugeot had worked hard to improve their cars and were clocking best times in pre-race practice sessions. The two Jaguars finished provisional third and fourth on the first day's qualifying, unable to match the new-found speed of the Peugeots. Final qualifying saw both Jaguars drop back one more place, starting the race in fourth and fifth spot, after they had also become out-timed by the number 2 Mercedes.

The race started with the second Peugeot immediately

overtaking its pole position team-mate, with Schumacher's Mercedes hot on their heels. The Jaguars stood little chance of reeling them in, and within six laps the lead cars were already up with the backmarkers. It looked as though the Silk Cut Jaguars would be fighting it out with the Mercedes for third and fourth, but Schlesser's number 1 car stopped on the track after only nine laps with a broken throttle linkage. Lap 23 saw the collapse of the Mercedes challenge when Schumacher followed suit with a disconnected water hose which forced him to abandon the steam-shrouded car.

From then on the Jaguars suffered irritating mishaps and delays, including a minor wiring fire which sent the pit crew into panic. Warwick nearly lost it altogether, spinning into the gravel, and only rejoined the race with the aid of the marshals. Brabham finished third, after the final round of relatively smooth laps. Warwick did well to bring car number 3 home in fifth place.

Venue: Magny Cours, France
Round 6, 15 September 1991
Race title: Championnat du Monde des Voitures de Sport

Chassis type	Chassis no.	Race no.	Drivers	Grid pos.	Finish position	Laps
XJR-14	591	T car				
XJR-14	691	4	Teo Fabi, David Brabham	4	3	99
XJR-14	791	3	Derek Warwick, David Brabham	5	5	94

Race winner: Peugeot 905, drivers Keke Rosberg and Yannick Dalmas, 101 laps

Round seven at **Mexico City** was extremely important for the Silk Cut Jaguar team, which needed only three points out of this race to take the Championship. Fabi and Warwick were also anxious to do well. If Fabi were to win, he could be certain of the Drivers' title.

Changeable weather conditions during qualifying hampered Jaguar's chances of gaining pole position, and for the second time in two races they were fourth and fifth on the grid, this time number 3 being ahead of Teo Fabi's number 4 car. The number 2 Mercedes of Wendlinger and Schumacher in second place was sandwiched between the first- and third-placed Peugeots. Disaster struck Teo Fabi at the start of the morning warm-up when his engine shed oil all over the pit floor, caused by a scavenge pump failure. The engine was changed, but to no avail, as further oil leakage problems kept the car in the pits with no chance of a start.

As had now become the norm, the Peugeots dominated most of the race, but for a period it seemed that the Wendlinger/Schumacher Mercedes might end their superiority, until it went out on lap 63 with oil pump failure. The other Mercedes lasted another 17 laps before succumbing to electrical gremlins. Warwick in Jaguar number 3 was just one of a number of cars caught out by heavy rain, spinning off onto the grass after gaining third place. After running to the pits to change tyres, he later reached second before events turned against him. As conditions improved, he returned to the pits on lap 89 for slicks, only to have his starter motor fail. Losing 10 minutes while a

The new formula Peugeot 905 was one of Jaguar's strongest competitors in the 1991 SWC season. (Peugeot)

Silk Cut Jaguar's final 1991 race at Autopolis in Japan concluded a six-year partnership with the tobacco company in which three Drivers' and Manufacturers' titles had been won in addition to two memorable victories at Le Mans. (Sutton Photographic)

replacement was fitted, he re-entered the race to finish in sixth place, bitterly disappointed after having the Championship lead almost within his grasp.

Venue: Mexico City, Mexico
Round 7, 6 October 1991
Race title: 1991 Trofeo Mexico

Chassis type	Chassis no.	Race no.	Drivers	Grid pos.	Finish position	Laps
XJR-14	691	4	Teo Fabi, David Brabham	5	Did not race, oil leaks	
XJR-14	791	3	Derek Warwick, David Brabham	4	6	92

Race winner: Peugeot 905, drivers Keke Rosberg and Yannick Dalmas, 98 laps

Not only was round eight at **Autopolis** in Japan the final SWC race for 1991, it was the last time Jaguar's XJR prototypes were to compete in Silk Cut colours. The XJR-14s began the year in stunning form, undisputed leaders of the new 3.5-litre non-turbo category, reigning long enough to be certain of the Championship. Now they were bowing out with a worthy second and third, finishing behind the Mercedes young guns who took the first place denied to them by Jaguar, and then Peugeot, for so long.

In qualifying, Teo Fabi made fastest time during day one. When the Peugeots' laps got faster during the final session, he out-paced them again to take his third pole position of the season. Warwick, balked by traffic, could only manage fourth place on the grid. On race day, early morning fog delayed warm-up, leaving the

Jaguar mechanics to play football while they waited for it to clear. Fuel leak problems forced Warwick to use the spare car (591) in the race.

The early race laps settled into a tussle for the lead between Fabi, the two Peugeots and Schumacher in the number 2 Mercedes. On lap 20, Dalmas in the lead Peugeot stopped on the track, leaving Schumacher to forge ahead, now firmly established in the leading position. From then on, Warwick did his best to catch up with the Mercedes, while Fabi remained content to finish Jaguar number 4 with enough points to clinch the Drivers' Championship, handing the car over to Brabham for the final stint.

Venue: Autopolis, Japan
Round 8, 27 October 1991
Race title: SWC in Autopolis

Chassis type	Chassis no.	Race no.	Drivers	Grid pos.	Finish position	Laps
XJR-14	591	3	T car, Derek Warwick	4	2	93
XJR-14	691	4	Teo Fabi, David Brabham	1	3	93
XJR-14	791	3	Derek Warwick, David Brabham		Did not race, tank failed, used 591	

Race winner: Sauber Mercedes C291, drivers Michael Schumacher and Karl Wendlinger, 93 laps

With Jaguar already Team Champion before this race, Teo Fabi's Drivers' Championship win made it a third-time double for the Silk Cut Team in only six full seasons of Group C Championship racing. A fitting end to a great period in Jaguar racing history.

Chapter 10

1991 All Japan Sportscar-Prototype Championship

Oriental excursion

Japan was an important export market for Jaguar, and in 1987 responsibility for sales had passed from the former British Leyland operation to Jaguar's own sales company, set up in collaboration with Seibu, an important Japanese commercial organisation. The Japanese market was not easy for imported cars, but Jaguar's image and racing heritage gave it a useful advantage in the eyes of customers looking for a car that was different from the products of the local manufacturers. The opportunity for the brand to make its mark on the active national racing scene was a welcome one. From TWR's viewpoint, the link with Suntec was valuable on many fronts, but the difficulties of operating so far from the home base in Oxfordshire were a drawback.

When TWR announced in April 1991 that two former Silk Cut XJR-11s would contest the All Japan Sportscar-Prototype Championship, it came as quite a surprise to many. One car would race, chassis 490, while the other, chassis 590, would be supplied as a spare, together with all the necessary service equipment, a TWR race engineer and the support team. This was part of a deal between TWR and the Japanese Suntec Racing Team, which also included entering an XJR-12 for the team in the 1991 Le Mans 24-hour Race. In both the AJS-PC events and at Le Mans, the cars would be raced in full Suntec sponsorship colours very unlike the factory Silk Cut, Castrol and Bud Light liveries.

Sundai Technologies Research and Development Inc (Suntec), first established in 1985, was set up to support the motorsports activities of the Sundai Automotive Technical College in Kofu, Japan. Involved in the manufacture and development of racing cars, and education of students in various aspects of motorsport in their car design centre, Suntec ran their own Formula 3000 race team and were also involved in Group A activities.

The 1991 AJS-PC race series for Group C cars consisted of seven races at three Japanese venues: Fuji, Suzuka and Sugo. During the season four races were held at Fuji, two at Sugo and one at Suzuka. Round one at Fuji in March took place before the TWR Suntec deal, so the XJR-11 participated in rounds two to six, with rather disappointing results. The two regular drivers, Mauro Martini (Italy) and Jeff Krosnoff (USA), had both previously raced in the Suntec Formula 3000 cars, but were inexperienced in Group C competition.

In the first race for the Suntec Jaguar, round two at **Fuji International Speedway**, practice and qualifying were not

This interesting picture of a JVC sponsored dark green liveried XJR-11 appeared in Jaguar Racing Review's first report of TWR's 1991 Suntec campaign in Japan.
(Ken Wells collection)

without problems. Starting from ninth on the grid, Mauro Martini made an encouraging start, moving up to third place. Soon after the first pit stop, with Jeff Krosnoff at the wheel, the car was black-flagged for having an unsecured door, requiring an unscheduled pit stop. Now back in ninth place it made good progress but suffered engine failure on lap 84 and was withdrawn. The race was mostly dominated by very strong works Nissan and Toms Toyotas, almost entirely manned by Japanese drivers.

Venue: Fuji, Japan
Round 2, 5 May 1991
Race title: Fuji 1000km

Chassis type	Chassis no.	Race no.	Drivers	Grid pos.	Finish position	Laps
XJR-11	490	18	Mauro Martini, Jeff Krosnoff	9	DNF, engine	83
XJR-11	590		Spare car			

Race winner: Nissan R91CP, drivers Kazuyoshi Hoshino and Toshino Suzuki, 224 laps

The Suntec XJR-11 Jaguar ran on Dunlop tyres but continued to use BBS three-piece wheels.
(Ken Wells collection)

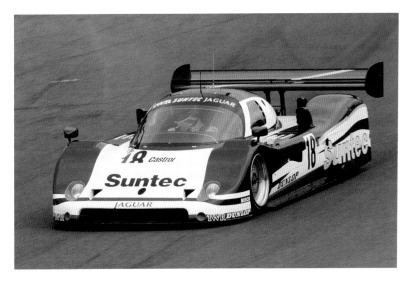

For the Suntec Jaguar XJR-11's second race at Fuji in July, John Nielsen joined the two regular drivers, but tyres were a problem, eventually putting the car out on lap 140. (Sutton Photographic)

John Nielsen joined the team for round three, also held at **Fuji**. Tom Walkinshaw made the journey to observe the race, which was run in uncomfortably hot weather. Tyres were the main problem, although this was not quite so apparent during qualifying, which was held in cooler conditions. Nielsen could only manage seventh place on the grid.

On race day, temperatures rose above 90° Fahrenheit, leaving everyone sweltering in rather unpleasant humid conditions. Nielsen moved up to sixth for a while, but soon experienced handling difficulties as the Dunlop tyres rapidly deteriorated in the heat. He was eventually reduced to running 20-lap stints before pitting to change tyres. All the team wanted was to finish, but even this was denied when one hour before the end a turbo failed. This problem was thought to have been brought about by vibrations and shock waves from the tyres as they deteriorated.

Venue: Fuji, Japan
Round 3, 21 July 1991
Race title: Fuji 500 miles, Japan 1991

Chassis type	Chassis no.	Race no.	Drivers	Grid pos.	Finish position	Laps
XJR-11	490	18	John Nielsen, Mauro Martini, Jeff Krosnoff	7	DNF, turbo	140
XJR-11	590		Spare car			

Race winner: Toyota 91CV, drivers Hitoshi Ogawa and Masanori Sekiya, 179 laps

John Nielsen was again present for round four at **Suzuka**, where the Jaguar fared no better, an electrical fault putting it out after only 46 laps. Only seven cars finished: two Toyotas, two Nissans, two Mazdas and one Porsche.

Venue: Suzuka, Japan
Round 4, 25 August 1991
Race title: 1000km Suzuka International

Chassis type	Chassis no.	Race no.	Drivers	Grid pos.	Finish position	Laps
XJR-11	490	18	John Nielsen, Mauro Martini, Jeff Krosnoff	7	DNF, electrics	46
XJR-11	590		Spare car			

Race winner: Toyota 91C, drivers Roland Ratzenberger and Pierre-Henri Raphanel, 171 laps

Round five at **Sugo** brought a first for the Suntec team - their first finish. Heavy rain washed out Saturday's practice session and disrupted the single car qualifying on Sunday morning. The Jaguar managed only ninth on the grid, but for once pole position went to a Porsche rather than to a Japanese car. There was little chance of mixing it with the leading Toyotas and Nissans, but the Suntec car completed a good race, finishing sixth and in the points at last.

Venue: Sugo, Japan
Round 5, 15 September 1991
Race title: 500 miles Sugo International

Chassis type	Chassis no.	Race no.	Drivers	Grid pos.	Finish position	Laps
XJR-11	490	18	John Nielsen, Mauro Martini, Jeff Krosnoff	9	6	129
XJR-11	590		Spare car			

Race winner: Toyota 91CV, drivers Geoff Lees and Eje Elgh, 135laps

One of the most active participants during round six, the fourth race this season to be held at **Fuji**, was the pace car, which was called out no less than five times on to the rain-lashed circuit. After the first 10 laps the circuit did dry out for a period, but rain returned after the second round of pit stops. From then on, the race settled into periods of wet, with cars spinning off and the pace car coming out again. To complete the misery, fog descended and combined with the rain to slow lap times down to 2min 45sec off pole time. Mauro Martini slid off the track on lap 166, managing to get back again just as the race was called to a halt. He was classified in seventh place overall, still in the points.

The two regular Suntec drivers, Jeff Krosnoff (USA) and Mauro Martini, were joined by John Nielsen for the mid-season races. (Ken Wells collection)

Venue: Fuji, Japan
Round 6, 6 October 1991
Race title: 1000km Fuji International

Chassis type	Chassis no.	Race no.	Drivers	Grid pos.	Finish position	Laps
XJR-11	490	18	Mauro Martini, Jeff Krosnoff	7	7	140
XJR-11	590		Spare car			

Race winner: Nissan R91CK, drivers Kazuyoshi Hoshino and Toshio Suzuki, 165 laps

With one more race to go and little to show for months of hard work, the desire to achieve a good result remained strong. One week before the final race, round seven at **Sugo**, the Silk Cut Jaguar team happened to be in Japan, where they were contesting the final SWC race at Autopolis with the Championship winning XJR-14s. Although at Autopolis they did not come home in first place, they added second and third places to their season's creditable tally of successes. Tom Walkinshaw, anxious to continue the TWR/Suntec partnership, had already pledged one or possibly two XJR-14s for the 1992 AJS-PC season, subject to

Rear view of the Suntec XJR-11. (Ken Wells collection)

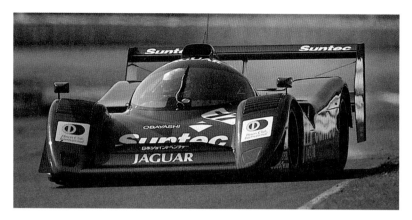

Entered at short notice, the XJR-14s raced to victory at Sugo, in 1991 Silk Cut colours but with Suntec stickers. (Autosport)

field, which they would have done but for deliberate lap-after-lap obstruction by peeved regulars, who were determined to make life difficult for the heavy-gang interlopers. Luckily, Teo saw the race through without serious mishaps due to his own skilful driving, although suffering a slight altercation with another driver along the way. The second Jaguar attempted to keep up, driving cautiously to avoid coming to grief while attempting to overtake resentful backmarkers. As the race neared the end, it seemed the Jaguars were in line for a splendid one-two finish when disaster struck number 18. Jeff Krosnoff pulled into the pits with smoke pouring from his car's tail, caused by a failed left rear wheel bearing. The pit crew set to replacing the assembly in record time. Teo took the flag four laps ahead of the Toms Toyota, with the Krosnoff/Martini Jaguar finishing a gallant, but disappointing, ninth.

a satisfactory agreement being reached. Meanwhile, in an effort to secure a satisfactory result at Sugo, the entire Silk Cut entourage stayed in Japan, including Sportscar World Champion driver Teo Fabi and David Brabham. Transferring the whole shooting match to Sugo was not to be acceptable to all, but such an opportunity was too good to miss.

The XJR-14s could not be repainted in Suntec colours in such a short time, so they remained in the Silk Cut 1991 corporate two-tone mauve/magenta livery, with Suntec stickers instead of the usual Silk Cut logos. Fabi and Brabham drove car 17, chassis 691, while Martini and Krosnoff were assigned to 791, carrying race number 18. Fabi managed an easy pole position, while Martini on his first-ever venture in an XJR-14 was only 1.2 seconds slower, taking second spot.

The Jaguars were expected easily to outrun the rest of the

Venue: Sugo, Japan
Round 7, 3 November 1991
Race title: 500 miles Sugo International

Chassis type	Chassis no.	Race no.	Drivers	Grid pos.	Finish position	Laps
XJR-14	691	17	Teo Fabi, David Brabham	1	1	217
XJR-14	791	18	Mauro Martini, Jeff Krosnoff	2	9	199
XJR-14	591	T car	David Brabham			

At last the Jaguars had made good in Japan, but perhaps not enough to secure a second AJS-PC season. If an agreement had been reached, maybe TWR would have built extra XJR-14 chassis in addition to those lined up to race in the 1992 IMSA series.

Nissan and Toyota won three races apiece during the first six rounds of the 1991 AJS-PC season. The last race went to Jaguar, although not with the XJR-11. (Ken Wells)

Chapter 11

1988 IMSA Camel GT Championship

An encouraging start, but...

Jaguar's return to Le Mans and the consequent entry into the World Sports-Prototype Championship resulted from two men's enthusiasm for racing. Mike Dale had profited from his position in sales with the American companies of BMC and later British Leyland by being able to race these companies' products as an amateur. In the course of his racing he had made the acquaintance of Bob Tullius, a fellow amateur who later made the preparation and racing of sportscars his business. When Dale got a budget to publicise British Leyland products through racing, it was natural he should give the work to Tullius and his Group 44 team. The success of the team brought bigger budgets and eventually the opportunity for Tullius and Dale to bring the team, which was by now running Jaguars, to Le Mans.

The return to the circuit whetted the appetite of the Coventry management for sports-prototype racing, and TWR, which had run a successful programme with the XJ-S in Europe, was given the task. The team's success on the world stage soon overshadowed Tullius's efforts in the USA, and it was decided to hand over American racing to a locally-based TWR operation from the beginning of 1988. It was the end of a long-standing business relationship between Dale, representing British Leyland and latterly Jaguar, and Tullius. But TWR had proved itself the more dynamic and successful organisation, and Dale, who had campaigned for so long for racing's place in the promotional scheme of things, could not argue against the change. Nevertheless, in the closed world of IMSA racing the TWR team was seen as the big-money interloper that had pushed Tullius's team out. This feeling was echoed in some parts of Jaguar USA, which did not feel the same closeness to TWR as it did to Group 44. The result was that TWR started its American journey needing to prove itself.

Commercially, racing was an important plank in Dale's marketing strategy, and the nationwide spread of the IMSA GTP series gave excellent local exposure, to the advantage of dealers in the region of each race. Nationally, however, the series had minimal exposure in a country where the media's sports coverage is traditionally limited to 'stick and ball' games.

From its inception back in 1969, the American International Motor Sports Association (or IMSA) grew to become one of the world's most important motor racing organisations. Sponsored since 1972 by Reynolds Tobacco, the IMSA Camel GT Championship attracted entries from works and private teams from around the

world, eager to participate in some of the most gruelling racing likely to be encountered outside their own borders. Second only to the 24-hour race at Le Mans, the annual 24-hour Daytona season opener is without doubt one of motor racing's greatest tests of men and machinery. During 1988 the IMSA Camel GT Championship season included races at 14 different venues, all within the USA, opening at Daytona in Florida and finishing at Del Mar in Southern California. For major motor manufacturers, the benefit of a win in their name in this most important market is enormous. Jaguar, anxious to capitalise on the WSPC successes of 1987, needed little persuasion to open a stateside second front, in partnership with the high-profile Castrol Oil as main sponsor.

Three IMSA specification XJR-9 chassis, numbers 188, 288 and 388, were built by TWR during the latter half of 1987. By the time they appeared at the Daytona 24-hour race, all three had been through a punishing series of track testing and evaluation outings in England and at various American circuits. Early publicity pictures of one XJR-9, seen in Castrol livery, showed the car

After what had been a demanding race for Martin Brundle, John Nielsen and Raul Boesel, Jan Lammers joined them to clinch victory in Castrol Jaguar number 60 (288) on its very first 1988 outing at Daytona. Here Martin Brundle heads for a well-earned rest after handing over to Raul Boesel. (Ian Norris)

*The Holbert/Bell/
Robinson Holbert Miller
Lite Porsche, seen here
at Road Atlanta behind
Daytona-winning
Jaguar, pursued the
Castrol Jaguars
through much of the
season, while they, in
turn, chased the
Nissans. (JDHT)*

*XJR racecar designer
Tony Southgate, seen
here talking to Danny
Sullivan (centre) and
Johnny Dumfries,
attended the race at
Daytona to advise on
set-ups and other
matters. (Ian Norris)*

bearing the race number 88. This probably referred to 1988 as the launch year, as there is no record of any Jaguar being raced as this particular number. Chassis 188 was used as the team's spare car, racing occasionally, and actually winning one race. Its most important appearance was in the 1988 Le Mans race, re-liveried as Silk Cut Jaguar 21, where it was rewarded with 16th place. The mainstays of Castrol Jaguar racing throughout the 1988 IMSA season were chassis 288 and 388.

Jaguar's stunning victory in round one at **Daytona** sent shock waves through the entire IMSA establishment and competitors alike. Castrol Jaguar's driver line-up read like a *Who's Who* of the finest names in International Sportscar racing. All of them were

doyens of one or another aspect of international motor racing, and would join the halls of fame as Sportscar World Champions, Daytona 24-hour winners and, last but not least, heroes of the Le Mans classic.

Racing at Daytona differed from anything TWR Jaguar had done before. Banked turns generate g-force levels beyond anything experienced on the diverse circuits raced at as part of the WSPC Championship. In addition to having to overcome this particular problem, the Sunbank 24-hour is run for almost twelve hours in darkness, due to being held so early in the year.

In WSPC racing, the Silk Cut Jaguars' main rivals up to and including 1987 were an abundance of teams equipped with the ubiquitous Porsche 956s and 962Cs, which had dominated the sport for years. In America it was much the same story, Porsche having taken the Daytona trophy for the last 11 years. The locals still had Porsche down to win in 1988 and Jaguar was not even considered as a possibility. What they thought when Jan Lammers careered around the circuit on the single qualifying day to take second position on the grid is anyone's guess. Eddie Cheever added to their dismay by capturing fourth place and, to consolidate Jaguar's upset of the establishment, Martin Brundle finished a superb run to start from sixth. A few rows further back was another Jaguar, immaculately turned out, racing under the name Group 44 Goodyear and entered by Bob Tullius and co-drivers. Sadly for Bob and a great many of his fans, this single Group 44 XJR-7 was to retire with a blown head gasket after only 122 laps. Of the Porsche teams pitted against the Castrol Jaguars, the favourite to win was the Al Holbert Miller Life Porsche 962, driven by Holbert himself, Chip Robinson and Britain's favourite sportscar Champion, Derek Bell.

The race started with Lammers taking an early but brief lead, then the three Jaguars settled into a moderate pace back in seventh, eighth and ninth places, allowing the Porsches to expend their energy in a battle for the lead. Boesel in Jaguar number 60 was first to hit problems as he ran into a backmarker; the Jaguar's rear end was torn off and it lost three laps while repairs and replacements were carried out. Two hours later, fuel pump problems caused the same car to lose more time. After several attempts to put it right, the car was four laps behind the leaders. The two remaining Jaguars were running strongly, and for several hours there was no pressure on them to take on the lead car. When rain fell in the early hours, Derek Bell brought the Miller Porsche in for 'wet' tyres, which enabled him to gain a full one lap lead, holding it until a faulty turbo wastegate kept him in the pits for 23 minutes. At the same time, Jaguar 61 suffered terminal engine failure and was withdrawn.

Dumfries took over the lead in Jaguar 66, but was soon passed by the BFG Porsche of Bob Wollek. Brundle's Jaguar was gaining fast as the teams' tactics changed. Eventually after 19 hours, Jaguar 60 took the lead while number 66, suffering from engine sickness, eased up slightly, the drivers preferring to just

finish if at all possible. Anxiety took over the number 60 drivers as braking became more precarious. They were also suffering the effects of fatigue. Tom Walkinshaw's answer was to put Lammers, now rested after number 61's withdrawal, into the driving seat. From that point on, Jaguar 60 remained firmly in the lead, Nielsen taking the final stint to bring it home one lap ahead of the Busby/BF Goodrich Porsche of Wollek, Baldi and Redman. With Jaguar 66 taking third place, the sceptics' forecasts had been proved thoroughly wrong.

Venue: Daytona, Florida
Round 1, 30-31 January 1988
Race title: Sunbank 24 at Daytona Camel Grand Prix

Chassis type	Chassis no.	Race no.	Drivers	Grid pos.	Finish position	Laps
XJR-9D	188	66	Eddie Cheever, Johnny Dumfries, John Watson	4	3	713
XJR-9D	288	60	Martin Brundle, Raul Boesel, John Nielsen, Jan Lammers	6	1	728
XJR-9D	388	61	Jan Lammers, Davy Jones, Danny Sullivan	2	DNF, engine	512

In round two at **Miami**, conditions on the tight-cornered street circuit were not going to be easy for the Castrol cars. However, the three XJR-9s raced in front of an appreciative crowd, anxious to see Tom's Cats exhibit the magic displayed four weeks earlier at Daytona. The race finished dramatically with an extraordinarily close-run final lap in which John Nielsen in Jaguar 60 raced neck

Chassis 188, racing as car number 66 at Daytona, was one of the two American-managed cars in the 1988 Le Mans, finishing 16th. (Jaguar)

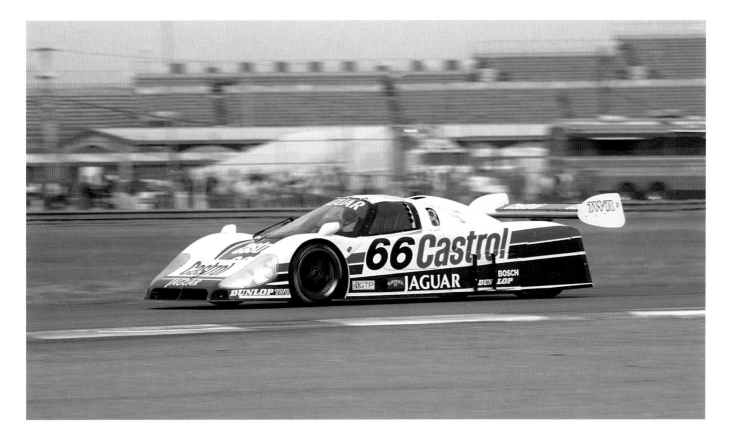

One of many refuelling and tyre-change stops for the Lammers/Jones number 61 XJR-9 (388) during the 12-hour Sebring race. (Ian Norris)

and neck with Price Cobb in the Blaupunkt Porsche. But he was unable to slip through, allowing the turbo Porsche to win by no more than a car's length.

Cheever and Boesel's Jaguar 66 was withdrawn after 32 laps after losing oil pressure. Martin Brundle was brought in for a stop-go penalty for overtaking under the yellow flag. It had been produced in front of him without warning, giving him little chance to ease up. Crashes and yellow flags were the order of the day, but the two remaining Jaguars maintained pressure at the front, each taking the lead at times.

Price Cobb's Porsche forged into the lead after the final round of pit stops, Nielsen in pursuit, followed by three other Porsche 962s and Jones in Jaguar 61. Although Nielsen managed to reduce the lead lap by lap, the three hours ran out a fraction too

soon for the Castrol Jaguar to take the win that the crowds wanted to see. Jan Lammers managed a sixth place finish following a couple of spins.

Venue: Miami, Florida
Round 2, 28 February 1988
Race title: 3 Hour Camel Grand Prix of Miami

Chassis type	Chassis no.	Race no.	Drivers	Grid pos.	Finish position	Laps
XJR-9	188	66	Eddie Cheever, Raul Boesel	14	DNF, engine	32
XJR-9	288	60	Martin Brundle, John Nielsen	3	2	124
XJR-9	388	61	Jan Lammers, Davy Jones	7	6	123

Race winner: Blaupunkt Porsche 962, drivers James Weaver and Price Cobb, 124 laps

Drivers used to the well-prepared and well-maintained race tracks of Europe need time to get accustomed to battling on some of the notoriously rough concrete circuits encountered when competing in the USA. Florida's former Air Force base, venue for the round three **Sebring** 12-hour race, came well within this category and tested chassis durability to the limit.

Initially the intention was to race only two Castrol Jaguars, but all three XJR-9s took part in practice sessions. During qualifying, Martin Brundle in car 60 and Jan Lammers in 61 both bettered the previous year's pole time by a full three seconds, good enough to put them on the grid front row - or so they thought - but they were up against strong opposition from Porsche 962C entries, two of which proved faster. Brundle's short-lived provisional pole was soon lost to Chip Robinson in the Holbert Miller Porsche. Another Porsche finally pushed him back into third, while the Lammers car 61 started from fifth spot.

From the beginning, the race developed into a Porsche v. Porsche duel, with Jaguar 61 running third for a while before Lammers made an unscheduled pit stop for repairs after being hit by one of the backmarkers. Brundle also ran third for a brief spell until a puncture sent him to the pits. On lap 31 his race ended with engine-related problems. Four hours from the finish, Davy Jones, at the wheel of car 61, suddenly lost use of all gears except first due to a broken input shaft. Rather than call it a day the team set about a complete rear-end rebuild, carried out in the remarkably short time of 42 minutes, allowing the car to continue racing and finish in seventh place. The 11 points gained helped to keep Nielsen's lead in the Camel GT Drivers Championship.

Venue: Sebring, Florida
Round 3, 19 March 1988
Race title: 12 Hours of Sebring Camel Grand Prix

Chassis type	Chassis no.	Race no.	Drivers	Grid pos.	Finish position	Laps
XJR-9D	188	60T	T car (Raul Boesel, Davy Jones)			
XJR-9D	288	60	Martin Brundle, Raul Boesel, John Nielsen	3	DNF, engine Classified 60	31
XJR-9D	388	61	Jan Lammers, Davy Jones, Danny Sullivan, John Nielsen	5	7	283

Race winner: Bayside/Havoline Porsche 962, drivers Klaus Ludwig and Hans Stuck, 318 laps

Round four at **Road Atlanta** saw the beginning of the record-breaking series of wins by Geoff Brabham, driving the new 1988 Nissan GTP ZX Turbo. This remarkably reliable car was kept out of the Daytona and Sebring events, but now it was set to leave the rest of the field reeling wherever it went. At Road Atlanta, the Castrol Jaguars were to prove that if they could not be winners they were worthy runners-up ahead of the remaining competition, not just once but many times in the forthcoming season.

Brabham and his co-driver John Morton took pole position with a record-breaking time, aided by the Electramotive Nissan's

new electronically-controlled turbo wastegate system, which gave them optimum boost throughout the rpm range. Nielsen in Jaguar 60 almost matched the Nissan's speed, earning him second place on the grid.

Brabham did not start from pole, having elected to race a much newer 1988 spare car instead of the 1987 car he had used in qualifying. Nielsen therefore headed the grid, from which he and Davy Jones in the second Jaguar led the early stages until the first round of pit stops. Brabham was gaining lap by lap, finally overtaking Nielsen on lap 24, only to lose the lead again during his next driver changeover pit stop. From then on it was Jaguar, Nissan, Jaguar, with the Chip Robinson/Derek Bell Miller Porsche elbowing for second place along the way. With seven laps to go, Brabham overtook Nielsen for the last time, both cars racing neck and neck to the line and finishing with just a few seconds between them. A similar duel was taking place between Jaguar 61 and the Robinson/Bell Porsche. Jones was set to finish third, only to spin 15 laps from the finish. He came home fourth, one lap behind the winning car.

Venue: Road Atlanta, Georgia
Round 4, 10 April 1988
Race title: 500 Km Atlanta Journal/Constitution Camel Grand Prix

Chassis type	Chassis no.	Race no.	Drivers	Grid pos.	Finish position	Laps
XJR-9	188	61T	T car (Andy Wallace, John Watson)			
XJR-9	288	60	John Nielsen, John Watson	1	2	124
XJR-9	388	61	Davy Jones, Andy Wallace	3	4	123

Race winner: Electramotive Eng. Nissan GTP-ZX Turbo, drivers Geoff Brabham and John Morton, 124 laps

Geoff Brabham and John Morton took their Electramotive Nissan to a second stunning win in round five at **West Palm Beach**, followed by Jaguar 61 of Lammers and Jones in second place. The season was clearly developing into a Jaguar v. Nissan contest, instead of Jaguar v. Porsche as predicted early on. In qualifying, the Jaguar times were just that little bit slower than the

At Road Atlanta Castrol Jaguar number 61 (388) and sister car 288 began a long series of races in which they were destined to follow Geoff Brabham's Nissan past the chequered flag. (Paul Skilleter)

Nissan's - not that it mattered to Jan Lammers, who started in second place and took the lead on the first corner. Nielsen moved up behind him on lap two and the two Jaguars then kept the rest at bay for several laps, pushed hard by Brabham, who eventually took the lead after the first yellow flag period. Lammers regained the lead after further cautions and pit stops, only to lose it again during the last pit stop, in which the pit crew lost time removing an errant wheel cover. The Nielsen/Brundle Jaguar 60 experienced fuel pressure problems earlier in the race, and dropped back to tenth place on lap 52. On lap 83 Nielsen had a near-miss accident when a seized gearbox locked the rear wheels, putting the car out of the race.

Venue: West Palm Beach, Florida
Round 5, 24 April 1988
Race title: 3 Hour Grand Prix of Palm Beach

Chassis type	Chassis no.	Race no.	Drivers	Grid pos.	Finish position	Laps
XJR-9	188	61T	T car (Davy Jones)			
XJR-9	288	60	John Nielsen, Martin Brundle	4	DNF, transmission	83
XJR-9	388	61	Jan Lammers, Davy Jones	2	2	149

Race winner: Electramotive Eng. Nissan GTP ZX Turbo, drivers Geoff Brabham and John Morton, 149 laps

In round six at **Lime Rock**, Martin Brundle was the hero of the day after qualifying on pole position, setting a new track record time of 44.885 seconds. The Lammers/Jones car number 61 managed sixth on the grid, with a lap time still quicker than the previous year's record time. Both Jaguars had undergone a series of improvements since their showing at West Palm Beach, including revised underbodies. Also seen for the first time were much deeper wing endplates, fitted to provide extra downforce.

The race had hardly begun when Brabham overtook Brundle, increasing the Nissan's lead by a second a lap. Brundle regained it after Brabham pitted for fuel, and then remained out front to the halfway point. Jaguar 61 stayed well in the running around fifth place after recovering from a spin. With Nielsen at the wheel of number 60 for the latter part of the race, Brabham could do little to get by until eight laps from the finish. Having nudged the Jaguar, causing it to run wide at the Esses, he quickly extended the lead to a full eight seconds at the finish. With the Castrol Jaguars' second and third places, Nielsen still led the Drivers' Championship with 80 points, while Jones and Lammers were in fifth and sixth places.

Venue: Lime Rock, Connecticut
Round 6, 30 May 1988
Race title: 150 Lap Camel Grand Prix

Chassis type	Chassis no.	Race no.	Drivers	Grid pos.	Finish position	Laps
XJR-9	288	60	Martin Brundle, John Nielsen	1	2	150
XJR-9	388	61	Jan Lammers, Davy Jones	6	3	150

Race winner: Electramotive Eng. Nissan GTP ZX turbo, driver Geoff Brabham, 150 laps

Looking at the result tables for round seven at **Mid Ohio**, one might be forgiven for thinking that the previous race result had been reprinted in error. The first three places were identical, except this time Geoff Brabham's team-mate was Tom Gloy. The Electramotive Nissan qualified first, followed by two Porsche 962Cs, then Jaguar 61 of Lammers and Jones. Another Porsche relegated Jaguar 60 of Brundle and Nielsen into sixth place.

The two Castrol cars were second and third past the flag at Lime Rock behind Geoff Brabham's Nissan GTP ZX turbo car. Tony Dowe (arms folded), Ian Reed (centre) and Martin Brundle appear to be ignoring it. (Ian Norris)

In this race, the Nissan led from start to finish, sometimes well ahead of the duelling Jaguars and Porsches, other times only a fraction in front when the Castrol cars had the better of the turbo rivals and were running second. Before the final pit stops the Lammers/Jones car was lying second when a spin by Jones put it third behind number 60. Lammers and Brundle took the final stints, in which Brundle gradually reeled in the Nissan, reducing its lead from 30 to eight seconds. Each time he achieved this, Brabham surged ahead to increase the gap. Unable to do more, the Jaguars finished second and third, with Brundle's drive being described as the best so far this season.

Venue: Mid Ohio, Ohio
Round 7, 5 June 1988
Race title: 500 Km Nissan Grand Prix of Ohio

Chassis type	Chassis no.	Race no.	Drivers	Grid pos.	Finish position	Laps
XJR-9	288	60	Martin Brundle, John Nielsen	6	2	129
XJR-9	388	61	Jan Lammers, Davy Jones	4	3	129

Race winner: Electramotive Eng. Nissan GTP-ZX Turbo, drivers Geoff Brabham and Tom Gloy, 129 laps

Neither Jaguar finished the race in round eight at **Watkins Glen**. Geoff Brabham, now rejoined by John Morton in the Electramotive Nissan, took pole position during qualifying, but not before a series of mishaps had befallen the car. A resurgence of Porsche power saw the next three places taken by a trio of 962Cs, with the two Jaguars occupying the third row. Jones made fastest time during the early morning warm-up session, but in the race both Jaguars ran into trouble long before the first scheduled pit stops. Brundle in Jaguar 60 was closing on the lead cars when he was forced into the pits on lap eleven with electrical problems. The mechanics were unable to diagnose what was wrong, so Brundle took a chance and went out again, only to return at the end of the lap. The car was unable to continue and the problem was eventually traced to an obscure wiring fault.

Meanwhile Lammers in Jaguar 61 had his own difficulties when the left rear tyre burst, causing him to limp back to the pits. The wheels were changed and the damaged bodywork replaced, allowing him to get back into the race, where he soon moved back up to seventh. Jones took over on lap 40, anxious to finish somewhere in the points, only to come to grief when he made contact with a Camel Lights-Spice Pontiac. Both cars hit the barriers and were put out of action. Brabham was now leading in the Drivers' Championship points standing.

Venue: Watkins Glen, New York
Round 8, 3 July 1988
Race title: 500 Km Camel Continental Camel Grand Prix

Chassis type	Chassis no.	Race no.	Drivers	Grid pos.	Finish position	Laps
XJR-9	288	60	Martin Brundle, John Nielsen	5	DNF, engine	12
XJR-9	388	61	Jan Lammers, Davy Jones	6	DNF, accident	55

Race winner: Electramotive Eng. Nissan GTP-ZX Turbo, drivers Geoff Brabham and John Morton, 92 laps

Now seemingly untouchable, and on course for yet another win, the Electramotive Nissan did not find it all that easy in round nine at **Road America**. In pre-race unofficial practice sessions Brabham was well ahead of the rest, but he lost out during official qualifying, in which pole position went to the Oscar Larrauri/Walter Brun Porsche. Jaguar 60 of Nielsen and Brundle took second

Deep wing endplates were featured at Lime Rock. Note also the extra large vent louvres on the engine cover. (Ian Norris)

Davy Jones at the control centre of the XJR-9. The dashtop computer monitors lap fuel consumption and tyre temperatures. By pressing one or other of the red buttons, one for each tyre, the driver can check if any are overheating. (Ian Norris)

place, while Jones and Lammers were fourth. Brabham started from fifth due to rain upsetting qualifying and to a heated dispute concerning the results recorded by the IMSA timekeepers.

For Lammers this was a race best forgotten as he clashed with Brabham on the warm-up lap, losing a rear wheel cover in the process. While Brundle moved up into the lead on lap two, the Dutchman became engaged in a no-holds barred battle to keep Brabham from overtaking, resulting in more serious contact which sent the Nissan back to the pits for repairs. Now back in 10th place, Lammers worked hard and finished fifth. In the meantime Brundle remained out in front until lap 24. From then on, number 60 was plagued with fuel pressure problems which slowed its progress, while Brabham climbed back up the field to take a sixth straight win.

Venue: Road America, Wisconsin
Round 9, 17 July 1988
Race title: Miller High Life Classic 500 Km Camel Grand Prix

Chassis type	Chassis no.	Race no.	Drivers	Grid pos.	Finish position	Laps
XJR-9	188	66	T car (John Nielsen, Davy Jones)			
XJR-9	288	60	Martin Brundle, John Nielsen	2	4	78
XJR-9	388	61	Jan Lammers, Davy Jones	4	5	77

Race winner: Electramotive Eng. Nissan GTP-ZX Turbo, drivers Geoff Brabham and John Morton, 78 laps

As at Road America two weeks earlier, there were three Castrol Jaguar XJR-9s present during practice and qualifying for round ten at **Portland**. Only two raced, but this time they were up against a pair of Electramotive Nissan GTP Turbo cars. From the

outset, the Japanese cars dominated practice, qualifying and the race itself, taking first and second places on the grid and past the chequered flag. The Jaguars qualified fifth and sixth behind a pair of Porsche 962s. The third Castrol car, chassis 188, qualified 11th, and early intentions were that it should race, but in the end Tony Dowe decided to concentrate on the two regular cars only.

The race started with Lammers in Jaguar 61 quite uncharacteristically slipping back to 15th place by the end of the first lap. Brundle kept up with the two Nissans as best he could, but with little chance of overtaking. Good weather helped to keep the race largely uneventful, although one by one the strongest Porsche contenders succumbed to engine problems. The two Jaguars were the only other cars to finish on the same lap as the leaders, Nielsen in number 60 in third place, while Jones in 61, having clawed back up the field, finished fourth.

Venue: Portland, Oregon
Round 10, 31 July 1988
Race title: GI Joe's Grand Prix 300 Km Camel Grand Prix

Chassis type	Chassis no.	Race no.	Drivers	Grid pos.	Finish position	Laps
XJR-9	188	66	T car (Martin Brundle)			
XJR-9	288	60	Martin Brundle, John Nielsen	6	3	97
XJR-9	388	61	Jan Lammers, Davy Jones	5	4	97

Race winner: Electramotive Eng. Nissan GTP-ZX Turbo, driver Geoff Brabham, 97 laps

Castrol Jaguar chances of turning the tide against the Nissan steamroller in round 11 at **Sears Point** appeared good, on a circuit where the normally-aspirated V12s were able to make the best times during Friday's practice session. As temperatures rose on qualifying day the Jaguars lost some of their edge, so Geoff Brabham took pole position for a seventh time. Martin Brundle's second fastest time was nearly one second slower than the Australian, while Jan Lammers in car 61 was third on the grid, already feeling the effects of higher track temperatures.

A number of drivers elected to drive the 75-lap race single-handed, Brabham included. From the start, he quickly forged ahead, lapping considerably faster than the two pursuing Jaguars before settling down to a steadier pace. A more determined Brundle caught up with him on lap 14, running nose to tail for a further 18 laps before finally slipping by, much to the delight of the 30,000 onlookers.

Nielsen took the car over on lap 41 but was troubled by understeer, a result of new tyres which had not been warmed up before the pit stop. Brabham was able to overtake before the car settled down, and there was nothing Nielsen could do to stop him making a clear run to the finish. Had the Lammers/Jones Jaguar 61 not suffered a puncture, requiring an additional pit stop towards the end of the race, the outcome might have been different. In finishing third, they were still ahead of the top three Porsche finishers.

Venue: Sears Point, California
Round 11, 14 August 1988
Race title: 300 Km Lincoln-Mercury Camel Grand Prix

Chassis type	Chassis no.	Race no.	Drivers	Grid pos.	Finish position	Laps
XJR-9	188	66	T car (Jan Lammers)			
XJR-9	288	60	Martin Brundle, John Nielsen	2	2	75
XJR-9	388	61	Jan Lammers, Davy Jones	3	3	74

Race winner: Electramotive Eng. Nissan GTP-ZX Turbo, driver Geoff Brabham, 75 laps

One of the saddest sights in the numerous press reports covering round 12 at **San Antonio** was a horribly mangled Castrol Jaguar XJR-9, chassis number 388, being transported from the track like a heap of scrap. Both regular cars were performing well at the start of qualifying, and again hopes were high that Nissan could be beaten. That is, until Jones crashed 388 heavily after a new set of tyres caught him unawares at the Esses. Fortunately he was not seriously hurt, and he and John Watson were able to race the spare chassis 188.

Brabham qualified in pole position yet again, but this time did not finish the race. He led a small group of top qualifiers away from the main pack during the first few laps of the race, which quickly became problematic for a number of drivers. John Nielsen in Jaguar 66, and Davy Jones in number 60, both became concerned about brake problems. Nielsen made several pit stops for his brakes to be bled and topped up, without any satisfactory improvement. On lap 121, with Andy Wallace now driving, the brakes locked, sending him smashing into the wall and inflicting considerable damage.

Now there was one Jaguar left to keep up the struggle, for once not against the all-conquering Nissan, which had retired seven laps earlier with a CV joint failure, but against Jaguar's old adversary, a Miller Porsche 962. The Watson/Jones Castrol Jaguar was a lap down, running third behind the Nissan at the time of its departure, still suffering difficulties with brakes. With the rest of the field fortunately well behind, number 60 cruised home to an easy second place. As chassis 388 had suffered the most extensive damage, the team had no alternative but to send this tub back to the UK for repairs.

Venue: San Antonio, Texas
Round 12, 4 September 1988
Race title: 3 Hour Nissan Grand Prix of San Antonio

Chassis type	Chassis no.	Race no.	Drivers	Grid pos.	Finish position	Laps
XJR-9	188	60	Davy Jones, John Watson	7	2	141
XJR-9	288	66	John Nielsen, Andy Wallace	3	10 (DNF, brakes)	121
XJR-9	388	61	Davy Jones, John Watson; Jones crashed in qualifying, car did not race			

Race winner: Blaupunkt/Dyson Porsche 962, drivers Price Cobb and James Weaver, 142 laps

Round 13 at **Columbus** took place four weeks after San Antonio, allowing plenty of time to put 288 back into shape again. Not that having two cars to race helped John Nielsen's chances in the Championship tables one bit. For the second time in the season there was a pair of Nissan turbo cars, and they took front row of the grid. All through the year, home-bred American cars stood little chance of qualifying in the top positions, but in this race the third grid spot was taken by a Goodwrench Corvette GTP car driven by local hero Bobby Rahal, who later became manager of

Road America had its problems for the number 61 Jaguar (388) of Lammers and Jones. Two clashes with the Brabham/Morton Nissan left them struggling to finish as well as they did. (Ian Norris)

Jaguar's Formula 1 team. The two Jaguars started from fourth and fifth positions.

Martin Brundle, now back in the team, was paired with Nielsen in Jaguar 66, but 23 laps into the race he fell foul of a backmarker running without wing mirrors and was shunted off the track. He made it back to the pits but 288 had suffered too much damage to continue. Nielsen now transferred to car 60, taking over from Lammers at the first pit stop, although not before the Flying Dutchman had run into Derek Daly's Nissan, causing damage to both cars. Time lost in the pits ended any hopes of top place finishes. The lone Jaguar fell back to 14th place before Davy Jones took on the last stint. He improved this to a 10th place finish, earning just one point for the team. Geoff Brabham took his ninth win, only three seconds ahead of the Bayside Porsche of Klaus Ludwig.

Venue: Columbus, Ohio
Round 13, 2 October 1988
Race title: 500 Km Columbus Ford Dealers Camel Grand Prix

Chassis type	Chassis no.	Race no.	Drivers	Grid pos.	Finish position	Laps
XJR-9	188	60	Jan Lammers, Davy Jones, John Nielsen	5	10	77
XJR-9	288	66	Martin Brundle, John Nielsen	4	DNF, accident	23

Race winner: Electramotive Eng. Nissan GTP-ZX Turbo, driver Geoff Brabham, 81 laps

Round 14 at **Del Mar** was by all accounts a fabulous race for Martin Brundle and Jan Lammers, who raced the only Jaguar left to compete with after chassis 288 once again became involved in an accident. Determined to make a good showing in qualifying, John Nielsen drove 288 through a gap that was not quite wide enough, sending himself and the Wynns Porsche of Jim Adams into the wall and denying both cars a start. Chassis 288 followed

In addition to winning at Daytona, chassis 288 as Castrol Jaguar number 60 achieved an impressive list of top four finishes in the 1988 IMSA season. The covers used to convert to single headlamps for sprint racing were as seen on Group C XJR-6s in 1986. (Jaguar)

388 back to the UK for a serious rebuild. Del Mar is but one of many street circuits raced on in the States and is lined by concrete walls. For drivers new to America they can be very challenging. Brundle was undeterred, relishing this particular challenge, especially after Lammers's best qualifying time had them starting from pole position.

Lammers shared Brundle's wholehearted enthusiasm, and at the end of lap one was already 6.59 seconds ahead of the second qualifying Porsche 962 of Bob Wollek. By lap 20 he was 14 seconds in front but was then slowed down by a pace car stint following an accident. Further cautions and pace car intervals eventually acted against the Jaguar, and at one point allowed Brabham to take the lead. Not for long though, with Brundle now in charge and gradually seeing off the competition. Brabham crashed his Nissan on lap 51, instigating yet another pace car session. With only half an hour left when the green flag was waved, it was a duel between Brundle's Jaguar and Wollek's Bayside Porsche. After pitting for badly needed new tyres, the Castrol car emerged 41 seconds behind the leader. Brundle set out on a race of a lifetime. In no time at all he was up to fourth place, then second, taking the lead with less than 10 minutes left and cruising home to a comfortable victory. This was described as the most exciting race of the season, and Brundle's and Lammers's first place helped Castrol Jaguar finish on a well-deserved high note. The winners' purse - at $145,000 the largest amount paid out at any of the races - was welcome too.

Venue: Del Mar, California
Round 14, 23 October 1988
Race title: 2 Hour Camel Grand Prix of Southern California at Del Mar

Chassis type	Chassis no.	Race no.	Drivers	Grid pos.	Finish position	Laps
XJR-9	188	61	Jan Lammers, Martin Brundle	1	1	88
XJR-9	288	60	John Nielsen		(crashed in qualifying, car did not race)	

For the Castrol team this particular result could not have been a better way to close the season. After starting magnificently, capturing the inaugural Daytona 24-hour race, much was expected of them. No one had foreseen the impact Geoff Brabham's amazing run of successes in the consistently reliable Nissan turbos would have on the series. Brabham richly deserved his 186-points GTP Championship title. Castrol Jaguar drivers took four of the next six places, with John Nielsen second best at 140 points.

The Manufacturers' Championship title went to Porsche, but bear in mind that for each Nissan and Jaguar entered there were two or three Porsche 962s spread over different teams. Porsche's total of 197 points was only just above Nissan's 196. Jaguar was placed third with 174 points. Overall Jaguar's tally of finishes in the top five put them way ahead of any individual Porsche team, which was particularly significant when taking into account that this was the team's first year of involvement in Camel GT Racing.

Chapter 12

1989 IMSA Camel GT Championship

Turbos fail to stem the tide

Americans love a winner, but they don't necessarily love a foreign winner. Yet as it went into 1989 the Castrol-Jaguar IMSA team was losing its 'foreign' image. With another American driver, Price Cobb, in the team along with Davy Jones, a predominantly American crew of mechanics and a 'can do' attitude that appealed to the locals, the TWR-Jaguar operation was better accepted into the IMSA family in 1989. The team had proved itself in the previous season, and the fears that it would sweep all before it following the Daytona win had not been realised. Despite the fact that the champion driver was Australian, the 1988 season-winning Electramotive-Nissan racing effort was seen as being similar to Group 44, an all-American team working for a foreign manufacturer. Its victory was therefore regarded as a home win which had shown that TWR-Jaguar wasn't the infallible interloper some had feared it would be. In a perverse way, Jaguar's valiant efforts to achieve elusive success had improved the team's credibility. But now it needed to win.

Commercially, Jaguar was benefiting from the improving image the company and its products were enjoying both internationally and in the US. With sales and profitability increasing, Jaguar Cars Inc., Jaguar's American arm, was able to maintain a credible challenge in IMSA, but only with the collaboration of Castrol, an active and supportive sponsor. The increased competitive element that Jaguar's presence had injected into IMSA racing was now helping raise the visibility of Jaguar, Castrol and IMSA to the benefit of all concerned.

For the second year running, the IMSA GT Championship season was dominated for most of the time by a phenomenal car-and-driver pairing: Geoff Brabham, now teamed up for some races with former Porsche 962 driver Chip Robinson, repeated his 1988 total of nine wins in the ultra-reliable Nissan GTP ZX Turbo. The Castrol Jaguars were foremost in helping to break them at other times.

All three IMSA XJR-9 chassis had been subject to extensive detailed improvement work during the winter close season, and were ready to repeat the previous year's debut success in the Daytona 24 Hours. The team had had the experience of a full season's racing on the diverse assortment of circuits visited in 1988 – some purpose-built, some street circuits of variable quality – and felt better prepared to hold off the competition until TWR's new turbo cars could be brought into play. Daytona had been conquered in 1988 by the reliable, normally-aspirated Jaguar V12

prototypes, against overwhelming turbo-powered opposition. The challenge now was to repeat the success.

Externally, the Castrol Jaguars looked nearly the same as before but had revised side-intake engine covers. Under the skin was a more refined suspension system, and the cars incorporated a greater number of US-manufactured components. Chief engineer Ian Reed said there was very little in the XJR-9s that had not been modified in some way.

The nine-man driver line up for **Daytona** included the 1988 Le Mans winners, Jan Lammers and Andy Wallace, and two newcomers to the team, the Frenchman Patrick Tambay and Martin Donnelly from the UK. As in 1988, car number 66 was chassis 188, last year's winning chassis 288 still retained race number 60, and similarly 388 ran as 61.

The Electramotive Nissans may have been masters of IMSA sprint racing up to now but they had shunned the longer endurance races, fearing they might not make the distance. However, the decision to enter two for Daytona in 1989 seemed well justified after Geoff Brabham qualified car number 83 on pole. Jan Lammers, in Jaguar 60, managed second, only seven-tenths of a second slower than Brabham but marginally faster than the other Electramotive Nissan. The other two Jaguars occupied fourth row of the grid.

Jaguar chairman and chief executive Sir John Egan spent

Pre-season 1989 was a time of intense activity for the Castrol team. Considerable improvements to all three XJR-9 chassis, followed by an exhaustive series of track tests, such as here at Talladega, raised expectations of a good year's racing. (Ian Norris)

Twelve hours racing in darkness at Daytona called for much night-time testing. (Ian Norris)

Price Cobb, John Nielsen, Andy Wallace and Jan Lammers almost produced another Daytona victory in the number 61 Jaguar, which was the only Castrol finisher. (Ian Norris)

much time in the pits, attired in Castrol green trousers and team shirt, taking a passionate interest in all the activities of the team. Regrettably he would not witness another great Jaguar win, as the previous year's favourite, the Busby/Miller Porsche 962, driven by Derek Bell, Bob Wollek and John Andretti, streaked past the flag 80 seconds ahead of Jaguar 61. In a 24-hour race, that could be considered very close indeed.

Misfortune befell Derek Daly in Jaguar 66 on the opening lap when he clashed with the second Electramotive Nissan 84, driven by fellow Irishman Michael Roe. Both cars made it to the pits. The Nissan was soon out again, but front suspension damage condemned the Castrol car to early retirement, much to the disappointment of Donnelly and Tambay, who were denied any involvement. The Nissan was to last another two hours before brake problems curtailed its race. The early hours were punctuated by mishaps which brought out the yellow flag, as well as by lead changes, with the different Porsche teams making a strong show. As the evening wore on, Jaguar 60 and Nissan 83 emerged as the principal front runners, swapping the lead each time the other pitted. Jaguar 61 was running third but not quite able to match the sister Jaguar's speed.

Around 2am on Sunday morning a heavy fog bank rolled across the circuit, prompting the organisers to impose what turned out to be well over three hours under the red flag. A little before the stoppage, Davy Jones in the lead Jaguar had his engine grind to a halt. Now all hopes rested on the remaining Cobb/Nielsen/Wallace Jaguar 61 to mix it with the Nissan and Porsche clique, all running on the same lap. Around 10am, with less than a minute between the three leading cars, Robinson brought Nissan 83 into the pits with a dropped valve. No one, including the Electramotive team members, had expected the Nissan turbo cars to survive for so long. For them it was a praiseworthy effort, certainly worth all the work put into it. Jaguar 61 was back in the lead although not running 100 per cent. Additional ducts had been fitted to help cool the engine and valuable time was lost while this was being done, which allowed the smooth-running Miller Porsche to take over the number one spot. In spite of strong pressure from the Jaguar, nothing could prevent a well-deserved win. Derek Bell, Bob Wollek and John Andretti made it quite clear that the ageing Porsche 962s were still fully capable of taking on, and beating, all comers. Had Jaguar 60 survived instead of number 61, things might have turned out very different.

Venue: Daytona, Florida
Round 1, 4-5 February 1989
Race title: Sunbank 24 at Daytona Camel Grand Prix

Chassis type	Chassis no.	Race no.	Drivers	Grid pos.	Finish position	Laps
XJR-9D	188	66	Derek Daly, Martin Donnelly, Patrick Tambay	8	DNF, accident	1
XJR-9D	288	60	Jan Lammers, Davy Jones, Raul Boesel	2	DNF, engine	288
XJR-9D	388	61	Price Cobb, John Nielsen, Jan Lammers, Andy Wallace	7	2	621

Race winner: Busby/Miller Porsche 962, drivers Derek Bell, Bob Wollek and John Andretti, 621 laps

Round two at **Miami** saw last year's winning Blaupunkt Porsche driver Price Cobb, teamed up with John Nielsen in Jaguar 61, all set to repeat his previous success, but this time for the Castrol team. Nielsen had finished second in the 1988 Camel GTP Drivers' Championship and Cobb third; together they made a formidable team. Jan Lammers and Davy Jones were paired together in number 60, while car 66 (chassis 188) would act as spare. Lammers completed a nail-biting qualifying lap, hugging the street circuit's concrete walls so close that had the Jaguar been given had another coat of paint, he would have scraped it off. Still unable to match the times of Brabham's Nissan and Wollek's Porsche, he started third on the grid with the Cobb/Nielsen Jaguar in fifth spot.

The first four cars raced the opening lap as they had started, Brabham soon pulling away from Wollek and Lammers. Twenty laps later Lammers overtook Wollek and held on to second place

for a further 12 laps. At this point, Lammers misjudged his braking at the end of the Biscayne Boulevard and dropped back several places. Cobb was now running third until a puncture sent him into the pits. On lap 44, oil from a damaged cooler spilled onto the tyre of number 60 and it slid into the barrier, sustaining severe damage. Now only the Cobb/Nielsen Jaguar remained to challenge the Nissan, already under much pressure from Wollek. The Porsche eventually took the lead and held it for much of the latter half until troubled by vibrations. Then the Nissan was back in front again, and although Nielsen was in hot pursuit of it for the final 20 minutes he was unable to get by. The Castrol Jaguar's second place finish repeated the previous year's result for Nielsen who, for the second year running, led the Drivers' Championship alongside Price Cobb.

A thick blanket of fog rolling in from the sea across the Daytona circuit halted night-time running for three hours. (Ian Norris)

Venue: Miami, Florida
Round 2, 5 March 1989
Race title: 3 Hour Nissan Grand Prix of Miami Camel Grand Prix

Chassis type	Chassis no.	Race no.	Drivers	Grid pos.	Finish position	Laps
XJR-9	188	66	T car (Davy Jones)			
XJR-9	288	60	Jan Lammers, Davy Jones	3	DNF, accident	44
XJR-9	388	61	Price Cobb, John Nielsen	5	2	131

Race winner: Electramotive Eng. Nissan GTP-ZX Turbo, drivers Geoff Brabham and Chip Robinson, 131 laps

The 12-hour race at **Sebring** (round three) was the only other endurance race in the Camel GT calendar, and this time Nissan made it, with the Cobb/Nielsen Jaguar finishing as the runner up. More often than not, Nissan kept their turbo car entry to one for most races, occasionally fielding a second car as they did here at Sebring. Both Nissans proved to be impressively faster in

Part of the roadshow fans rarely see - the Jaguar pits at Sebring. Note the scuttle panel allowing access to the spring-damper assemblies. (Ian Norris)

qualifying than the Castrol cars and they occupied front row of the grid, while the Jaguars took the second row.

Price Cobb and Davy Jones took the first stints. They drove a cautious race behind the Nissans, losing a second a lap and biding their time until the latter hours. Dutch driver Arie Luyendijk in the second Nissan 84 completed an astonishing fastest lap of the race before losing a wheel on lap14, which reduced Electramotive to their usual single car running. On lap 20 Chip Robinson, leading in Nissan 83, was being chased hard by Cobb's Jaguar 61, and 20 laps later these two cars were the only ones still on the lead lap. Shortly afterwards a faulty body latch caused the Nissan to make a couple of unscheduled pit stops, allowing Nielsen to take a brief lead, while the second Jaguar moved up to third place.

Some time later Jones had the misfortune to come across a wandering Camel Lights car. He was unable to avoid running into it and the Jaguar was badly mauled, necessitating a 1¾-hour pit

stop for repairs. In the meantime the race settled into a duel between Jaguar 61 and the Nissan, which swapped the lead from time to time until a delayed pit stop cost the Castrol car three laps. Both cars finished the race with no further problems. Electramotive Nissan's win ended a record number of 13 consecutive victories at Sebring by Porsche, and was the first by a Japanese car.

Venue: Sebring, Florida
Round 3, 18 March 1989
Race title: 12 Hours of Sebring Camel Grand Prix of Endurance

Chassis type	Chassis no.	Race no.	Drivers	Grid pos.	Finish position	Laps
XJR-9	188	66	T car			
XJR-9	288	60	Jan Lammers, Davy Jones	4	14	281
XJR-9	388	61	Price Cobb, John Nielsen	3	2	328

Race winner: Electramotive Eng. Nissan GTP-ZX Turbo, drivers Geoff Brabham, Chip Robinson and Arie Luyendijk, 330 laps

into the pit after 25 laps with a broken valve. Cobb in Jaguar 61 began to feel the effects of rising temperatures, which increased tyre pressures and caused excessive wear. After pitting for new tyres, he set out to overtake the Nissan. The Toyota had already expired with turbo problems, but not before impressing everyone by maintaining the lead over the other Japanese car for the first 32 laps. With only 10 laps to go Cobb took the lead when Brabham's Nissan made a quick pit stop for new tyres. Back out again, the Nissan's fresh tyres gave it a definite edge over the Jaguar. Cobb could do nothing to prevent it streaking by, leaving him to settle for second place once again.

Venue: Road Atlanta, Georgia
Round 4, 2 April 1989
Race title: 500 Km Nissan Camel Grand Prix

Chassis type	Chassis no.	Race no.	Drivers	Grid pos.	Finish position	Laps
XJR-9	188	66	Davy Jones (crashed in practice, car did not race			
XJR-9	288	60	Jan Lammers, Davy Jones	4	DNF, engine	25
XJR-9	388	61	Price Cobb, John Nielsen	2	2	124

Race winner: Electramotive Eng. Nissan GTP-ZX Turbo, drivers Geoff Brabham and Chip Robinson, 124 laps

Six different manufacturers' cars were in the first seven grid placings in round five of the Championship at **West Palm Beach**, two of which were Castrol Jaguars. Not surprisingly, Geoff Brabham had out-qualified all others in Electramotive Nissan 83 to take another pole position. Jan Lammers's time put Castrol Jaguar 60 in fourth place, while John Nielsen could only manage sixth in number 61. Second place went to another Japanese car, an All-American Racers Toyota which was now threatening to usurp some of the Porsche entries as they vied with Jaguar for the best-of-the-rest placings behind the all-conquering Nissans.

This race was not to be another success for Nissan 83, which

There was also plenty of action in the pits. Here the second-placed XJR-9's radiator is being checked. (Ian Norris)

Looking at the result for round four at **Road Atlanta**, one could be forgiven for assuming it was just as before, but here things were rather different. Pole position went to a Toyota, not the Nissan, and Price Cobb/John Nielsen in Jaguar 61 seemed the likely winners near the end of the race, only to have victory snatched from their grasp five laps from the flag. Price Cobb had qualified second fastest in Jaguar 61, while for the second race in a row Jaguar 60 started from fourth. The regular spare XJR-9 chassis 188 was severely damaged in practice while driven by Davy Jones, and was subsequently returned to Kidlington for repairs. 188 was not listed again in any race.

A starter flag mix-up at the beginning of the race allowed Cobb to dash into the lead, only to be called back to the pits for a stop-go penalty. The starter happened to be a Nissan dealer. Tony Dowe and Tom Walkinshaw were less than pleased, especially when their complaints fell on deaf ears. The Castrol team's frustrations were further deepened when Lammers brought car 60

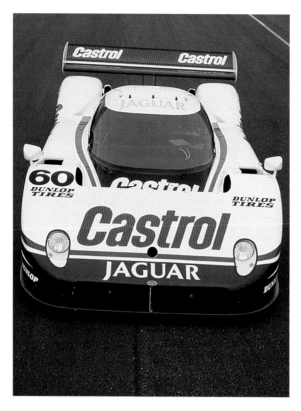

An early picture of the new Castrol XJR-10 turbo car, in which the short-lived monocoque ducts behind the wing mirrors are clearly visible. They were soon replaced by periscope ducts fixed further back on the engine cover panel. (JDHT)

The Castrol Jaguar team had something new for round six at **Lime Rock**, namely the all new 3-litre V6 turbocharged Southgate-designed XJR-10. Given the chassis number 389, it was the first of the new-generation prototypes with which Jaguar hoped to compete on level terms with the dominant forced-induction cars such as the Electramotive Nissans and the up and coming Toyota Eagles. Jan Lammers marked the debut of this radically different Jaguar in stirring fashion by gaining number two spot on the grid. However, the All-American Racers Toyota was faster still. For once the two Nissans struggled to make good progress, and when rain disrupted qualifying they were left in seventh and ninth places.

Davy Jones was absent for this race as he was competing in the Indianapolis 500, so Lammers raced the turbo car solo. He and the Toyota broke away from the rest of the field, increasing their lead lap by lap. The Dutchman was unable to reel in the All-American Racers front runner, whose advantage of lighter weight allowed it to open up the gap by one second per lap to a full 20 seconds. In the meantime Brabham had moved up the field to third place, challenging Lammers for second. Nielsen in the XJR-9 came next, while much of the field were already a lap down on the lead car.

On lap 66 Lammers, fearing he was using a little too much fuel, dashed into the pits determined not to be ousted by running dry. By this time only Brabham and Nielsen were on the same lap as Olsen. Shortly afterwards, Nielsen pitted the XJR-9, which was taken over by Cobb. Olsen, still in the lead, called in for a routine pit stop, only to be held up by the officials, who insisted that a faulty brake light must be put right. Now Brabham led, with Lammers next. Olsen rejoined in third place but later went out altogether with a broken engine. Lammers's second place finish was only eight seconds behind Brabham, excellent for the turbo car on its first time out. Nielsen came third in spite of a collision with another car in the closing stages.

Venue: Lime Rock, Connecticut
Round 6, 29 May 1989
Race title: Lime Rock Toyota Trucks Camel Grand Prix

Chassis type	Chassis no.	Race no.	Drivers	Grid pos.	Finish position	Laps
XJR-9	388	61	Price Cobb, John Nielsen	8	3	150
XJR-10	389	60	Jan Lammers	2	2	150

Race winner: Electramotive Eng. Nissan GTP-ZX Turbo, driver Geoff Brabham, 150 laps

went out on lap four with a broken engine, leaving the Toyota to lead with Lammers hot on its tail. Nielsen could not match Lammers' pace and was running fourth. Lammers lasted only 22 laps before being brought to a halt by a rare transmission failure in which some of the pinion teeth had been stripped off.

The Toyota continued to run well, while the Cobb/Nielsen Jaguar battled it out for second place with the Daytona-winning Busby Miller Porsche of Bob Wollek and John Andretti. When Drake Olsen in the Toyota pitted for fuel under a yellow flag, Nielsen led for a while. From then on there were five different leaders, including a one-time rare opportunity for an American-manufactured car to lead the pack. Greek driver Costas Los in the 5-litre Spice Pontiac Firebird thrilled the local crowds, going on to finish fifth in the GTP class. The final laps saw the Jaguar-Porsche battle increasing in intensity. The TWR pit crew's turnaround times were far superior, helping to get the Castrol car out in double-quick time. In the end the superiority of the Miller Porsche's tyres was the factor which allowed Wollek to manoeuvre past Cobb and take a very hard-won first place.

Venue: West Palm Beach, Florida
Round 5, 23 April 1989
Race title: Pontiac Grand Prix of Palm Beach

Chassis type	Chassis no.	Race no.	Drivers	Grid pos.	Finish position	Laps
XJR-9	288	60	Jan Lammers, Davy Jones	4	DNF, transmission	22
XJR-9	388	61	Price Cobb, John Nielsen	6	2	162

Race winner: Miller High Life Porsche 962, drivers John Andretti and Bob Wollek, 162 laps

The new Castrol turbo car's promising debut race led to disappointment in round seven at **Mid Ohio** when it seemed on course to make another impressive showing. Indeed, during qualifying it flew around the circuit in a quick time, only 0.051sec slower than Brabham, who captured pole position yet again in the Nissan. The normally-aspirated XJR-9 was fourth, behind the increasingly competitive Toyota of Drake Olsen and Chris Cord.

The XJR-10 lagged slightly behind in the early stages of the race, suffering tyre problems, although later it picked up remarkably well, becoming easily the fastest car on the circuit. Overheating was destined to bug the turbo Jaguars, but on this occasion the car was forced out after Lammers had scythed into the grass, picking up enough cuttings to block his radiator, with the inevitable consequences. Number 60 was retired after 82 laps. Jones transferred to join Cobb and Nielsen in the V12, making good progress amongst the front runners. The final round of pit stops was made under a yellow flag, brought out after the Toyota caught fire while leaving the pit lane after its scheduled refuelling and driver changeover.

On re-starting, Brabham exited later than the Jaguar and the Busby Porsche, due to problems with a troublesome wheel nut. Cobb, now in charge of number 61, was leading, hoping to hold on until the finish. Brabham was back to third behind the Wollek/Andretti Porsche, which he soon reeled in, and then followed this by slipping past Cobb on lap 108. The Castrol team was still very happy to finish second, proving the V12s were far from throwing in the towel, and they were now more than confident that the turbo cars would change the team's fortunes very soon.

Venue: Mid Ohio, Ohio
Round 7, 4 June 1989
Race title: Nissan Camel Grand Prix of Ohio

Chassis type	Chassis no.	Race no.	Drivers	Grid pos.	Finish position	Laps
XJR-9	388	61	Price Cobb, John Nielsen, Davy Jones	4	2	129
XJR-10	389	60	Jan Lammers, Davy Jones	2	DNF, cooling	82

Race winner: Electramotive Eng. Nissan GTP-ZX Turbo, drivers Geoff Brabham and Chip Robinson, 129 laps

Round eight at **Watkins Glen** appeared all set to produce a great result for the Lammers/Jones XJR-10, as Lammers actually made better qualifying times than Brabham in the Nissan. Unfortunately, the Australian's team-mate did better still, capturing pole position yet again for the Electramotive team. By now Lammers was well used to starting from the number two spot - he had been there so many times already. The Castrol Jaguar team still had only one turbo car prepared for racing so, as before, 389 was accompanied by the regular XJR-9 chassis 388. The latter qualified sixth, regrettably completing only six laps before succumbing to engine problems, which brought it to a halt in front of the pits.

Lammers on the other hand took XJR-10 number 60 into the lead, passing Brabham just after turn one and holding on until the first round of pit stops, which were taken rather early, on lap 17. When he was back on the track a disastrous blow-out of the left rear tyre on the back straight sent him spinning this way and that, although luckily not off the track. With pieces of shattered bodywork scattered everywhere, the Castrol crew had no option but to pack up and return home. Jaguar was not alone in having a rotten day, as the popular Busby Miller Porsche car lasted well until lap 69, when engine problems ended its race. The second

All-American Toyota Eagle fared even worse as it was involved in an accident on lap 45.

Venue: Watkins Glen, New York
Round 8, 2 July 1989
Race title: Camel Continental

Chassis type	Chassis no.	Race no.	Drivers	Grid pos.	Finish position	Laps
XJR-9	388	61	Davy Jones, John Nielsen	6	DNF, engine	6
XJR-10	389	60	Jan Lammers, Price Cobb	2	DNF, puncture	32

Race winner: Electramotive Eng. Nissan GTP-ZX Turbo, drivers Geoff Brabham and Chip Robinson, 92 laps

From one bad race Castrol Jaguar progressed to a much more satisfying result in round nine at **Road America**. Yes, the Electramotive Nissan did win, but the Jaguars took second and third, in addition to having claimed the front row of the grid. Davy Jones's pole time of 1min 55.970sec in the XJR-9 smashed IMSA's longest-standing qualifying record by two seconds. Jan Lammers in the XJR-10 was only 0.151sec slower. The V12s were not ready to be put out to grass yet and it was very satisfactory to have two of the wonder Nissans behind on the second row, rather than in front as had become the norm.

Lammers and Jones took off side by side, but by the end of the first lap Brabham had slipped past Jones in the XJR-9. From then on the race became the familiar duel between one or other Castrol car and Brabham, ahead of a similar tussle between the Olsen/Fangio Toyota and the Busby Miller Porsche of Wollek. Olsen was delayed after being run off the track by a GTO car. Brabham made it past Lammers on lap 23, losing out again by stalling on the first round of pit stops. In all, 48 cars started the race, inevitably causing traffic problems for the fastest runners. Surprisingly there were few major incidents, but one car stalled on the track, bringing out the pace car. Cobb was called in for a brake pad change, putting him behind the leading XJR-9 and Nissan at the re-start. Later he fought hard with Bob Wollek in the Porsche for third place, before Nielsen made an unscheduled pit stop due to a puncture.

Brabham was in the lead and Lammers second, having taken over from Cobb, with the XJR-10 no longer under pressure from Wollek. When the Frenchman made his second pit stop he was delayed in the pits while a faulty stoplight was seen to. Nielsen's extra pit stop did not prevent him from running home third, making this a satisfactory race for the Castrol Jaguars.

Venue: Road America, Wisconsin
Round 9, 16 July 1989
Race title: Miller High Life 500 Km

Chassis type	Chassis no.	Race no.	Drivers	Grid pos.	Finish position	Laps
XJR-9	388	61	John Nielsen, Davy Jones	1	3	78
XJR-10	389	60	Jan Lammers, Price Cobb	2	2	78

Race winner: Electramotive Eng. Nissan GTP-ZX Turbo, drivers Geoff Brabham and Chip Robinson, 78 laps

XJR-10 chassis 489, seen here in its one and only race at Portland, was destroyed by fire during a practice session at Grattan. (Paul Skilleter)

Round ten at **Portland** will be remembered for a blunder by the official starter, who prematurely waved the chequered flag three laps from the finish while Price Cobb in XJR-10 number 60 was leading. The Jaguar and Brabham's Nissan were neck and neck at that moment, then the mistake was realised and the flag withdrawn. The chase continued for another three laps before the flag was brought out again just after Brabham had nudged Cobb sideways, running past to take the win for the Electramotive team. Three days later, after a protest from Castrol Jaguar, Lammers and Cobb were declared rightful winners. The rules were clear: when a chequered flag is shown, even in error, the race is over.

Portland saw the appearance of a second Jaguar XJR-10, chassis 489, only recently completed and still largely untested. The team concentrated on this car alongside the XJR-9 during the first two days' practice, but in the end Lammers used chassis 389 to good effect, making best qualifying time to put him in pole position, the first time for an XJR-10. Brabham's time was less than a second quicker than the third place XJR-9, so he stood alongside the XJR-10 on the front row. The new XJR-10 did race, having started from 14th position, but went out after only 10 laps with mechanical problems.

Lammers' pole start allowed him to catapult away from the pack, rapidly pulling away from the Nissan and well clear of the *mêlée* affecting the mid-field runners. One of the Toyotas had spun on turn three, causing other drivers to take avoiding action. Nielsen also took a spin, but order soon reigned and everyone settled down to the job in hand. After 40 laps of the race Lammers was still ahead of Brabham and remained so until lap 52, when he made his first routine pit stop and handed over to Cobb. Brabham inherited the lead for three laps before his own pit stop. Choosing to remain in the driving seat, he was soon passed by Cobb and held at bay most of the time until the premature flag incident. Davy Jones's last stint in the XJR-9 included the fastest lap of the race. His fourth place made it Jaguar-Nissan-Nissan-Jaguar, with the Drivers' Championship top four places also

shared by the two teams: Brabham first followed by Robinson, Cobb and Nielsen.

Venue: Portland, Oregon
Round 10, 30 July 1989
Race title: GI Joe's Camel Grand Prix

Chassis type	Chassis no.	Race no.	Drivers	Grid pos.	Finish position	Laps
XJR-9	388	61	John Nielsen, Davy Jones	3	4	94
XJR-10	389	60	Jan Lammers, Price Cobb	1	1	94
XJR-10	489	66	Davy Jones	14	DNF, mechanical	10

Round eleven took place at the brand-new **Heartland Park** circuit at Topeka, Kansas. Of the several race reports examined, some call the venue Heartland Park while others refer to it as Topeka. Four XJR prototypes were present during the period of practice and on race day, two XJR-9s and two XJR-10s. XJR-10 chassis 489 was used for practice only, and XJR-9 chassis 288 acted as the T car, supporting the two regulars 388 and 389. In qualifying, the XJR-10 managed second place on the grid, sandwiched between the first and third placed Nissans of Robinson and Brabham. Lammers started the session, making fastest time, but lost out during official qualifying after a spin, which meant that he had to settle for fifth spot.

On the rolling start, Brabham steamed past both the Nielsen/Jones XJR-9 number 60 and his team-mate Chip Robinson, and then for much of the race the two Nissans remained fully in charge. On a circuit suited to the turbo-powered cars even the Jaguar XJR-10 was unable to match the superior performance of the Japanese cars. Not only were the Nissans permanently just out of reach but the Castrol drivers were also struggling to fend off Olsen's Toyota, which at one point towards the end slipped by Nissan number 2 into second, followed by Lammers in Jaguar 61. Robinson soon regained station behind the lead car, and a spin by Olsen cleared the way for Lammers to run home a worthy third. Olsen came fourth, and the only other car still on the same lap was the Nielsen/Jones XJR-9, which finished in fifth place.

Venue: Heartland Park, Topeka, Kansas
Round 11, 13 August 1989
Race title: 300 Km Camel Grand Prix of Heartland Park

Chassis type	Chassis no.	Race no.	Drivers	Grid pos.	Finish position	Laps
XJR-9	388	60	John Nielsen, Davy Jones	2	5	75
XJR-10	389	61	Jan Lammers, Price Cobb	5	3	75
XJR-10	489	66	Price Cobb, Jan Lammers (practice only, not raced)			

Race winner: Electramotive Eng. Nissan GTP-ZX Turbo, driver Geoff Brabham, 75 laps

The 1989 Camel GT Championship season was more than two-thirds through, yet the Castrol team was still fielding one of the ageing V12s, long after the new generation of turbo cars had been introduced. XJR-10 chassis 389 had showed considerable promise so far, and it was hoped that its newly introduced sister car chassis 489 could also be amongst the front runners. Sadly this was not to be. Following a brief debut outing at Portland lasting only 10 laps, and the race practice sessions at Topeka, 489 was taken to Grattan circuit for testing. Davy Jones was unfortunate enough to be driving when the car went off the track and hit an incorrectly installed Armco safety barrier which, in addition to wrecking the car, ripped the fuel cell open. Chassis

489 was destroyed in the ensuing fire.

The two regular cars, XJR-9 chassis 388 and XJR-10 chassis 389, were present for round twelve at **San Antonio**, but this was one of those awful occasions when both retired quite early on. No prizes for guessing which two cars started from the front row: Brabham in Nissan 83 on pole position, and Robinson's car 84 by his side. An engine water leak prevented what might have been better timing for Price Cobb in the XJR-10 on third, with Nielsen qualifying fourth.

San Antonio, though a popular venue, is not the easiest track to race on, and to make things even harder this time, the organisers decided to run the race in the opposite direction to usual. For the race, Nielsen was partnered with Frenchman Michel Ferte. Jones, who had spent most of his practice time in the V12, began the race in the XJR-10 and soon took the lead when the Nissans bumped into each other and spun off. Hardly able to believe his luck, Jones remained out in front up to and through a full course caution, only threatened for the lead by James Weaver in the Bayside Porsche 962C. At the end of the caution, while still well up front, the Jaguar's engine lost boost, leaving Jones no option but to return to the pits. His race was over.

Ferte also enjoyed a moment of glory, having seen off Weaver and one of the Toyotas, but lost control on lap 29 as he negotiated the final chicane and unhappily spun into the wall. Weaver was unable to avoid the Jaguar and also came to grief. It was Chip Robinson's turn to take victory for Nissan, Brabham having gone out with engine problems on lap 82.

After two DNFs and two second places, XJR-10 chassis 389 as Castrol Jaguar 60 was soon to take the very first TWR turbo car win at Portland, Oregon. (Paul Skilleter)

Price Cobb (right), shown with Andy Wallace, was the highest Jaguar points scorer in 1989, came third in the Drivers' Championship behind Nissan drivers Geoff Brabham and team mate Chip Robinson. (Ian Norris)

Venue: San Antonio, Texas
Round 12, 3 September 1989
Race title: 2 Hour Nissan Camel Grand Prix of San Antonio

Chassis type	Chassis no.	Race no.	Drivers	Grid pos.	Finish position	Laps
XJR-9	288	66	T car (Davy Jones, Michel Ferte)			
XJR-9	388	60	John Nielsen, Michel Ferte	4	DNF, accident	28
XJR-10	389	61	Davy Jones, Price Cobb	3	DNF, engine	20

Race winner: Electramotive Eng. Nissan GTP-ZX Turbo, driver Chip Robinson, 94 laps

In 1989 the performance of the Nissans and the Jaguars resembled that of Ferrari and McLaren in Formula 1 Grand Prix races some 10 years later, as they hogged the grid front row race after race to the exclusion of almost every other car. The same could be said for podium places. Round thirteen at **Sears Point** saw little change in the status quo. Lammers made a brilliant fastest qualifying lap in the turbo Jaguar, putting him in pole position ahead of the two Nissans, with Nielsen in fifth place still in the XJR-9. Jaguar now had three poles to its credit.

During the race warm-up the Jaguars were easily the fastest cars on the track, raising hopes of a possible triumph over the Nissans. Cobb reinforced these sentiments by building up a superb lead of over five seconds by the seventh lap. Gradually Brabham edged the Electramotive Nissan closer, running neck and neck by lap 17. As the two leaders caught up with the race traffic Brabham saw his chance to slip by. Cobb handed over to Lammers on lap 33, while on the track the Nissans swapped places out in front. Now it was a battle, between Robinson in the second Nissan and the Dutchman, which lasted until lap 53. Lammers, suffering a lack of positive grip, was unable to prevent Robinson steaming by and building up a sizeable distance between them. Lammers was called into the pits for new tyres during a full caution, earning himself a stop-go penalty by overtaking slower cars before the green flag. Now he found

himself running fifth behind Jochen Mass in a Porsche 962 and the Nielsen/Jones Jaguar XJR-9 in third place. The race seemed set to finish in that order but Mass was forced to pit with a loose front wheel. Castrol Jaguar once more had to settle for being the runners-up behind the Nissans.

Venue: Sears Point, California
Round 13, 10 September 1989
Race title: Lincoln-Mercury California Grand Prix

Chassis type	Chassis no.	Race no.	Drivers	Grid pos.	Finish position	Laps
XJR-9	288	60	John Nielsen, Davy Jones	5	3	75
XJR-10	389	61	Jan Lammers, Price Cobb	1	4	75

Race winner: Electramotive Eng. Nissan GTP-ZX Turbo, driver Geoff Brabham, 75 laps

For round fourteen at **Tampa**, the team was fully confident that the continued development of the turbo cars would improve on the capabilities of the XJR-9s, and yet it was 'old faithful' which surprised everyone by being first past the post. Not that poor performance or a failed engine affected the XJR-10 - just the opposite. Lammers had qualified second behind Brabham's Nissan, while Price Cobb was way back starting from sixth slot. The first two hours of the race, according to one report, were routine if not rather dull. Brabham led most laps, exchanging for a time with team-mate Robinson's Nissan, Lammers's XJR-10 and Wayne Taylor in his Spice Pontiac.

Lammers thrilled the crowds with some stunning skid school antics after spinning during the latter part of the race. This memorable incident came on lap 94 when, hard on the heels of the two Nissans, he accelerated too soon upon clearing the last turn. The turbo car pitched into a 180-degree about-turn. Lammers immediately selected reverse, hit the pedal accelerating backwards down the pit straight and then, effecting another 180-degree spin, changed back into third and roared away. The whole grandstand and the pit personnel were on their feet - who said this race was dull?

A little later, Lammers was caught unawares when Brabham spun ahead of him. Forced to take avoiding action, he left the track and was unable to stop the turbo Jaguar from ramming into the tyre barrier. The contretemps with Brabham's car occurred just seven laps from the end. Other cars were involved, but through it all Cobb passed unscathed into the lead, safely holding it under a yellow caution flag period. The green flag was waved with only one lap left. Cobb stepped on it, narrowly outmanoeuvring Robinson's Nissan, to take victory. One thing was for sure: the V12s still had magic when it was most needed. Tampa was the last time a normally-aspirated V12 Jaguar competed alongside a turbo Jaguar in any IMSA sprint race. A few weeks later, two Silk Cut XJR-9s saw action in the WSPC final race in Mexico, although unsuccessfully. From now on, as the XJR-12s, the V12s would be confined to endurance racing only, in 12- and 24-hour events.

Venue: Tampa, Florida
Round 14, 1 October 1989
Race title: 360 Km GTE World Challenge of Tampa Grand Prix

Chassis type	Chassis no.	Race no.	Drivers	Grid pos.	Finish position	Laps
XJR-9	288	60	Price Cobb	6	1	117
XJR-10	389	61	Jan Lammers	2	DNF, accident	110

Round fifteen at **Del Mar** was the debut race for the third XJR-10, chassis number 589. In 1988, Jaguar had ended a long period without a win by taking first place at this circuit. After the magnificent result at Tampa, the team were in the right mood to do it again. Neither Jaguar nor Nissan made pole position, the fastest time being achieved by a Spice Pontiac. It was obvious that the track suited the Spice cars, as the other front row spot was taken by a Chevrolet-engined Spice. The new XJR-10 chassis started from fourth place alongside Brabham, who was third fastest in the Nissan. Lammers, complaining of poorly balanced tyres, could only manage seventh.

The lightweight Spice cars enjoyed a lengthy period of glory out front during the first 39 laps until the first yellow flag period rearranged the field. At the re-start Brabham led with Lammers third. Three more yellow flags mixed up the runners even more, but Lammers and Brabham emerged to make it a duel to the finish. The Jaguar took the honours after Brabham locked up on turn one, allowing Lammers to slip by and home for the last time. Cobb, like Lammers, drove solo in the new, still unrefined chassis, unable to keep up with the leaders of the pack but finishing well in seventh place. For the second year running Castrol Jaguar scooped the largest purse, this time $180,000.

Venue: Del Mar, California
Round 15, 22 October 1989
Race title: 2 Hour Nissan Camel Grand Prix of Southern California

Chassis type	Chassis no.	Race no.	Drivers	Grid pos.	Finish position	Laps
XJR-10	389	60	Jan Lammers	7	1	85
XJR-10	589	61	Price Cobb	4	7	82

Geoff Brabham won the 1989 Drivers' Championship with 230 points, team-mate Robinson was second with 219, then came Cobb with a very worthy 193. Nielsen was fourth with 154, while, for all his achievements, Lammers came lower down the list with 103 points. Jaguar was second in the Manufacturers' Championship with 206 points against Nissan's top score of 247.

Tony Dowe stands in front of assembled drivers, engineers, pit crews and related personnel with two Castrol XJR-9s and one of the new XJR-10s (389) in September 1989. Jaguar Inc. Vice President of Sales and Marketing Mike Dale, standing by the turbo car with Davy Jones, was a great supporter of Jaguar racing in America. (Jaguar)

Chapter 13

1990 IMSA Camel GT Championship

The going gets tougher

With Jaguar now under Ford ownership there was a new atmosphere in the company. Although there was a 'hands-off' policy that saw Jaguar executives left in charge and no mass influx of Ford people, there was a change of attitude at the top. The major manifestation of this change was the arrival of Bill Hayden to replace Sir John Egan in mid-1990. Despite the distance from Coventry to Jaguar's US headquarters in New Jersey, Hayden's relentless emphasis on quality and efficiency soon made itself felt. Improving quality was a major priority as warranty costs were a major headache for Jaguar in the US, where the recession was biting hard and luxury cars were becoming more difficult to sell. The racing programme was an obvious candidate for cost cutting, but with the Castrol contract in place until the end of the year the 1990 season was business as usual for TWR-Jaguar.

Once again the team was wearing the mantle of the plucky

Castrol Jaguars continued to use modified engine covers in 1990 but were up-to-date with the revised noses with NACA brake ducts. (Jaguar)

underdogs as the season opened, for Geoff Brabham and Nissan had triumphed again in 1989. Castrol-Jaguar had achieved more wins, but the overall title had eluded them and the turbocharged XJR-10 had not given the team the advantage it had hoped for. In addition, while the challenge from the privateer Porsche teams diminished, Gurney's Toyotas were becoming a major threat.

Castrol Jaguar's back-to-back wins in the last two races of the 1989 season raised expectations of better things to come in 1990. The sponsorship deal with the oil company still had one year to run, and now the team had formed a new partnership with the Goodyear tyre company. Henceforth all Jaguars would run on Goodyear rather than Dunlop tyres, and Goodyear decals appeared on the cars and team clothing.

Considerable improvements had been made to the V12 chassis, now upgraded and listed as XJR-12s, although for the time being they retained their original XJR-9 chassis numbers. The turbos, still on their learning curve, were also subject to a long list of modifications. They had proved faster than the best forced-induction competitors at times, but whenever the engineers had wrung a little extra performance from them the rival teams did likewise. Reliability was the key to success, and until now the Electramotive Nissans, which now raced under the title Nissan Performance, had reigned supreme in this respect. The challenge for the improved turbo Jaguars was to counter their superiority and capture the elusive IMSA titles, or the team would finish as runners-up yet again.

The 1990 driver line-up for sprint racing remained much as before: Price Cobb with John Nielsen, and Davy Jones with Jan Lammers. Driver changes and substitutions were made during the season, and later on a decision was made to cut down to single-driver entries, following a number of occasions when the team's number one driver Davy Jones had driven solo. In January TWR announced that Martin Brundle and Andy Wallace would join the regulars for Daytona.

Departing from earlier practice, only two cars were entered in the round one **Daytona** 24-hour race, after having been extensively modified to endurance specification. There was no question of attempting to race with the still unproven turbo cars. Throughout winter testing the team's new Goodyear Eagle tyres won much praise from the drivers, who declared them less prone to 'going off' towards the end of stints. Tom Walkinshaw's edict was teamwork and strategy above all else, knowing he could rely

In seven years of prototype racing the Allan Scott Jaguar V12 engine changed little in general appearance. (Ken Wells collection)

The Daytona-winning Castrol Jaguar XJR-12 in the pits for fuel, tyres and a driver change (Jones to Wallace). (Jaguar)

absolutely on the skills and leadership of chief engineers Ian Reed and Dave Benbow, to whose care the two cars were entrusted.

Qualifying was not to be an all-out run for the grid front row, as this was left to the turbos. The two Nissans took second and third places behind the pole winning Bayside Porsche 962. The two Jaguars started from the fifth row, running a controlled race while all around their strongest competitors suffered delaying mishaps. They emerged from the first rounds of pit stops in fourth and sixth places and gradually saw off the lead cars until it was their turn to head the race. From then on the Castrol Jaguars took control

through the hours of darkness, pursued by one of the Nissans, a Toyota Eagle and a brand new Dauer Porsche. None of these would survive the night, while the Jaguars continued to build up an impressive lead.

One incident will always stand out in the minds of everyone in attendance, especially those still in the main grandstand and pit straight after nightfall. Derek Bell's Momo Porsche 962C suffered a tyre blow-out as it came off the exit banking. He lost control and the car flipped over, skidding some distance on its roof before it came to rest in the centre of the track. Derek momentarily lost

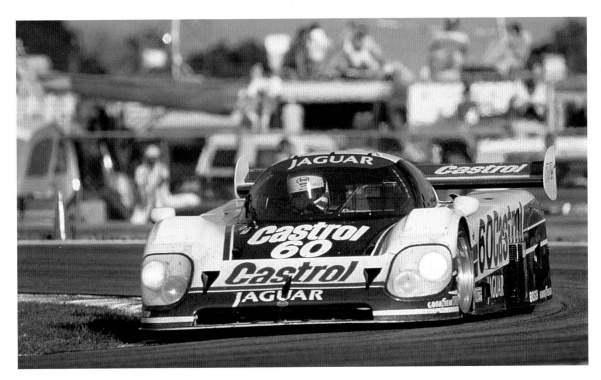

The second-placed number 60 Jaguar (288) scooped a $25,000 prize. (Jaguar)

consciousness, then 'came to' trapped upside down with fuel pouring out all around him. Fortunately the emergency crew arrived to extract him from this perilous predicament before the fuel ignited. All agreed he had had a very lucky escape, but for him and his co-drivers the race was over, though not in the way they would have preferred.

As morning dawned the two Jaguars were running clear of the third place Porsche by a very comfortable 16 laps. However, worrying problems started to develop as daytime temperatures increased. First one engine and then the other began to overheat, losing valuable time in the pits while the radiator systems were flushed. The Bayside Porsche began moving up, endeavouring to add first place to its pole start.

The last hours were a time of great anxiety for the TWR pit crews, but when Jan Lammers finally cruised past the chequered flag in Jaguar 61, followed shortly after by number 60, albeit four laps down, their lack of success at Daytona one year earlier faded to a distant memory. In taking this spectacular one-two finish Castrol Jaguars set up a number of records including the greatest distance covered in the event, with a winning speed of 112.857mph for 761 laps.

Venue: Daytona, Florida
Round 1, 3-4 February 1990
Race title: 1990 Sunbank 24 At Daytona Camel Grand Prix

Chassis type	Chassis no.	Race no.	Drivers	Grid pos.	Finish position	Laps
XJR-12D	288	60	Martin Brundle, Price Cobb, John Nielsen	9	2	757
XJR-12D	388	61	Davy Jones, Jan Lammers, Andy Wallace	10	1	761

A delighted Sir John Egan, with Davy Jones (left), Jan Lammers (centre) and Andy Wallace, holds the winning trophy, while Tony Dowe takes charge of the $66,000 prize money cheque. (Jaguar)

The winning Castrol Jaguars had worn down their main rivals to breaking point at Daytona, including the Championship title holders Nissan. Now in round two at **Miami** it was the Japanese cars' turn, coming home one-two just as Jaguar had done, with no finish at all for the Castrol cars.

Qualifying was best described as dismal for Martin Brundle and Davy Jones in car 60. After both cars appeared to be on course for top places, their XJR-10 developed a head gasket problem. With no time to change the engine, attempts were made to qualify the car with one bank turbocharged and the other without boost. Nothing could be done, and number 60 finally started from ninth place. Things initially looked much better for the Cobb/Nielsen Jaguar 61, which should have started alongside the pole position Nissan of Geoff Brabham, but it suffered an engine mishap during pre-race warm up. Debris thrown up from the track had damaged the cam belt, a problem discovered only as the cars were being taken to the grid. This day only one Jaguar would start the race.

Davy Jones knowing he faced a tough task as he set about

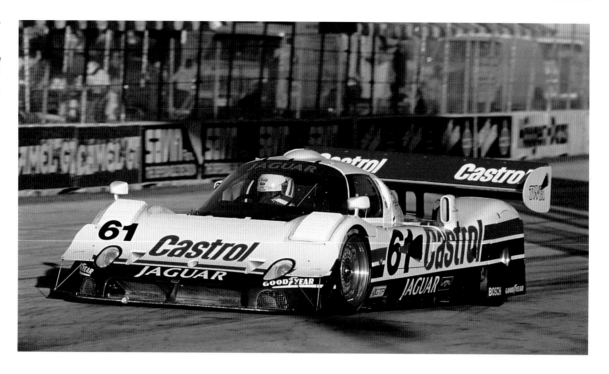

The number 61 Jaguar XJR-10 of Cobb and Nielsen qualified on the grid front row at Miami but a warm-up mishap kept it out of the race. (LAT Photographic)

reeling in the Nissan, Spice, Toyota and other higher-placed runners. He just managed to slip by one of the Nissans when disaster struck. The V6's oil pump lost drive, sending smoke streaming out of the back and forcing the Jaguar into very premature retirement on lap 14. After a run of three straight wins this was a bitter pill for the team to swallow.

Venue: Miami, Florida
Round 2, 25 February 1990
Race title: Nissan Grand Prix of Miami Camel Grand Prix

Chassis type	Chassis no.	Race no.	Drivers	Grid pos.	Finish position	Laps
XJR-10	589	60	Martin Brundle, Davy Jones	9	DNF, engine	14
XJR-10	389	61	Price Cobb, John Nielsen; car suffered damaged cam belt prior to race, so did not race			

Race winner: Nissan Performance Nissan GTP-ZX Turbo, drivers Bob Earl, Geoff Brabham and Chip Robinson, 120 laps

Round three at **Sebring**, with a duration of 12 hours, should have been an easy nut for the normally-aspirated V12 Jaguars to crack, although up to now success in this half-distance endurance race had eluded them. The previous year's second place had been a good result and there was no shortage of enthusiasm in the Jaguar camp this time. Price Cobb, still paired with Nielsen, would drive XJR-12 chassis 288 as car number 60, while Lammers would race the sister Jaguar chassis 388 as car 61 with his regular co-driver Davy Jones. Andy Wallace joined the team as reserve driver.

Cobb considered Nielsen better suited to qualify in number 60 and was quite satisfied with the Dane's fourth place start position. The second Jaguar's attempts to get on the front row were thwarted by a blown engine during Thursday's shoot-out for the top 10 places. Lammers made reasonably good time during the final session, starting the car from 11th spot. Derek Daly's Nissan 84 was first on the front row, which it shared with Bob Wollek's Porsche 962.

In what had become the norm in endurance racing, the Jaguars started on a cautious note, keeping up with the leaders but declining to go for broke in the early stages. Avoiding the mishaps affecting this or that leader, they gradually edged up to third and fourth, Cobb leading Jones and both now ahead of Bob Earl's Nissan. Later, when Nielsen had taken over Jaguar number 60, he came under pressure from the Nissan and suddenly the hardworking V12 engine started to complain. Nielsen steered the stricken Jaguar back to the pits but nothing could be done and the car had to be retired. Now the team was down to single-car racing again, with a long way to go.

Jan Lammers and Davy Jones, instructed to ease back, ran steadily while two of the leading Porsches succumbed to engine failures. Both Nissans took over the lead, losing it on occasions to Bob Wollek's Porsche, and Brabham's car had to pit to have a damaged radiator replaced. Jaguar 61 stayed with the leaders most of the time and even managed to regain fourth place after losing time when Andy Wallace brought it into the pits to have a brake calliper changed.

After the mid-race round of pit stops Wollek's Porsche was in the lead by half a lap but lost out again to Nissan 83 when it was left immobilised with a flat battery after a spin. Veteran driver Henri Pescarolo in the Joest Porsche enjoyed a brief 10-lap lead, only to crash out rather violently, taking a GTO Nissan with him. At the end of the resulting pace car stint, Wallace handed over to Lammers, who soon caught up with the leading Nissans. When Brabham pitted, Lammers was left running second to Daly's Nissan 84. Brabham returned with an all-out drive to catch the

Jaguar, which was now running perilously low on fuel. Lammers, with one eye on the fuel reserve and with only minutes to go, could not hold him off and had to settle for third, still nine laps ahead of the fourth place Porsche.

Venue: Sebring, Florida
Round 3, 17 March 1990
Race title: 12 Hours of Sebring International Camel Grand Prix

Chassis type	Chassis no.	Race no.	Drivers	Grid pos.	Finish position	Laps
XJR-12D	288	60	Price Cobb, John Nielsen	4	DNF, engine	56
XJR-12D	388	61	Davy Jones, Jan Lammers, Andy Wallace	11	3	301

Race winner: Nissan Performance Nissan GTP-ZX Turbo, drivers Derek Daly and Bob Earl, 301 laps

From round four at **Road Atlanta** onwards, Castrol Jaguar's racing would be confined to the turbocharged XJR-10s. The Nissan GTP cars still continued to dominate, while the Toyota Eagles gradually eased out the once almighty Porsche brigade in the battle for best-of-the-rest honours. The Nissans could still be pipped though, as in qualifying at Atlanta, where Price Cobb completed a nail-biting best time to take pole position in Jaguar 61. Davy Jones's time of 0.898sec slower left him two rows back in fifth place. The Cobb/Nielsen Jaguar shared the front row with Olsen's Toyota, relegating Robinson's Nissan to the second row. A total of 23 cars started the race, all led by Nielsen up to the first round of pit stops. He made the fastest race lap in the process.

Davy Jones' Jaguar 60 was less fortunate, spinning into the barrier on turn six and causing damage to the front end. Even after a new nose was fitted the car's handling was seriously affected by a bent track rod, although Jones did manage to gain the lead while the front runners made routine pit stops, only to

spin off once again, leaving him no choice but to pit for suspension repairs. The smooth performance of Jaguar 61 waned a little due to an unaccountable electrical problem. Nielsen soldiered on, keeping in second place to the flag, by which time Brabham had built up a two-lap lead. Fortunately for Nielsen, he was still a similar distance ahead of the third Toyota. The Jones/Lammers XJR-10, which had lost so much time earlier on, could only manage seventh.

Venue: Road Atlanta, Georgia
Round 4, 1 April 1990
Race title: 500 Km Nissan Grand Prix of Atlanta

Chassis type	Chassis no.	Race no.	Drivers	Grid pos.	Finish position	Laps
XJR-10	589	60	Davy Jones, Jan Lammers	5	7	113
XJR-10	389	61	Price Cobb, John Nielsen	1	2	122

Race winner: Nissan Performance Nissan GTP-ZX Turbo, drivers Geoff Brabham and Derek Daly, 124 laps

Both Jaguars finished at Road Atlanta, the Cobb/Nielsen number 61 car (389) taking second after a pole start.
(LAT Photographic)

The different engine cover exhaust exits on this XJR-10 were necessary because of regulations concerning side-exit exhausts as used on the XJR-11.
(LAT Photographic)

Venue: West Palm Beach, Florida
Round 5, 22 April 1990
Race title: Toyota Grand Prix of Palm Beach

The number 64 Chevrolet Spice of Wayne Taylor and Jim Miller fought hard with one Jaguar and then the other at Palm Beach, eventually finishing fourth behind the third placed Cobb/Nielsen XJR-10. (LAT Photographic)

Opinions at **West Palm Beach** for round five favoured Jaguar or Toyota to win, but Davy Jones went out in Jaguar 60 following a collision with a slower car after less than one third of the race. Jones had made a good impression, putting his car second on the grid alongside the Olsen/Fangio Toyota. A second Toyota Eagle occupied fourth place, ahead of the Brabham Nissan. Olsen's Toyota darted into the lead under heavy pressure from Jones, who himself soon came under attack from Wayne Taylor's Miller Spice. Nielsen moved forward to join in and was soon ahead of Jones.

After the first hour, two Toyotas, two Jaguars and the Spice were running almost as a group, oblivious to all others, until Jones's collision. Two hours on, Olsen was still leading, with Nielsen in Jaguar 61 keeping station in second place, but now the Nissan 83 was third, with the 84 sister car behind. Shortly after the third round of pit stops, Price Cobb, who had taken over from Nielsen, found himself in the lead when the Toyota's clutch failed. Cobb could have made it but for a problematic seat belt buckle that just would not stay fastened. On top of that, the engine began misfiring. Both Nissans caught up and slipped by, leaving Nielsen and Cobb to settle for third.

Chassis type	Chassis no.	Race no.	Drivers	Grid pos.	Finish position	Laps
XJR-10	589	60	Davy Jones, Jan Lammers	2	DNF, accident	53
XJR-10	389	61	Price Cobb, John Nielsen	6	3	171

Race winner: Nissan Performance Nissan GTP-ZX Turbo, drivers Geoff Brabham and Derek Daly, 172 laps

Round six at **Heartland Park** saw the list of GTP entries down to 10, with one lone Porsche 962 to remind spectators of past glories. In addition to the regular factory campaigners from Jaguar and Toyota, Nissan fielded a brand new chassis, the Nissan NPT90, to run alongside one of their usual GTP ZX turbos. Derek Daly and Bob Earl were given the honour of driving the new car, which was soon to show its potential by qualifying second. The two Jaguars started well during practice, Jones and Brundle making fastest times in number 60. Qualifying was rather disappointing though, after fluctuating boost pressures kept them back in seventh and eighth places.

and Jim Miller's Spice Chevy, was also a triumph for the entire TWR team, who were much praised for their efficient pit strategy. In a race where a number of top drivers opted to drive solo, Cobb and Nielsen weighed up the potential problems, such as higher than normal g-forces sapping energy towards the end, and decided to share the driving. Davy Jones in Jaguar 60 set out on a solo run, making good progress and getting the better of Fangio's Toyota, only to retire with turbo failure.

Price Cobb took first stint in Jaguar 61 from fourth place on the grid. He was content to shadow the leaders rather than fight for the front, and held third position for the first 20 laps. Jones made his way forward into fourth, so the two Jaguars followed the two Toyota leaders. After lap 34, both Castrol cars moved ahead of the second Toyota and ran second and third until Jones had turbo problems which put him out of the running. The time advantage of the leading Toyotas over Cobb's Jaguar was greatly reduced during their respective pit stops - when Nielsen took over, he was back in the race much faster than Olsen could turn around. On lap 100, Olsen misjudged an overtaking manoeuvre and came to grief on the barriers, allowing the Jaguar to claim the lead all the way to the flag. This was one race in which the Nissans did not excel, although Brabham managed third, while the remaining Toyota of Rocky Moran and Juan-Manuel Fangio II came fifth.

Venue: Lime Rock, Connecticut
Round 7, 28 May 1990
Race title: Toyota Trucks Lime Rock Camel Grand Prix

Chassis type	Chassis no.	Race no.	Drivers	Grid pos.	Finish position	Laps
XJR-10	589	60	Davy Jones, Jan Lammers	8	DNF, engine/turbo	48
XJR-10	389	61	Price Cobb, John Nielsen	4	1	150

The star of the race was undoubtedly Juan-Manuel Fangio II in the Toyota Eagle, who led from his pole start all the way to the chequered flag. The two Jaguars ran most of the time around their starting positions. Cobb, making the most of his better soft-compound tyres, challenged one or two of the front runners at times, and eventually finished fifth, but it just was not Jaguar's race. Jones in number 60 might have done better than his sixth place finish had he not spun off course on two occasions, and if Brundle had not got a puncture near the end of the race.

Venue: Heartland Park, Topeka, Kansas
Round 6, 6 May 1990
Race title: Camel Grand Prix of Heartland Park

Chassis type	Chassis no.	Race no.	Drivers	Grid pos.	Finish position	Laps
XJR-10	589	60	Davy Jones, Martin Brundle	8	6	73
XJR-10	389	61	Price Cobb, John Nielsen	7	5	75

Race winner: All-American Racers Toyota Eagle HF89, driver Juan-Manuel Fangio II, 75 laps

Price Cobb's and John Nielsen's tremendous victory in round seven at **Lime Rock**, finishing one full lap ahead of Wayne Taylor's

It seemed that each time the Jaguar team enjoyed a memorable success in IMSA racing, the next race brought nothing but disappointment. The new Nissan NPT90 took its first victory in round eight at **Mid Ohio**, but before his retirement with engine problems Davy Jones proved in the early laps that the XJR-10 was capable of outpacing the newcomer. John Nielsen's Jaguar was unable to take on the challenge, having expired with similar problems much earlier on. The two Castrol cars should have performed well, especially after measures had been taken to improve the XJR-10's handling. They were still incredibly fast, but rain during qualifying prevented them making better times than the two Nissans and the James Weaver/Hurley Haywood number 1 Porsche 962.

Brabham started from pole position and immediately came under pressure from a forceful Jones, who had already dispatched the intermediate runners in double quick time. As the Nissan slowed behind a Camel Lights car Jones snatched his chance to overtake and held Brabham at bay until the first round of pit stops. Cobb, who had been made redundant when the

other Jaguar dropped out with an oil pump pulley failure, took over, but now the gremlins struck once again, putting the second Jaguar out of action. The race continued with a duel between the two Nissans and Olsen's Toyota in which the latter finished third.

Venue: Mid Ohio, Ohio
Round 8, 3 June 1990
Race title: 500 Km Nissan Camel Grand Prix

Chassis type	Chassis no.	Race no.	Drivers	Grid pos.	Finish position	Laps
XJR-10	589	60	Price Cobb, Davy Jones	4	DNF, engine	45
XJR-10	389	61	John Nielsen, Price Cobb	5	DNF, engine	13

Race winner: Nissan Performance Nissan GTP-ZX Turbo, drivers Geoff Brabham and Derek Daly, 129 laps

At **Watkins Glen** in round nine Davy Jones came third, even though a last-minute engine failure prevented a run past the chequered flag. The rules in IMSA GT racing differed from those of the WSPC competition in that distances covered at the moment the flag was waved were decisive in determining finish positions and points awarded. Thus even early retirements could be listed as 'classified' in the results. Jones was set to take second place as the race ended, but his retirement allowed the Porsche of James Weaver and Hurley Hayward to snatch it from him.

Both Jaguars had qualified well, Jones being second fastest to put him alongside Olsen's Toyota on the front row. After a wet start in which some of the top qualifiers were soon slipping back places, Davy Jones took over the lead when the track became dry and after everyone had changed to 'slicks'. By the time all cars had finished their regular pit stops, Jaguar 60 with Alain Ferte in control still held a commanding lead, losing it briefly later on as Jones took over during the second round of stops. Number 60

was now second behind the pole-winning Toyota but came to a standstill just off the racing line with electrical problems. A full course yellow caution flag reduced the Jaguar's lead over the next runner, Robinson's Nissan. Soon it was neck and neck, but Robinson charged by to take the win. Jones would have taken second with certainty, had his engine not failed. John Nielsen in Jaguar 61 was a lap down at the time but still managed to come home in fourth place.

Venue: Watkins Glen, New York
Round 9, 1 July 1990
Race title: Camel Continental VII

Chassis type	Chassis no.	Race no.	Drivers	Grid pos.	Finish position	Laps
XJR-10	589	60	Davy Jones, Alain Ferte	2	3	91
XJR-10	389	61	Price Cobb, John Nielsen	4	4	91

Race winner: Nissan Performance Nissan GTP-ZX Turbo, drivers Bob Earl and Chip Robinson, 92 laps

For round ten at **Sears Point** rule changes due in 1991 were brought forward. These meant that some cars could shed weight, with the result that one or two cars appeared on the grid front row for the very first time - in this particular case two Spices. The next few rows would be shared by the usual crop of front runners: Nissan, Jaguar, Toyota and the lone Porsche of James Weaver. Both Spices failed to make the finish line as they went out with engine problems on laps 22 and 65.

The race was dominated by the number 99 Toyota Eagle of Juan-Manuel Fangio II, and for once the Jaguars struggled to keep up, let alone move up to make a strong challenge for the lead. Grip, or lack of it, was their problem, Nielsen complaining that it was like driving on glass. Alain Ferte in number 60 spun the car, prompting him to pit for softer-compound tyres. He did well to finish fourth on the same lap as the leader. The second Cobb/Nielsen Jaguar 61 advanced to fourth at one stage but bad handling problems dropped it down to sixth at the finish.

Venue: Sears Point, California
Round 10, 15 July 1990
Race title: California Camel Grand Prix

Chassis type	Chassis no.	Race no.	Drivers	Grid pos.	Finish position	Laps
XJR-10	589	60	Davy Jones, Alain Ferte	9	4	75
XJR-10	389	61	Price Cobb, John Nielsen	8	6	75

Race winner: All-American Racers Toyota Eagle, driver Juan-Manuel Fangio II, 75 laps

Round eleven at **Portland** saw major changes in Jaguar strategy. From now on there would be one driver only for each car except in the long-distance endurance races. Top of the tree now in Jaguar's driver standings, Davy Jones took over as the number one driver and showed a mastery that was destined to keep the Jaguar name on everybody's lips even when the cars were not outright winners. Portland was to be one of those occasions. Having made second-best qualifying time, Jones put his stamp on the race from lap one and led throughout to take first place. John Nielsen, less fortunate, started from sixth on the grid and soon eased forward into fourth, only to be denied a chance to make further headway when his engine failed on lap 13.

Venue: Portland, Oregon
Round 11, 29 July 1990
Race title: GI Joe's Camel Grand Prix presented by Nissan

Chassis type	Chassis no.	Race no.	Drivers	Grid pos.	Finish position	Laps
XJR-10	589	60	Davy Jones	2	1	97
XJR-10	389	61	John Nielsen, Price Cobb	6	DNF, engine	13

Rain, threats of rain, mist and uncertain weather prospects hung like the sword of Damocles over round twelve at **Road America**. IMSA had planned two separate 250km races with the points total split between them. The weather put paid to that, resulting in a single 250km race, which was considered the best solution for all concerned. Brabham and Robinson qualified their Nissans to take the grid front row. Jones was third and Nielsen fourth. This was their starting order and much of the race developed into a contest between the two teams. The track was never really either wet or dry enough to make the choice of tyres an easy matter. Geoff Brabham chose to run on warmed 'slicks' when the weather worsened, while Jones opted for wets. In the circumstances, either was suitable.

Jones took Jaguar 60 into an early lead, leaving Brabham to fend off Nielsen for second place. Brabham's decision to run on 'slicks' paid off later when he gained a moderate lead. Jones was determined to make a run for it and almost succeeded, but three laps from the finish his over-eagerness caused him to spin.

Brabham was free to run to the flag, while Jones recovered just in time to beat Fangio's Toyota and Weaver's Porsche, taking second place. Nielsen in number 61 was a lap down but still managed sixth.

Venue: Road America, Wisconsin
Round 12, 19 August 1990
Race title: Nissan Camel Grand Prix of Road America

Chassis type	Chassis no.	Race no.	Drivers	Grid pos.	Finish position	Laps
XJR-10	589	60	Davy Jones	3	2	39
XJR-10	389	61	John Nielsen	4	6	38

Race winner: Nissan Performance Nissan GTP-ZX Turbo, driver Geoff Brabham, 39 laps

At **San Antonio** in round thirteen, Price Cobb piloted Jaguar 61, regrettably not to a good result as both Jaguars crashed out. They had qualified well, Jones second, Cobb fourth, with Brabham in Nissan NPT 83 yet again on pole position. San Antonio's street circuit was regarded as being very fast, and in the first half of the race speed was all-important. Davy Jones's pursuit of Brabham lasted no more than three laps before he crashed Jaguar 60 on Bowie Street. From then on it was a constantly changing tussle for top places between the works Nissans, the All-American Racers Toyotas and James Weaver's lone Porsche 962. Juan-Manuel Fangio II in Toyota Eagle 99 won after an amazing series of lead changes. Cobb's Jaguar XJR-10 featured well in the lead pack, getting up to second before its unfortunate exit on lap 71 after spinning on turn one.

Venue: San Antonio, Texas
Round 13, 2 September 1990
Race title: Nissan Grand Prix of San Antonio

Chassis type	Chassis no.	Race no.	Drivers	Grid pos.	Finish position	Laps
XJR-10	589	60	Davy Jones	2	DNF, accident	3
XJR-10	389	61	Price Cobb	4	DNF, accident	71

Race winner: All-American Racers Toyota Eagle, driver Juan-Manuel Fangio II, 98 laps

Another difference in IMSA rules permitted the use of much deeper diffuser tunnels, as used on WSPC XJR-6s and XJR-8s before 1988. The rear air-jack installation on this XJR-10 was common to all TWR prototypes except XJR-14s. (Paul Skilleter)

Round fourteen at **Tampa** finished on lap 89 for Davy Jones in Jaguar 60, not because of mechanical failure but because of driver fatigue brought about when his coolsuit failed. The circuit is demanding at the best of times, and in addition the unpleasantly high humidity levels encountered in the climate of a Florida summer can sap the energy of even the fittest drivers. Qualifying for Davy in this debilitating environment was exacerbated by understeer, while for Nielsen tyres were the problem. They were placed fourth and seventh respectively. Chip Robinson in his still relatively new Nissan NPT90 took pole position, ahead of team-mate Geoff Brabham in the sister car.

Both Nissans started well, but Jones soon pulled Jaguar number 60 into second place, then took the lead when the Nissans dived into the pits. By lap 40, Jones was still in the lead, three seconds ahead of Fangio's Toyota. John Nielsen was running third, with the Nissans endeavouring to catch up. Nearing the halfway mark, both front runners made their pit stops, taking advantage of a yellow flag. Now Nielsen led for a few laps only before he was obliged to pit for re-fuelling, dropping back several places in the process. From then on, both Jaguars struggled to keep up with the top five or six runners; even the Nissans were experiencing difficulties at times.

Problems were brewing up for Jones when his coolsuit malfunctioned. Conditions within the car became unbearable. His feet were burning, added to which his drink bottle was empty. Struggling to keep his concentration, he hit the wall and lost the rear wing, continuing for a couple of laps before throwing in the towel on lap 89. As if the heat was not enough, rain started to fall later on in the race, sending cars in all directions, including Brabham's Nissan. Derek Bell's Porsche followed suit. Nielsen was not allowed to get off lightly either, losing Jaguar 61's wing, which joined the growing miscellany of debris scattered all around the circuit. Many cars ceased racing, compelled to crawl through the mess to the pits if possible, and the organisers finally called a halt seven laps early. James Weaver had successfully guided his Dyson Porsche through the obstacle course, inheriting the lead as the chequered flag appeared. Nielsen, still running wingless, was declared fourth ahead of Brabham.

Venue: Tampa, Florida
Round 14, 30 September 1990
Race title: Nissan World Challenge of Tampa Camel Grand Prix

Chassis type	Chassis no.	Race no.	Drivers	Grid pos.	Finish position	Laps
XJR-10	589	60	Davy Jones	4	DNF, driver fatigue	89
XJR-10	389	61	John Nielsen	7	4	109

Race winner: Dyson RCG Porsche 962C, driver James Weaver, 110 laps

The Castrol Jaguars' two previous wins at **Del Mar**, venue for round fifteen, the season's final race, raised hopes of a hat-trick. Indycar Champion Al Unser just beat Brabham's Nissan to pole

position in one of the 6.3-litre Chevrolet Spice cars, while the two Jaguars shared the second grid row. Martin Brundle was driving Jaguar number 61 in this race. Davy Jones in Jaguar 60 almost missed the start of the race as he had the misfortune of a blown engine during warm-up. Frantic efforts by the mechanics allowed him to join the last parade lap before the start. Not that this affected the start, since a Camel Lights car crashed on the first corner, resulting in a re-start. The pole Spice car crashed out on lap 18 after being obstructed by a slower car.

Martin Brundle took the lead shortly after the re-start when Brabham missed a downshift and spun off. Brundle's joy lasted only one lap as his alternator drive belt broke and he he was from then on plagued by electrical problems. He stayed in the race to finish a dismal eleventh, requiring four battery changes to keep going. To the delight of Castrol pit crews and the Jaguar buffs in the stand, Davy Jones threaded through the field to reach the number one spot, which he held for an encouraging 23 laps. His most serious challengers were John Paul junior in a privateer Nissan and James Weaver's Porsche 962.

Jones pitted 30 minutes from the finish and had dropped back to third when he rejoined the race. Though determined to regain the lead, his progress faltered as one of the turbos went off. Now Fangio led in the All-American Racers Toyota with John Paul junior's Nissan next. Weaver had been delayed in the pits by the marshals due to his car's excessive noise levels. The flagging turbo did little to retard Jones's Jaguar too seriously: he not only caught up with the Nissan but nudged it, sending both cars into a spin. Quickly recovering, Jones set off after Fangio and finished a good second. If only the car had not needed a new engine prior to the start... but these things happen in motor racing, however frustrating.

Venue: Del Mar, California
Round 15, 11 November 1990
Race title: Camel Grand Prix of Greater San Diego Presented by Nissan

Chassis type	Chassis no.	Race no.	Drivers	Grid pos.	Finish position	Laps
XJR-10	589	60	Davy Jones	3	2	87
XJR-10	389	61	Martin Brundle	4	11	78

Race winner: All-American Racers Toyota Eagle, driver Juan-Manuel Fangio II, 87 laps

For the third year running, Geoff Brabham was Drivers' Champion, with 196 points. Team-mate Chip Robinson was second with 175 and Davy Jones third with a hard-earned 132. John Nielsen was fifth with 115. Jaguar, with 187 points came second in the Manufacturers' Championship, against Nissan's first place with 251 points. Del Mar marked the end of Castrol Oil's sponsorship of the TWR Jaguars. First place wins may have been thin on the ground, but the impressive tally of finishes in the top four or five positions during the three-year period kept eyes firmly on the Jaguars.

Chapter 14

1991 IMSA Camel GT Championship

'We was robbed'

Despite a policy of cutting costs, Jaguar's racing activities continued on both sides of the Atlantic, with a new sponsor, Bud Light beer, taking over in the US from Castrol. Sales continued to drop and morale within Jaguar, where the workforce was being reduced, was low. The sales company in the US was affected by the downturn in sales and the reduction in staff numbers; a few wins from the racing team would help bolster spirits internally, as well as boosting Jaguar's image with the public.

The new XJR-16 development of the turbocharged car, which was being prepared for action after the faithful old V12-powered cars had contested the early-season long-distance races, was seen as the weapon that could deliver those wins. At the Valparaiso headquarters of TWR Inc. morale was high - the fact that the American team had prepared and pit-crewed the Le Mans winner in 1990 gave a great confidence boost.

The competition the team faced still came mainly from Nissan, but the All-American Racers Toyotas were a growing threat, while a change in the IMSA rules gave the cars powered by stock-block American engines a better chance of competing with the turbocharged 'screamers'.

For 1991 the TWR Jaguar IMSA team switched from Castrol Oil to Anheuser-Bush Inc. as principal sponsor, the cars now appearing in the eye-catching Bud Light livery. Budweiser's beers had been involved in various aspects of motor racing in America for several years including Indycar, Nascar and Drag racing. The legendary Mario Andretti was Indycar Champion for them in 1984. Two years later, Bobby Rahal also won the Championship in Budweiser colours, and followed this with a repeat win in 1987. Budweiser's entry into GT sponsorship brought a good measure of luck for the Valparaiso outfit, although regrettably not immediately.

Jaguar's excellent total of six wins during the forthcoming season was to be double the score of the reigning champions, the Nissans. Juan-Manuel Fangio II's All-American Racers Toyota also managed three firsts. The other two race wins in this slightly shorter 14-race season were taken by a Joest/Blaupunkt Porsche 962 at Daytona and by an Intrepid Chevrolet at New Orleans. Early-season sprint racing for the Bud Light team relied on the now improved XJR-10 turbo cars, which were superseded later in the season by the more more refined XJR-16s, making this the best year to date.

Each hour of action is bought at the cost of many days, weeks or months in the workshops. The large black radiator hanging down the left side cools the engine oil.
(Ken Wells)

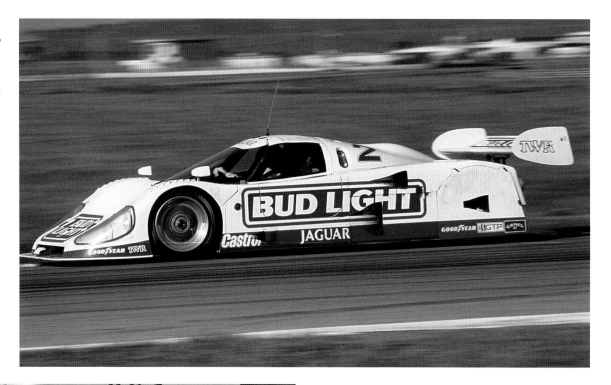

Only one Bud Light Jaguar XJR-12D made it to the start line at Daytona in 1991. Here the car, chassis 290, is being put through a pre-race practice session. (Ken Wells)

The lone Bud Light Jaguar started from grid spot no. 2, completing 379 laps before retirement. That was 19 laps better than the pole starter number 6 Joest Porsche, which went out with engine-related problems on lap 360. (Ken Wells)

The season opened with round one, the Sunbank 24 at **Daytona**, which was tipped to be an epic contest between the Bud Light Jaguars and the Nissan Performance R90C turbo cars. Three of the Japanese cars were entered, and Jaguar's intention was to field two XJR-12Ds as in 1990. These were the two new 1990 cars, with chassis numbers 190 and 290.

Seven of the finest drivers in the sport were listed in Bud Light's pre-race press releases. Davy Jones would lead car number 2 with co-drivers Scott Pruett, the 1987 WSPC World Champion Raul Boesel, and ex-Mercedes and Nissan driver Kenny Acheson. Ex-Silk Cut driver Derek Warwick would be the principal driver of Bud Light Jaguar number 3, sharing with John Nielsen and Raul Boesel's 1987 WSPC co-driver Eddie Cheever. With such a formidable reservoir of driving talents and back-up skills, Tony Dowe expressed confidence that the team would repeat the previous year's magnificent victory.

New rules for 1991 permitted an increase in engine capacity for the V12 power units to 6.5 litres. As was usual, the closed season during the winter was devoted to implementing a range of improvements. Although basically unchanged in general appearance, the XJR-12s now appeared with the 'camel' (humped) tails.

For all the superb planning and preparation in the months leading up to Daytona, the Bud Light Jaguars should have won on merit alone, if not for being first past the flag. That they did not was an undeserved and cruel blow. Three of the seven drivers did not even get a race. This was partially due to heavy rain, which created dangerous driving conditions during the first day's practice session. John Nielsen, driving Jaguar number 3, took his chances, only to lose control on the back straight chicane. While braking, his foot caught the accelerator, causing the car to skid, and the XJR-12's rear end impacted hard into the grass banking, inflicting extensive damage that was well beyond trackside repairs. John received a blow to the head, hard enough to crack his helmet and require a hospital check-up. For him, Eddie Cheever and Kenny Acheson, their race hopes had ended.

Derek Warwick was transferred to Jaguar number 2 with Davy Jones in control, setting out on a damage limitation exercise. They achieved a very fast time in qualifying to take second on the grid. Two Nissans bettered this time, but they were now racing in the Group C class - new for IMSA - and thus were not eligible for the front row, which was strictly reserved for GTP cars. The lone Jaguar was destined not to have an easy time of it, suffering a sequence of irritating problems during Thursday evening's practice. Worst of all, during the pre-race warm up the water pump bearing seized as a result of a broken alternator belt.

Derek Warwick duelling with the number 98 All American Toyota Eagle, which was destined to suffer engine failure on lap 408.
(Sutton Photographics)

The race started with no hanging back on Davy Jones's part this time. Bob Wollek's Porsche raced ahead from pole, chased hard by Jones and even harder by Michael Andretti in another Porsche, who quickly relegated the Jaguar to third. The next few laps saw all three playing musical chairs at the front, soon joined by Arie Luyendijk in one of the Nissans. Jones's bid for the lead gradually became more difficult, but he made it again on lap 28 before diving in for a scheduled pit stop four laps later. Twenty laps on, rain returned to Daytona, causing the inevitable series of sideways departures, with cars pitting for replacement noses and wet-weather tyres. Scott Pruett was in control of the Jaguar after a lengthy yellow flag period ended on lap 56, and was still in the lead, but he was now firmly in the sights of Derek Daly in Nissan number 83, who was bearing down on him at an alarming rate.

This was a routine pit stop, but as the race wore on the Jaguar was to spend much time in the pits following a series of water pump failures.
(Ken Wells)

The Irishman went into the lead on lap 63 and soon the Jaguar began to drop back down the field.

It was Warwick who eventually went back up to the front after lap 133, holding on for a good 50 laps before it was the turn of Nissan 84. Jones commandeered the lead back once again on lap 202 for a further 34 laps. The see-saw between Jaguar and Nissan was to last some while, their drivers seemingly content to hand over to each other as long as no one else had a chance to muscle in.

From around 1.15am things started to go wrong for the Jaguar. First a water pump failed, then unbelievably, another. Just when it seemed the Bud Light Jaguar might be a safe bet for taking the chequered flag, it remained static in the pits for 110 minutes while the problem was being rectified. Now more than 50 laps down, all hopes of success had faded. Warwick took the Jaguar out again for a couple of stints, running reasonably well, but eventually came back with yet another water pump gone. By 7.45am, the tortured cat moved no more.

No less than five drivers shared victory in the Joest/Blaupunkt Porsche including Bob Wollek and his fellow countryman Henri Pescarolo, veteran of many 24-hour races including Le Mans.

Davy Jones took advantage of a mid-race yellow flag to make his one and only pit stop at Palm Beach before going on to take a magnificent win. (JDHT)

Venue: Daytona, Florida
Round 1, 2-3 February 1991
Race title: Sunbank 24 at Daytona

Chassis type	Chassis no.	Race no.	Drivers	Grid pos.	Finish position	Laps
XJR-12D	190	3	John Nielsen, Eddie Cheever, Kenny Acheson		Crashed in practice, did not race	
XJR-12D	290	2	Davy Jones, Scott Pruett, Derek Warwick, Raul Boesel	2	DNF, engine	379

Race winner: Joest Porsche 962, drivers John Winter, Frank Jelinski, Henri Pescarolo, Hurley Haywood and Bob Wollek, 719 laps

Round two at **West Palm Beach** contrasted completely with Daytona, being a resounding victory for Davy Jones in Bud Light Jaguar XJR-10 number 2. The weather during qualifying was hot and humid, adding discomfort to driving on what is a tricky circuit at the best of times. Davy Jones qualified second even with a slightly misfiring engine. Raul Boesel could not match his time or those of the Nissan and Chevrolet contenders, having to start from seventh.

Davy Jones stayed behind the pole Spice of Tom Kendall as

Luck deserted chassis 290 after it failed to finish at Daytona. Davy Jones's unfortunate crash in practice after this picture was taken at Sebring kept it out of the 12- hour race. Later, racing as the number 36 Suntec Jaguar at Le Mans in June, it was plagued with problems and once more failed to finish. (JDHT)

far as the first hairpin on lap one and then overtook him to lead the rest of the race all the way to the flag. He took advantage of the one and only mid-race yellow flag period to make his routine pit stop. Boesel in Jaguar number 3 kept well up with the leaders, challenging the Nissans, along with one or two other likely contenders from time to time, until gearbox problems put him out on lap 61. With the majority of cars entered in the GTP class, Jones's stunning victory was a very praiseworthy achievement for him and for all of the team, universally recognised as being one of the most efficient in the business.

Venue: West Palm Beach, Florida
Round 2, 3 March 1991
Race title: Toyota Camel Grand Prix of Palm Beach

Chassis type	Chassis no.	Race no.	Drivers	Grid pos.	Finish position	Laps
XJR-10	389	3	Raul Boesel	7	DNF, transmission	61
XJR-10	589	2	Davy Jones	2	1	115

The TWR Jaguar team suffered another disastrous blow in pre-race practice for round three at **Sebring**. This 12-hour event is one of the oldest road races in America, and the last time a Jaguar had won was 35 years before. Then it was a D-type driven by Mike Hawthorn and Phil Walters.

Two cars were entered, XJR-12s chassis numbers 190 and 290, but only the former survived to start the race. Davy Jones had just started the Thursday practice session. On his first lap taking turn 14, a fast left-hand kink, he came across a slower GTU car to his right, which turned in on him as he took the inside line. The Jaguar was forced up the kerb and hurtled into the concrete retaining wall. Such was the impact that four of the heavy

concrete blocks were dislodged, and one fractured. The front end of the car was extensively damaged, which ruined its chance of starting in the race.

The wrecked number 2 Jaguar would have been driven by Davy Jones and Raul Boesel, while the number 3 car would have been piloted by John Nielsen with Kenny Acheson. Both Nielsen and Acheson should have taken part in the Daytona season opener, had not the team had the misfortune to lose one of the Jaguars in pre-race practice. With only one car left to compete in the race, Jones, Nielsen and Boesel shared the driving. Acheson was given the opportunity to take stints, but declined on the grounds that this would be overkill. John Nielsen qualified the car sixth but one of the faster-qualifying Nissans was withdrawn, moving him up a place to start from fifth.

Conditions at the outset were wet and decidedly miserable.

It would be hard to imagine a more distinctive racecar transporter than this striking Bud Light vehicle. (Ken Wells)

Jones took the first stint, still a little sore after his practice mishap but running steadily and maintaining Jaguar's strategy of not going all-out for the lead in the early stages. When Boesel took over after midday the engine developed a worrying misfire. This was to bug the car for hours and defied numerous pit stops to correct it. If that wasn't enough, two engine covers became detached and lost. Added to these misfortunes, the car suffered a flat tyre.

By the fifth hour the Bud Light Jaguar number 3 was trailing in 17th place when the drivers set about improving on this lowly position. The final hour or so was blighted by heavy rain but this did not deter the gallant drivers, who edged the car forward to finish in a very creditable fifth place. The valuable points earned were sorely needed because at this point in the Championship tables the Jaguars were well down from where they had been in the previous three years.

Venue: Sebring, Florida
Round 3, 16 March 1991
Race title: The Nissan Camel Grand Prix 12 Hours of Sebring

Chassis type	Chassis no.	Race no.	Drivers	Grid pos.	Finish position	Laps
XJR-12D	190	3	John Nielsen, Davy Jones, Raul Boesel	5	5	284
XJR-12D	290	2	Davy Jones (crashed in practice, car did not race)			

Race winner: Nissan Performance Nissan NPT-90, drivers Geoff Brabham, Derek Daly and Gary Brabham, 298 laps

Tom Walkinshaw and Tony Dowe's decision to bring Raul Boesel back into the TWR fold paid off handsomely in round four at **Miami**. Raul brought his Bud Light Jaguar XJR-10 number 3 home to a nail-biting victory. The Brazilian started from third place on the grid behind his team-mate Davy Jones in Jaguar number 2. Wayne Taylor's Chevrolet Intrepid had taken the pole position.

On the first lap Jones jumped into the lead on turn three, easily overtaking Taylor's Chevrolet. He was soon followed by Boesel, making it a Jaguar one-two, while some of the stronger competitors had their race hopes terminated, mostly through engine-related problems. The first to exit was Fangio's Toyota Eagle, which caught fire after an engine failure.

Jones lead the race for the first 44 laps before his engine expired, but Jaguar's hopes remained high, knowing that Boesel's Jaguar number 3 was still out in front. After the mid-race pit stops the lead was taken over very briefly by James Weaver's Dyson Porsche 962C, then for a longer 14-lap period by Bernd Schneider in a Joest Porsche 962C. Boesel had one or two near misses but managed to get through unscathed although other cars eliminated themselves. He eventually regained the lead, but Tom Kendall in the Spice Chevrolet 64 seemed determined that he would not keep it. The gap between them narrowed to 1.9 seconds on the penultimate lap, and to nothing during the last lap. However, Boesel successfully balked all attempts by the American to pass, and both streaked past the chequered flag neck and neck. The winner's purse for this race was $50,500, with a further $3,000 awarded to Davy Jones.

Venue: Miami, Florida
Round 4, 7 April 1991
Race title: Nissan Camel Grand Prix of Miami

Chassis type	Chassis no.	Race no.	Drivers	Grid pos.	Finish position	Laps
XJR-10	389	3	Raul Boesel	3	1	91
XJR-10	589	2	Davy Jones	2	DNF, engine	44

The Bud Light Jaguar team unveiled its newest secret weapon for round five at **Road Atlanta**, and what a stunner it was. This was the revolutionary turbo-powered XJR-16. During qualifying Davy Jones actually beat Price Cobb's previous track record time, but this was not recognised when official qualifying was cancelled due

Davy Jones in XJR-16 chassis 191 stunned the crowds by winning at Road Atlanta on the car's first outing. He took further wins at Mid Ohio, Laguna Seca and Road America, although here at Lime Rock he finished seventh. (JDHT)

to heavy rain. Jones was awarded pole position, sharing the grid front row with Raul Boesel in the number 3 Jaguar XJR-10.

Boesel led the race for the first lap only, then Jones took over and remained up front for a full 73 laps before taking the win at a new record speed of 120.932mph. Boesel on the other hand had to duel with Chip Robinson in his brand new Nissan NPT91, now also powered by a V6 four-valve turbo engine. Geoff Brabham in another new Nissan lasted only three laps, and his early departure reduced some of the pressure the XJR-10 might otherwise have been under. Boesel finally lost out to Robinson after making a slower pit stop which prevented what might have been a Jaguar one-two. Nevertheless, his and Jones's mounting points total was beginning to look promising.

Venue: Road Atlanta, Georgia
Round 5, 28 April 1991
Race title: Nissan Camel Grand Prix of Atlanta

Chassis type	Chassis no.	Race no.	Drivers	Grid pos.	Finish position	Laps
XJR-10	589	3	Raul Boesel	2	3	73
XJR-16	191	2	Davy Jones	1	1	74

By round six at **Topeka** the Bud Light Jaguars had won three of the first five races, and prospects for another stunning victory looked good when Davy Jones captured pole position for the second consecutive race in the XJR-16. Raul Boesel, still in the XJR-10, started the race from sixth.

On his second time out in the Nissan NPT91, Chip Robinson won the race, but it was Wayne Taylor's 6.0 litre Chevrolet Intrepid which harried Davy Jones the most, as he led much of the race. The pair raced as one until Taylor, who was desperate to overtake, finally came too close, made contact and sent both of them off. The Chevrolet was quicker to recover but became stuck in third gear. Robinson took over where Taylor left off, chasing hard until two laps from the end, when a momentary lapse of concentration by Jones sent the XJR-16 into a spin. Robinson streaked by, leaving Jones to settle for second. Raul Boesel moved up from his sixth place start to fourth, maintaining this position for many laps before having to pit with radiator problems. Upon investigation, a three-inch chunk of metal had embedded itself in the radiator, thereby draining the system. Jaguar number 3 (chassis 589) was retired, and was used as a spare or T car in the later races.

Venue: Heartland Park, Topeka, Kansas
Round 6, 5 May 1991
Race title: Camel Grand Prix of the Heartland

Chassis type	Chassis no.	Race no.	Drivers	Grid pos.	Finish position	Laps
XJR-10	589	3	Raul Boesel	6	DNF, mechanical	66
XJR-16	191	2	Davy Jones	1	2	75

Race winner: Nissan Performance Nissan NPT-91, driver Chip Robinson, 75 laps

Round seven at **Lime Rock** saw the introduction of the second XJR-16, chassis number 291, driven by Raul Boesel as car number 3. This was a last-minute appearance as Boesel started practice in the XJR-10 but damaged it on the Saturday. The new XJR-16 was brought in on the Sunday, too late for the team to set it up well enough for a worthwhile place near the front of the grid. It started back in 15th place, while Jones stood on the front row alongside pole winner Tom Kendall in the Chevrolet Intrepid.

Kendall quickly took a five-second lead, with Jones hard on his heels. For much of the race Jones worked to get the better of the Intrepid while also holding off Chip Robinson in the Nissan NPT91 after Kendall's team-mate Taylor in the other Intrepid had dropped back into fourth position. Jones was finally leading when a too hasty overtaking manoeuvre to get around a Spice Pontiac proved his undoing. He made contact, suffering front end damage including a break to the left-hand steering linkage. Pit repairs were quickly carried out and he got back in the race to finish seventh. Boesel's race did not run too smoothly either, as he too was involved in an accident when he was hit by a Camel Lights car. His pit stop only involved changing a wheel but the delay kept him back to finish one better than Jones in sixth.

Venue: Lime Rock, Connecticut
Round 7, 27 May 1991
Race title: Toyota Trucks Presents the Lime Rock Camel Grand Prix

Chassis type	Chassis no.	Race no.	Drivers	Grid pos.	Finish position	Laps
XJR-10	589	3	Raul Boesel - damaged in practice, did not race, used XJR-16 291 instead			
XJR-16	191	2	Davy Jones	2	7	129
XJR-16	291	3	Raul Boesel	15	6	131

Race winner: Nissan Performance Nissan NPT-91, driver Chip Robinson, 133 laps.

The Bud Light Jaguar team was well on form again during round eight at **Mid Ohio**. Davy Jones fought off the Chevrolet Intrepids, placed first and second on the grid, to take his third IMSA Camel GTP victory of 1991, gaining joint second place in the Drivers' Championship with Geoff Brabham, both at 102 points. Jones started from third on the grid, overtaking Wayne Taylor. On lap seven he took the lead and kept it all the way to the flag.

Raul Boesel started from sixth in the still comparatively new XJR-16. Both Jaguars ran with extra front wings, first tried in practice. They were a considerable aid as they provided additional downforce for high-speed cornering. Raul was slowed early in the race by a blistered front tyre, but his fourth-place finish put him in front of Brabham's and Robinson's Nissans. Mid Ohio circuit was well known to the team, who had used it for track testing and development on a number of occasions. Winning here brought an extra level of satisfaction.

Venue: Mid Ohio, Ohio
Round 8, 2 June 1991
Race title: Nissan Camel Grand Prix of Ohio

Chassis type	Chassis no.	Race no.	Drivers	Grid pos.	Finish position	Laps
XJR-16	191	2	Davy Jones	3	1	83
XJR-16	291	3	Raul Boesel	6	4	82

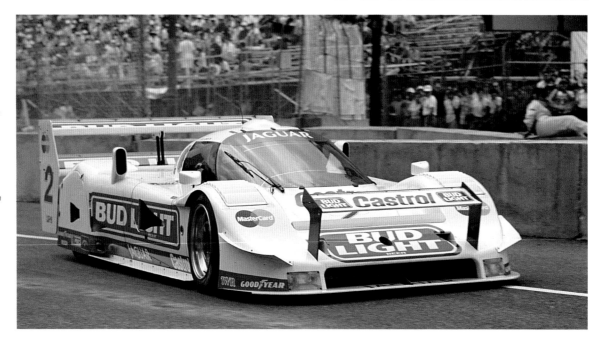

The need for extra downforce at some circuits was catered for in different ways. The nose of Davy Jones's XJR-16 at New Orleans was fitted with an extra front wing, winglets or bibs at the sides and a radiator exit panel extension, in addition to the widely used gurney flap fitted along the trailing edge of the rear wing. (Author)

Wayne Taylor and his Intrepid Chevrolet had been up at the front and challenging for the lead on numerous occasions this season, so his forceful win in round nine at **New Orleans** came as no great surprise. The two Jaguar XJR-16s had made a good impression so far but here on this new circuit both retired with rear suspension problems. If having to endure hot, humid conditions while negotiating the notoriously rough surface of this 1.5-mile track was not enough, rain was on hand to complete an afternoon of misery. Construction work delayed practice and qualifying, and the latter was put back to the Sunday morning. Davy Jones qualified fifth while Raul Boesel was slower, starting from eighth place on the grid.

Jones took Bud Light Jaguar number 2 into the lead during a shower on lap 11 while everybody else pitted for wet-weather

The much cleaner lines of the XJR-16 are evident in this picture of Davy Jones's number 2 Jaguar at Watkins Glen. (JDHT)

tyres. His spell at the front lasted only a few laps before a spin put him right at the back. Undeterred, Davy set out to claw his way back through the field, only to become plagued by suspension problems. The team, unable to put the car right, retired it on lap 44. Raul Boesel made good progress, moving up to third behind Geoff Brabham's Nissan and Wayne Taylor's Chevrolet before being affected by similar problems. His race ended on lap 49. Following this race, Davy and Raul flew to France to join the Silk Cut Jaguars at Le Mans. The car they drove there came home second, ahead of the other Jaguars in third and fourth places.

Venue: New Orleans, Louisiana
Round 9, 16 June 1991
Race title: Nissan Camel Grand Prix du Mardi Gras

Chassis type	Chassis no.	Race no.	Drivers	Grid pos.	Finish position	Laps
XJR-16	191	2	Davy Jones	5	DNF, suspension	44
XJR-16	291	3	Raul Boesel	8	DNF, suspension	49

Race winner: EDS/ICI Chevrolet Intrepid, driver Wayne Taylor, 81 laps

Back in America, the two drivers hardly had time to recuperate when it was off to **Watkins Glen** for round ten. They felt confident that the XJR-16s would find this fast circuit considerably easier to perform on than New Orleans. Davy Jones regarded this as his home track and was eager to get going. He started from fourth on the grid in Bud Light Jaguar number 2, and was quick to move into second place as the race got under way. On lap nine he took the lead and stayed out front until lap 50. Kendall's Chevrolet Intrepid was involved in a severe accident, and the extended mid-race yellow flag period which followed allowed Jones to stop for fuel twice, the second time to top up just before the green flag. Back in fourth place, he knew the front runners still needed to pit for fuel and was confident of taking the lead to the end.

Trouble struck on lap 88 when a rear suspension upper wishbone failed. The mechanics replaced it, allowing Jones to return to the job in hand but, in spite of running the fastest race lap, he could do no more than finish in 13th place. Raul Boesel's race ended on lap 10 after he was hit by Geoff Brabham's Nissan. Boesel had started from sixth and soon moved up to fourth, choosing to bide his time for a while. Brabham had started from the back and was soon picking off the middle runners. He attempted to pass Jaguar number 3 on turn five but made contact and sent the car spinning hard into the wall. The XJR-16 suffered severe rear end damage. Boesel was taken to the hospital unit for a check-up and was found to be uninjured. Brabham apologised publicly and personally for his lack of judgement.

Venue: Watkins Glen, New York
Round 10, 30 June 1991
Race title: Camel Continental VIII

Chassis type	Chassis no.	Race no.	Drivers	Grid pos.	Finish position	Laps
XJR-16	191	2	Davy Jones	4	13	107
XJR-16	291	3	Raul Boesel	6	DNF, accident	10

Race winner: All-American Racers Toyota Eagle, driver Juan-Manuel Fangio II, 122 laps

The Bud Light team had only a single car to field in the round eleven race at **Laguna Seca**, as Jaguar number 3 (chassis 291) could not be repaired in time after the Watkins Glen smash. However, Davy Jones won the race, although not in exactly the way it should have been. Fangio in the brand new Toyota Eagle Mark III number 99 looked set to win, only to lose out by default.

Jones had qualified third behind Wayne Taylor's Chevrolet Intrepid and Fangio's Toyota on the front row. Fangio streaked into the lead almost immediately, and built up a good distance between him and the next front runners before a full course caution closed up the field. Jones took the lead after the green flag was shown, and hung on before experiencing tyre deterioration problems. Fangio took over the lead again and this time built up a lead of one lap as the race neared the finish. With only eight laps left, his team called him into the pits for a last minute top-up just as the pace car took to the track to clear a stranded car. Fangio exited the pits at full speed, thereby incurring the wrath of the exit flagman and earning himself a 35-second penalty and, even more serious, the loss of one lap.

The beneficiary of this incident was Bud Light driver Davy Jones, now leading in Jaguar number 2 although under pressure from Geoff Brabham and from Perry McCarthy in a Spice Chevrolet. Jones eventually won with a margin of 31.573 seconds.

Venue: Laguna Seca, California
Round 11, 21 July 1991
Race title: Grand Auto Supply Camel GT Presented by Toyota

Chassis type	Chassis no.	Race no.	Drivers	Grid pos.	Finish position	Laps
XJR-16	191	2	Davy Jones	3	1	84

Round twelve at **Portland** saw the number of entries down to 17 as compared to 20 in 1990 and 24 in 1989. While the grids were getting smaller year by year, the quality of competition had improved considerably, particularly with homebred entries such as the Chevrolet Intrepids. Wayne Taylor qualified his to good effect, as he captured pole position for the second consecutive race.

Davy Jones in the lone Bud Light Jaguar was third on the grid, behind Geoff Brabham's Nissan. He had won at Portland in 1990 but this time the XJR-16 could do no better than fifth. The first half of the race was not the usual dash to the lead for Jones, who started on hard compound tyres in the belief that these would be the best choice in the light of conditions experienced during practice. He dropped back to fifth place before changing to softer tyres, but it was too late to make a difference. His fifth place finish put him behind two Toyotas and two Nissans. His points standing in the Drivers' Championship was such that if he won the last two races and if the Nissans failed to score he would become Champion.

Venue: Portland, Oregon
Round 12, 28 July 1991
Race title: GI Joe's Camel Grand Prix Presented by Nissan

Chassis type	Chassis no.	Race no.	Drivers	Grid pos.	Finish position	Laps
XJR-16	191	2	Davy Jones	3	5	97

Race winner: All-American Racers Toyota Eagle MK III, driver Juan-Manuel Fangio II, 97 laps

Raul Boesel was back again for round thirteen at **Road America** with the repaired XJR-16, joining Davy Jones who was on sparkling form throughout the entire weekend. Jones made fastest time in every practice session, and qualified on pole position in the record time of 1min 51.822sec at 128.776mph. Raul missed qualifying when his car needed a last-minute engine change and had to start from the back of the grid. Nissan driver Geoff Brabham was absent from the race. He had unfortunately been involved in a serious pre-race test session accident in which he suffered several fractures to his vertebrae and to various other

Davy Jones in the number 2 XJR-16 leads the Chevrolet Spice of Brian Bonner and Jeff Kline in the GI Joes race at Portland on 28 July 1991. Tyre problems affecting the Jaguar slowed him down to a fourth-place finish. (Paul Skilleter)

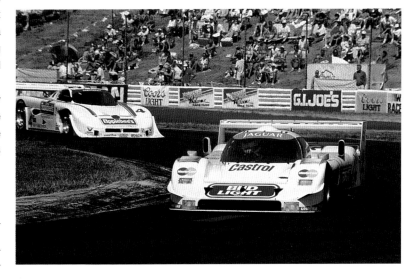

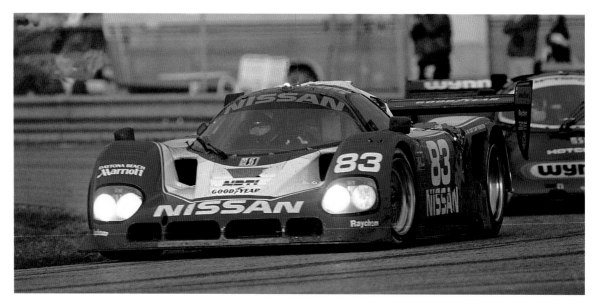

Geoff Brabham in the ultra-reliable Nissan took the Drivers' Championship title for a third year running but Toyota Eagles ruled the roost in 1992. (Sutton Photographics)

small bones. He spent the weekend in the care of specialists.

From the start Jones took command, leading every lap except 25 when he made a scheduled pit stop. He was determined to get maximum points but so was Nissan driver Chip Robinson, who needed a good score to secure top place in the points table. He achieved this by following Jones home to take second place. This put Robinson at 166 points, only 3 more than Jones's score of 163. His second place, along with the other Nissan driver Bob Earl's fifth place finish, clinched the Manufacturers' title for Nissan. Boesel's fourth place finish came after a long, steady haul through the field from his starting position at the back of the grid.

Venue: Road America, Wisconsin
Round 13, 25 August 1991
Race title: Nissan Camel Grand Prix of Road America

Chassis type	Chassis no.	Race no.	Drivers	Grid pos.	Finish position	Laps
XJR-16	191	2	Davy Jones	1	1	47
XJR-16	291	3	Raul Boesel	19	4	47

The last race of the season, round fourteen at **Del Mar**, was important for Davy Jones and the two top Nissan drivers, Chip Robinson and Geoff Brabham. Brabham was still feeling the effects of his accident at Road America but did not want to miss this last chance of gaining a fourth successive Drivers' Championship. He wore a special metal chest brace to ease his pain and his Nissan was fitted with a specially adapted seat. Brabham commented: 'Once the race is under way the pain will quickly be forgotten.'

Martin Brundle was brought in to race XJR-16 number 3, but both Jaguars experienced handling difficulties during qualifying which kept them at the back on the grid in fourth row. Their efforts were not helped when Jones hit the barrier on the Friday and lost his rear wing. The race itself was just as difficult and dramatic for Jones on the tightly walled circuit. He was not able to mix it with those at the front, so it was left to pole winner Wayne Taylor to

fend off the crowd of Nissans and Toyotas. Jones had enough on his hands duelling with the Spice Chevrolet of John Paul junior, who actually got up to third when two of the lead pack went out with problems. Paul got by as Jones locked up and hit the wall, causing damage to the rear wing assembly of the Jaguar. On pitting, the team was unable to fix the wing so he went out again but was not able to finish higher than a very disappointing 13th.

Martin Brundle was running relatively smoothly until his clutch pedal broke. After it was made temporarily safe he drove on to finish in fourth place. The team had hoped to do much better, especially following the previous race success. Geoff Brabham came home third, earning enough points to be IMSA GT Drivers' Champion once more, with a top score of 175. Team-mate Chip Robinson was second with 170 points, while Davy Jones came third with 158 points. Despite six wins against three apiece for Nissan and Toyota, for the third time Jaguar had to be content with second place in the Manufacturers' Championship, leading to understandable disappointment in the TWR Jaguar camp.

Venue: Del Mar, California
Round 14, 13 October 1991
Race title: Camel Grand Prix Of Greater San Diego Presented By Nissan

Chassis type	Chassis no.	Race no.	Drivers	Grid pos.	Finish position	Laps
XJR-16	191	2	Davy Jones	7	13	79
XJR-16	291	3	Martin Brundle	8	4	91

Race winner: All-American Racers Toyota Eagle Mk III, driver Juan-Manuel Fangio II, 92 laps

Just for the record Geoff Brabham's total winnings for the season were $332,421. Davy Jones collected $284,508. In the world of prototype sportscar racing this kind of money probably covered only a few broken front ends and smashed wing assemblies. The potent XJR-16s had finished their last race and next year would bring many changes, including better prospects of winning the Championship with the so far highly successful Jaguar XJR-14s.

Chapter 15

1992 IMSA Camel GT Championship

Keeping the flag flying

From a business point of view Jaguar's situation continued to deteriorate. At some points during 1992 the company was said to be losing a million dollars a day, and there is no doubt that without Ford's backing Jaguar would have gone to the wall. The American giant was investing heavily to cover costs and to provide for future models but the economies it demanded were stringent. The world championship race programme had finished but there were contractual requirements to fulfil in the United States.

However, Europe's ill wind blew the US racing team some good in the shape of the XJR-14 that had dominated the World Championship in 1991. With this radical car as its main weapon the Bud Light Jaguar team had every right to be confident of success. The team was so confident - and so affected, like everyone else at Jaguar, by the need for economy - that only one car was to be fielded. Sadly, however, IMSA was suffering from the same declining appeal as world sportscar racing. Crowd figures went down as grids were reduced, and although there was fierce competition between Jaguar, Nissan and Toyota, there was little else, particularly after GM pulled the plug on a Corvette GTP project.

TWR Jaguar's fifth year of competition in IMSA Championship racing was destined to be the last full season for a number of reasons. The two main crowd pullers, the Daytona 24-hour and Sebring 12-hour races, still attracted large entries, but all other

events in the 13 race season saw less than 20 cars lined up on the grid. The major manufacturers, Nissan, Toyota and Jaguar, continued to support all events for the time being, although few believed that the series could survive much longer at the same level as in previous years. With the factory teams dominating every race to the point of tedium the privateer entries dwindled and the fans stayed away in their droves.

When TWR announced that the team would be running XJR-14s in the 1992 season, Davy Jones immediately became the bookies' favourite to win the Championship. Silk Cut Jaguar's tremendous success in the 1991 SWC season, winning both the

Of the two Jaguars entered in the 1992 Daytona 24-hour race, the number 3 XJR-16, chassis 191, achieved second fastest qualifying time and should have started alongside the pole-winning Toyota Eagle. Engine-related problems kept it out of the race, putting an end to Jaguar's turbo car era. (Ken Wells)

XJR-12 chassis number 891 competed at Le Mans in 1991, where it came fourth, and then took the class win at Daytona in 1992. A few weeks later, another fourth place at Sebring ended its short but excellent race history. (Ken Wells)

Bud Light Jaguar number 2 (891) completes another routine pit stop. Here it is ready to leave the temporary pits erected specially for the annual 24-hour race. (Sutton Photographics)

Manufacturers' and the Drivers' Championships with the superfast Ross Brawn-designed racers, was a subject for much discussion by Jaguar's competitors. They considered the car much too light, giving it a worryingly unfair advantage.

As before, normally-aspirated V12 XJR-12s would contest the two endurance races, although the Daytona 24-hour race featured one of the turbo XJR-16s in qualifying. The rest of the season was made up of single driver and car entries, except at Laguna Seca where two XJR-14s raced. All three XJR-14 chassis were shipped over to Valparaiso and were listed during the season as chassis numbers 591, 791 and 192. The highest point-scoring Silk Cut car, chassis 691, was not listed during the season due to having been re-numbered as chassis 192 after upgrading and improvement works carried out to suit IMSA racing.

The two Jaguars entered for the opening race of the season, round one the Rolex 24 Hours at **Daytona**, were a single XJR-12D chassis number 891, a relatively new car built for the 1991 Le Mans 24-hour race, and one of the 1991 XJR-16s. Davy Jones qualified the turbo car only four tenths of a second slower than the pole winning All-American Racers Toyota Eagle 99 of Juan-Manuel Fangio II, with co-drivers Kenny Acheson and Andy Wallace. The XJR-16 should have started the race from the grid front row alongside Fangio with Scott Goodyear as its nominated

driver, but it was withdrawn just before the race because of engine problems. Goodyear joined up with Davy Jones, Geoff Brabham's younger brother David and Scott Pruett to drive the lone XJR-12 as a four-man team.

With nearly 50 cars on the grid, the number 2 Jaguar XJR-12 did well in qualifying to start from seventh place. Less than half the starters made it to the finish line, and amongst those that did there was a very strong Japanese presence. New for Daytona was an all-Japanese Nissan - or NISMO - factory team, which competed against the Nissan Performance and other privateer Nissan teams, and raced an in-house lookalike version of the former Lola-built Nissan NPT-91 used so successfully by Geoff Brabham and fellow drivers during the previous season. The Nissan R91 CP factory car number 23 did battle with Brabham's number 83 Nissan throughout much of the race, both cars taking turns to lead until the Nissan Performance car retired with engine failure on lap 272. The new NISMO car remained at the front all the way to the flag and won decisively, a feat which until then no other Nissan had achieved at Daytona.

The Bud Light Jaguar number 2 may not have led a single lap but it had an excellent race and came home second behind the factory Nissan. In doing so it came first in the GTP class. The winning NISMO Nissan was entered as a Group C car and thus despite its victory was not eligible for points. For finishing in first place in the GTP class the Jaguar was awarded maximum points.

Few cars ever complete a 24-hour race without one or two little problems along the way. Davy Jones took the first two stints in the XJR-12D. He moved up the field to tail the lead Nissans, at times taking one or other of them on yet maintaining a steady and controlled race during the early hours. Around 7.30pm David Brabham, on leaving the pits with new tyres, hit the exit barrier. This damaged the front end of the Jaguar and broke its steering arm. Repairs and replacements were hurriedly carried out with the loss of just five laps. Another of the Brabham brothers, Gary, who drove the second Nissan Performance NPT-91, came to grief at the same spot shortly afterwards, but he wrote his car off.

One by one the four Bud Light drivers had moved Jaguar number 2 back up to third place when a more serious fault developed in the gearbox. The mechanics set to and replaced the entire gear cluster in only 24 minutes. Davy Jones rejoined the race, determined to cut down on their 18-lap deficit. He clawed the Jaguar back up to third but another excursion into the pits to remedy a faulty front brake set it back a further seven minutes. This was the final unscheduled stop, and from then on an all-out push towards the front narrowed the gap between the Jaguar and the smooth-running NISMO Nissan to a mere nine laps at the finish. Had the V12 engine not experienced increasing temperatures during the latter stages, Jones might have made a last-minute run for it. Knowing that coming second would earn maximum points anyway, he wisely declined taking risks. TWR Jaguars had taken part in the Daytona 24-hour race five times,

claiming two outright wins and one all-important class win, not by any means a poor record.

Venue: Daytona, Florida
Round 1, 1-2 February 1992
Race title: Rolex 24 at Daytona

Chassis type	Chassis no.	Race no.	Drivers	Grid pos.	Finish position	Laps
XJR-12D	891	2	Davy Jones, David Brabham, Scott Pruett, Scott Goodyear	7	2, and 1 in GTP class	753
XJR-16	191	3	Scott Goodyear was the nominated driver, but Davy Jones qualified this car		Qualified second but withdrawn	

Race winner: Nissan Motorsport International Nissan R91 CP, drivers Masahiro Hasemi, Kazuyoshi Hoshino and Toshio Suzuki, 762 laps

Having scored maximum points, the class-winning team look pleased with themselves. Tony Dowe gives the thumbs-up sign, while Ian Reed appears glad it's all over. The team's great supporter, Jaguar Inc. Vice-President Michael Dale, on the left, shares their moment of glory. (Sutton Photographics)

The Bud Light Jaguar proved superior to the All American Racers Toyota Eagle at Daytona, but the Japanese cars were to dominate much of IMSA racing in 1992. (Sutton Photographics)

The first outing for the XJR-14 (791) at Miami was not quite the runaway success expected, as Davy Jones spun the single Jaguar entry out on lap 91. Geoff Brabham took the win in the Nissan. (JDHT)

Round two at **Miami** was the first outing for the XJR-14 in Bud Light livery. Chassis number 791 had been flown to America at the beginning of February and had undergone testing at Phoenix, Arizona, before its appearance at Miami. Changes were made to comply with IMSA's permitted noise levels, and also in response to complaints from other teams. Following similar modifications carried out to the XJR-10 turbo Jaguars, the V8's exhaust pipe positions were altered from side exit to rearward facing. The most significant visible bodywork change concerned the roof-mounted engine air intake, now cut back and reshaped to twin lower-profile scoops situated either side of the centre line.

Great things were expected from the new TWR supercats. Davy Jones far from disappointed the crowds when he captured pole position with a record-breaking fastest lap of 1min 5.402sec, which was 0.825sec better than Geoff Brabham's 1min 6.247sec. Brabham's time was three seconds better than his previous year's best, so the XJR-14 was certainly living up to expectations. It was quite another matter whether this car, substantially lighter in weight than any previous Jaguar, could survive two hours on Miami's tricky and bumpy circuit while also having to endure Florida's hot and humid conditions.

Brabham was fully aware that the XJR-14 was faster than his new Nissan NPT-91, and realised that the most effective way to get the better of Jones was to push him to the limit. The closely-fought opening laps saw the two cars engaged in a battle of their own, free from the *mêlée* of crashed cars which had spread themselves across the track on lap one. This had been caused when Davy Jones's namesake, P J Jones, spun his Toyota Eagle across the path of the middle field. At the end of a caution period Davy Jones still led, but only just, keeping Brabham at bay until lap 33 when a gearchange error sent him spinning. After a pit stop to change tyres and re-fuel, the Jaguar was in third place behind Brabham's Nissan and Tom Kendall's Chevrolet.

Brabham built up a sizeable lead, only to hit trouble when an oil-smeared windscreen drastically reduced his vision. He pitted on lap 54 for cleaning and shortly afterwards Jones took the lead until his own pit stop on lap 63, when Brabham, now with a clean windscreen, took over again. Jones did his best to catch up with the Nissans, but was forced to make an additional stop for fresh

tyres. After spinning on lap 92 the XJR-14's engine failed to re-start, thus ending the team's hopes for a debut win with the much-vaunted Jaguar supercat.

Venue: Miami, Florida
Round 2, 23 February 1992
Race title: Toyota Grand Prix of Miami

Chassis type	Chassis no.	Race no.	Drivers	Grid pos.	Finish position	Laps
XJR-14	791	2	Davy Jones	1	DNF, spin	91

Race winner: Nissan Performance Nissan NPT-91, driver Geoff Brabham, 99 laps

The fourth place finish of number 2 Bud Light Jaguar XJR-12 in round three in the **Sebring** 12-hour race was sufficient to keep Davy Jones at the top of the Drivers' Championship table with 52 points. Juan-Manuel Fangio II was next with 47. In the Manufacturers' Championship, Jaguar was third, but at this very early stage of the game anything could happen. Bud Light Jaguar's single XJR-12 entry, chassis 891, with only two drivers, was their smallest commitment to an endurance race so far. The general feeling amongst team members was that concentrating all their resources on this lone car might bring about a first win at this circuit for TWR. Nissan had taken the last three wins following a staggering 13 successive Porsche victories from 1976 to 1988. Bud Light Jaguar hoped to change the team's fortunes this time around.

Davy Jones qualified Jaguar number 2 in 10th place and it was never to challenge the lead cars during much of the race. He

Bud Light XJR-14s differed from when they raced as Silk Cut Group C cars in having twin roof engine intakes. Note the addition to the front wing, used on both sides of the Atlantic where extra downforce was required. (LAT Photographic)

The number 2 Bud Light Jaguar's fourth-place finish here at Sebring maintained Davy Jones' early-season Championship lead. (Sutton Photographics)

moved the XJR-12 up to fourth after two hours, only to come to a standstill on the track with a loose right rear wheel. Crew members were sent out with a spare wheel and wheel nut, and with all the necessary tools for Jones to fix it himself. This allowed him to get the Jaguar back to the pits. Here it was checked over but eight laps had been lost.

With little chance of overwhelming the Japanese Nissans and Toyotas, Jones and Brabham were further hampered by oil cooler and brake line problems which kept the Jaguar away from the sharp end. Geoff Brabham's Nissan 83 and the number 84 sister car dominated most laps, occasionally allowing the All-American Racers Toyotas to grab a few, until the Toyota 99 of Juan-Manuel Fangio II and Andy Wallace moved up front for the last time on lap 251. They never let go, finishing five laps ahead of Brabham's Nissan. Nissan 83 did not actually finish the race as it was caught in the pits with wheel problems while lying second as the flag waved. The Bud Light Jaguar's fourth place finish came after hours of steady but determined effort by Davy Jones and David Brabham. They survived in a race where half of the cars entered failed to finish.

Venue: Sebring, Florida
Round 3, 21 March 1992
Race title: Contac 12 Hours of Sebring Presented by Camel

Chassis type	Chassis no.	Race no.	Drivers	Grid pos.	Finish position	Laps
XJR-12	891	2	Davy Jones, David Brabham	10	4	338

Race winner: All-American Racers Toyota Eagle MKIII, drivers Andy Wallace and Juan-Manuel Fangio II, 360 laps

If round four at **Road Atlanta** had been great for Jaguar in 1991, it was absolutely fabulous for Davy Jones and the team this year.

Jones qualified the XJR-14 with a new track record time of 1min 7.418sec at 134.563mph to take pole position. During the race he set a new race lap record of 1min 8.639sec at 132.170mph, and also led the field from start to finish.

The two All-American Racers Toyotas were deemed to be the XJR-14's strongest competitors, with Geoff Brabham's Nissan NPT-91A also in the running, but not one of the Nissan and Toyota brigade could match the Jaguar's tremendous speed. It was quicker in all pre-race practice sessions, so everybody knew that an interesting race lay ahead of them. Fangio's Toyota 99 stood alongside Davy on the grid front row and surprisingly leapt into the lead at the start. Fangio kept it past turn one but the Jaguar slipped past before turn two.

Only one Toyota finished, way back in 14th place, and both Nissans crashed. The race was still on its warm-up lap when a multi-car accident occurred in front of the starter's stand. Chip Robinson's Nissan was the first of the front runners to exit after a disastrous tyre blow-out sent the Nissan rolling over and over, just before the right-hand kink and the main straight. The car was wrecked and Robinson was taken to hospital with a suspected broken shoulder. Geoff Brabham followed suit with a similar accident on lap 55. His car was also wrecked but he escaped with light bruising.

While all this was going on Davy Jones continued to build up his lead, and so was able to take a leisurely pit stop on lap 44. His nearest rival was Tom Kendall in a Chevrolet, who followed into second place as the flag brought the race to a close a few laps early. Davy Jones now led the Drivers' Championship with 77 points to Fangio's second place with 49. Jaguar was top in the manufacturers' listing.

Stricter noise level regulations at IMSA circuits called for muffler devices as seen on this XJR-12D. (Ken Wells)

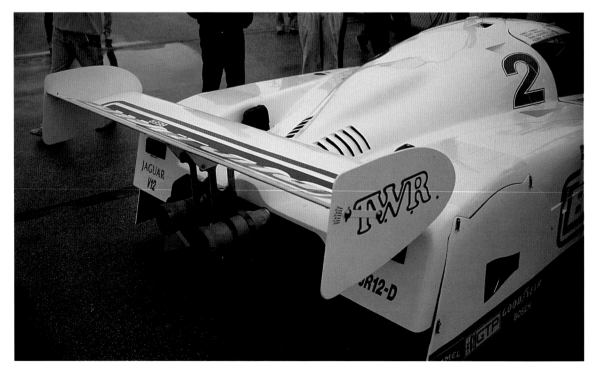

Venue: Road Atlanta, Georgia
Round 4, 26 April 1992
Race title: Nissan Grand Prix of Atlanta

Chassis type	Chassis no.	Race no.	Drivers	Grid pos.	Finish position	Laps
XJR-14	791	2	Davy Jones	1	1	63

Round five at **Lime Rock** started much like the previous race for Davy Jones and Bud Light XJR-14 number 2. Jones set a new record in qualifying after being fastest in all practice sessions. He qualified on pole with a time of 43.985sec at 126.043mph. Juan-Manuel Fangio II's Toyota 99 shared the grid front row.

This time pole starter Jones was not to take the same commanding lead in the opening laps but had to follow Fangio before gaining the lead on lap 12. Jones completed a fastest race lap record on lap 14 in 45.857sec or 120.897mph. He continued to lead until lap 19 when an undetermined mechanical failure sent Jaguar number 2 hard into the tyre barrier, inflicting severe damage. The car was taken back to Valparaiso for a thorough investigation and some components were dispatched to the UK

for examination and testing at TWR headquarters.

Fangio in Toyota Eagle 99 won the race, followed home by Nissan 83 driven jointly by Geoff Brabham and Chip Robinson. The XJR-14 Jaguar's unfortunate accident put Jaguar down to joint second in the Manufacturers' Championship, but Davy Jones still led the driver standings.

Venue: Lime Rock, Connecticut
Round 5, 26 May 1992
Race title: Toyota Trucks Presents the Lime Rock Grand Prix

Chassis type	Chassis no.	Race no.	Drivers	Grid pos.	Finish position	Laps
XJR-14	791	2	Davy Jones	1	DNF, accident	19

Race winner: All-American Racers Toyota Eagle MKIII, driver Juan-Manuel Fangio II, 140 laps

Disappointment at Lime Rock was soon turned around in round six at **Mid Ohio**, where Davy Jones took a brilliant win in the team's replacement XJR-14. This increased his drivers' points tally to 104. Fangio in his Toyota Eagle 99 came second, in front of Geoff Brabham's Nissan.

Davy Jones led from start to finish in 192 at Road Atlanta, breaking both qualifying and race lap records. (LAT Photographic)

Jones earned pole position in yet another qualifying record time of 1min 9.856sec at 115.952mph. He also made the fastest race lap of 1min 25.728sec, but this was not a record. Unlike some of the American circuits, Mid Ohio was comparatively smooth and better suited to the lightweight Jaguars. In rather wet and drizzly conditions Jones quickly moved ahead of Fangio and led every lap up to the finish flag. Even after causing a few heart flutters in the TWR pit by spinning off the slippery circuit, he was able to make his scheduled pit stop and re-join the race 26 seconds ahead of Fangio. This aside, Davy ran a trouble-free race to claim another superb victory. The chassis which he used is thought to be the former Silk Cut XJR-14 chassis number 691 re-numbered to 192, the only Jaguar prototype car given a 1992 chassis number.

Venue: Mid Ohio, Ohio
Round 6, 31 May 1992
Race title: Nissan Grand Prix of Ohio

Chassis type	Chassis no.	Race no.	Drivers	Grid pos.	Finish position	Laps
XJR-14	192	2	Davy Jones	1	1	82

Round six at Mid Ohio had been led from flag to flag by the number 2 XJR-14, but in round seven at **New Orleans** it was Fangio's turn to be out front throughout the race. Fangio qualified first and finished first, while Davy Jones qualified second but was fourth past the flag.

Jones took off at the start slightly ahead of Fangio as they approached turn one. While braking, Jones found himself sliding away and made for the escape road, allowing Fangio to take Toyota 99 into the lead, followed by team-mate P J Jones in the number 98 sister car. David Tennyson came next in the Spice Chevrolet. By the time Jones rejoined the race he was running last, 37 seconds behind Fangio. Gradually he worked the Jaguar back up the field into seventh, when a first full course yellow flag enabled him to make a short pit stop and then rejoin in sixth. Towards the finish, Jones advanced up to third before being struck by P J Jones's Toyota, which caused him to hit the wall. Undeterred, he finished the race in fourth place behind his namesake. He earned enough points to stay at the top of the Drivers' Championship, including a single point for fastest lap of the race.

Venue: New Orleans, Louisiana
Round 7, 14 June 1992
Race title: Grand Prix du Mardi Gras

Chassis type	Chassis no.	Race no.	Drivers	Grid pos.	Finish position	Laps
XJR-14	192	2	Davy Jones	2	4	89

Race winner: All-American Racers Toyota Eagle MKIII, driver Juan-Manuel Fangio II, 89 laps

Watkins Glen, the venue for round eight, is Davy Jones's declared home circuit and his greatest wish was to take a decisive win here to make up for the catalogue of failures the TWR Jaguars had at the Glen during the previous four years. He started the weekend with another fastest qualifying lap record for the circuit of 58.669sec at 150.334mph. He also added a new record fastest race lap of 59.920sec at 147.196mph.

From his pole start he had led the first 109 laps with ease when the Watkins Glen gremlins struck, as the XJR-14's left front wheel bearing failed. In only six minutes the upright was replaced but Davy was now six laps behind Fangio's number 99 Toyota, and in fourth place. In his gallant effort to catch up with the leader, Jones completed the fastest race lap time on lap 116. He moved up to third but Fangio's Toyota and Price Cobb's Mazda RX-792P remained out of reach at the flag. Jones's third-place points and those he earned from the fastest qualifying and race laps were enough to keep him ahead in the Drivers' Championship by just three points.

Venue: Watkins Glen, New York
Round 8, 28 June 1992
Race title: Camel Continental IX

Chassis type	Chassis no.	Race no.	Drivers	Grid pos.	Finish position	Laps
XJR-14	192	2	Davy Jones	1	3	142

Race winner: All-American Racers Toyota Eagle MKIII, driver Juan-Manuel Fangio II, 147 laps

Two Bud Light Jaguar XJR-14s competed in round nine at **Laguna Seca**, but at the finish two of the All-American Racers Toyota Eagles beat them to the flag. The second XJR-14, chassis number 591, was driven by Dutchman Arie Luyendijk, whose first task was to get accustomed to left hand gear changing. Both cars performed well during Friday's practice session, in which Jones made fastest time. Saturday was by contrast plagued by problems. Jones suffered one drivetrain failure, then another, losing valuable track time while changes were made. Luyendijk in number 3 XJR-14 fared even worse, missing a full session while his engine and gearbox assembly was replaced after a mishap.

Davy Jones was back in form again during qualifying, where he broke the previous best time only to be out-timed a little later by P J Jones in Toyota Eagle 98, which took pole position. Juan-Manuel Fangio II's Toyota 99 shared the front row with another faster time, so Jones' number 2 Jaguar was back on the second row. It was quite clear that the All-American Racers Toyotas were now the equal of the XJR-14s, relegating the Championship-holding Nissans further back in the line-up for top honours.

The race was completely dominated by Fangio and his Toyota 99, who passed team-mate P J Jones on turn one and kept the lead all the way to the finish. Davy and P J Jones swapped places on lap two, then back again 15 laps later. This short spell in second place was the nearest Davy Jones got to the front, and he was left to settle for third place at the finish. Luyendijk started from sixth on the grid and ran a steady race, dicing with Chip Robinson's Nissan NPT-91B along the way. He finished fourth, which for a first time in the XJR-14 could be considered a good result. Fangio's win put him seven points ahead of Jones in the drivers' standing.

Venue: Laguna Seca, California
Round 9, 19 July 1992
Race title: Grand Auto Supply Camel GT Presented by Toyota

Chassis type	Chassis no.	Race no.	Drivers	Grid pos.	Finish position	Laps
XJR-14	192	2	Davy Jones	3	3	94
XJR-14	591	3	Arie Luyendijk	6	4	92

Race winner: All-American Racers Toyota Eagle MKIII, driver Juan-Manuel Fangio II, 94 laps

Pre-race press releases announced that round ten at **Portland** would also see two Jaguar XJR-14s entered, driven as they were at Laguna Seca by Jones and Luyendijk. However, on race day Davy Jones was the only Bud Light representative in Jaguar number 2. For Jones this was a disappointing race which ended all his hopes of recovering the Championship lead, especially if Fangio's Toyota 99 continued to perform so well in the remaining races of the season.

The All-American Racers team claimed the grid front row, and this time it was Fangio who broke the qualifying lap record. Jones was third on the grid, from where he ran a troubled race, fighting understeer and then suffering a dead engine after a spin. He eventually got the Jaguar going again and immediately made for the pits for new tyres and refuelling. Back out again, the tyres were still giving him problems, so he returned to the pits once

more for different compounds. By now he was back in 11th place, and embarked on a desperate bid to get back up the field. He made it to sixth but a couple of spins proved too much for the XJR-14's drivetrain and its race ended on lap 70. Fangio led the race up to the time when Davy went out, and then team-mate P J Jones in the second Toyota took over to finish first. Davy Jones's failure to complete 70 per cent of the race denied him any points.

Venue: Portland, Oregon
Round 10, 26 July 1992
Race title: GI Joe's Camel Grand Prix Presented by Nissan

Chassis type	Chassis no.	Race no.	Drivers	Grid pos.	Finish position	Laps
XJR-14	192	2	Davy Jones	3	DNF, mechanical	70

Race winner: All-American Racers Toyota Eagle MKIII, driver P J Jones, 109 laps

A pre-race warm-up disaster resulted in no Jaguar participation in round eleven at **Road America**. Davy Jones's XJR-14 suffered a catastrophic wheel failure as he turned into the Carousel, sending the car straight into the guard-rail to finish on top of the tyre barrier at turn ten. Severe damage to the left front of the car resulted in the team's withdrawal. Davy suffered no more than a bruised left shoulder, but the crash ended any possibility of a last-minute change of fortunes for him in the Drivers' Championship tables. Jones had qualified third once again behind the two AAR Toyotas,

Chassis 192 (691) scored many points for Davy Jones but not enough to win the longed-for Drivers' Championship. (LAT Photographic)

Not quite a Jaguar but just as important to the hardworking pit crews for moving wheel sets and other gear around the pit area. Note the markings on the tyres behind, all intended for Jaguar number 2 and arrowed to show direction of rotation. (Ken Wells)

which finished one-two after total domination of the race. The winner Fangio streaked ahead in the drivers' standing to 186 points.

Venue: Road America, Wisconsin
Round 11, 9 August 1992
Race title: Nissan Grand Prix of Road America

Chassis type	Chassis no.	Race no.	Drivers	Grid pos.	Finish position	Laps
XJR-14	591	2	Davy Jones		Crashed on last lap of warm-up, did not race	

Race winner: All-American Racers Toyota Eagle MKIII, driver Juan-Manuel Fangio II, 63 laps

The penultimate round twelve at **Phoenix** was more encouraging for the Bud Light team in that Davy Jones finished in a good second place, behind Fangio's Toyota Eagle MKIII. For the third race in a row Davy started from the grid second row, and as before the front row was occupied by the seemingly unstoppable AAR Toyotas. The Jaguar team had not participated in any of the earlier race practice sessions, but having spent some time here earlier in the year they used the data gathered then for pre-race preparation.

In uncomfortably hot weather which made tyre wear a problem the race was totally dominated by the Toyotas. For the first 24 laps P J Jones led the field, after which Fangio took command all the way to the flag. Davy Jones did well to keep up with them, and at the finish the XJR-14 was the only other car on the same lap as Fangio.

Venue: Phoenix, Arizona
Round 12, 4 October 1992
Race Title: The Checker IMSA Camel GT Grand Prix

Chassis type	Chassis no.	Race no.	Drivers	Grid pos.	Finish position	Laps
XJR-14	192	2	Davy Jones	3	2	127

Race winner: All-American Racers Toyota Eagle MKIII, driver Juan-Manuel Fangio II, 127 laps

Round thirteen, the final race of the season at **Del Mar**, was convincingly won by Jones, but for Bud Light Jaguar it was the wrong Jones. The TWR Jaguars had done well on this circuit in earlier days and the team always looked forward to racing here. Their appearance this time must have been tinged with a little

sadness as there was so much speculation about the future of the series. The near-total domination of the all-powerful factory teams, one after the other, had stifled interest in the series, and now it was certain that some teams were on their last season in GTP racing.

Unless both of the mighty Toyota conquerors succumbed to mechanical failure or got involved in damaging mishaps, they would already be making space in the trophy cupboard long before the race got under way. When Fangio qualified on pole and P J Jones claimed third place, the Toyota team already had the cupboard door open. They might have wondered a bit, as Davy Jones's XJR-14 Jaguar split them up by qualifying fast enough to sit beside Fangio on the front row. Davy Jones had also made best time during Friday's unofficial practice session, so he was certainly not to be ruled out.

The race started in near perfect weather conditions, Fangio leading the first eight laps with Davy Jones hard on his heels. Then an overheating engine forced the Toyota back to the pits, where a water leak was diagnosed. After getting out again, the All-American Racers' Champion lasted but a handful of laps before retirement became inevitable. Davy Jones now held the lead in the XJR-14, a position not enjoyed by him for a number of races. His P J namesake in the number 98 Toyota was close behind, along with long-reigning IMSA Drivers' Champion Geoff Brabham in Nissan 83.

Around the halfway stage, while cars were making their first round of pit stops, Davy Jones was approaching turn 10 when his rear brakes locked up. The resultant spin caused him to hit the wall, damaging the front end. He came to the pits for a new nose plus fuel and tyres. The time lost put P J Jones in the lead. Davy was unable to prevent him from running home first and had to content himself with the prospect of second place. But even that was not to be, for on the very last lap a driveshaft broke, allowing Brabham to capture the number two place, which was the best result for the outgoing Champion since he had finished second in June at New Orleans. Davy was awarded third place in this, the very last sprint race in which TWR prototype Jaguars would compete.

Venue: Del Mar, California
Round 13, 11 October 1992
Race title: Vons Grand Prix Of San Diego Presented By Nissan

Chassis type	Chassis no.	Race no.	Drivers	Grid pos.	Finish position	Laps
XJR-14	192	2	Davy Jones	2	3 (DNF, driveshaft)	112

Race winner: All-American Racers Toyota Eagle MKIII, driver P.J. Jones, 114 laps

Fangio's points score rose to 215 while Davy Jones was second, though well down, with 169. At least he had surpassed his former Championship-winning rival Geoff Brabham, who finished in third place with 132 points. Toyota became Manufacturers' Champion for the first time with 224 points. Nissan was second with 158 and Jaguar scored 153 points for a third place.

Chapter 16

1993 IMSA Camel GT Championship

Last hurrah: Rolex 24 Hours at Daytona

By 1993 Jaguar was a very different company from the one that had started in Group C in 1985. When first privatised, Jaguar had been a glowing example of Thatcherite Britain. Its cars were a part of the lifestyle that typified the growing entrepreneurial spirit in the country, and its renaissance was encouraging overseas buyers. The 20 years that followed the war had made Jaguar a household name in the rest of the world, especially in America, but the 1970s and the lacklustre image of British Leyland had tarnished the brand. Many foreign buyers wanted to buy Jaguars, but the quality and reliability problems associated with the big combine's stewardship of the marque had made them wary. When Jaguar regained its independence the higher quality standards that John Egan had introduced rebuilt the confidence of potential customers. They felt able to buy the car they had wanted but had not dared to buy, and improving export sales figures provided evidence of their renewed faith.

Racing success was a part of Jaguar's growing confidence, and the 1988 Le Mans win had marked a peak. But one of the major elements that would change Jaguar had already developed before the 24-hour victory. In late 1987, the US stock market had fallen disastrously, taking markets across the world with it. Luxury car sales were a victim of that collapse, and although it took some time for the full effects to be felt, as the 1990s started Jaguar was

reeling from the shock. The result of this and other influences was the Ford take-over, and by 1993 racing looked like an expensive luxury to a company that had to concentrate on improving quality and efficiency, and developing new models. Not for the first time, Jaguar's racing activities had to give way to planning the cars that would ensure the company's future. Daytona 1993 was the last gasp of the second era in which Jaguar wrote its name on the racetracks of the world.

The last prototype TWR V12, chassis 193, appeared as car 3T during pre-race practice at Daytona, then changed to race number 32 for the start. (Don Law)

Davy Jones, lead driver in Jaguar XJR-12D number 2 (190). Note the blue-coloured exhaust system and the chassis number inside the door. (Don Law)

All three Bud Light Jaguar XJR-12Ds lined up in the temporary pits constructed for the race. (Don Law)

The new chassis 193 looked promising but proved a difficult car to handle. (Sutton Photographics)

The 1993 Rolex 24-hour race at **Daytona**, while entertaining in several aspects, was a highly poignant moment for TWR drivers and the dedicated engineers, mechanics and all other personnel who had worked so hard for so long to keep Jaguar's name to the fore in international sportscar racing. This final throw of the dice brought down the curtain on a fascinating chapter in Jaguar's illustrious history. It had all begun in North America at Mosport in August 1985, and now it was to conclude on the same continent, albeit at one of the most successful and important venues in the entire series. Exactly five years earlier the newly established Valparaiso TWR team had raced the 1988 model XJR-9s to a historic victory at this very circuit. Taking the chequered flag here just once more, this time in an XJR-12D, would mark a memorable exit for Jaguar.

Three XJR-12Ds raced at Daytona, no longer as GTP cars but entered in the Le Mans category. Jaguar was the only team running cars in this particular group, but the Le Mans 24-hour race was only a few months away and there was still talk of Jaguar V12 participation. Reputedly designed with Le Mans in mind, a brand new XJR-12D chassis was sent over from the UK in late January after a brief test session at Silverstone on 15 January, driven by John Nielsen and David Brabham. Given the chassis number 193, its combination of XJR-12 and XJR-14 features gave the car a very impressive businesslike appearance. Work on 193 started early in 1992, probably with Le Mans that year as the intended target. Had it been completed early enough, the intention was to give it chassis number 192LM. A consequence of this might have been re-numbering 691 to 292 for IMSA racing instead of 192.

TWR entered it as Bud Light Jaguar number 32, intending to complete a limited number of laps to test the car's Le Mans potential rather than to embark on a full-blown 24-hour race. The car was too new and untried for that, but a limited amount of track experience would have great value in future projects. Indeed, no mention was made in Bud Light's pre-race press releases of Jaguar 32 or of intended drivers. However, the proposal was for Davy Jones to complete a short stint, after which the car would be parked behind the wall while the team concentrated all resources on the two main entries.

These were chassis 190 and 990, racing as Bud Light Jaguars numbers 2 and 3. Chassis 990 had last raced at Le Mans in 1991 driven by Davy Jones, Raul Boesel and Michel Ferte, coming home second with two other XJR-12s in third and fourth places. Chassis 190 had raced at Sebring in 1991, where it had come home in fifth place, and also once at Le Mans in 1990, where it had failed to finish. In 1993 Davy Jones was the principal driver in the number 2 Bud Light Jaguar, sharing it with Scott Pruett and Scott Goodyear. The drivers for Jaguar number 3 were John Nielsen, David Brabham and John Andretti.

Davy Jones qualified Jaguar number 2 sixth on the grid, while number 3 started from seventh, and to complete a close bunched trio the new Jaguar 32 took eighth. Dan Gurney's All-American Racers Toyota Eagles 98 and 99 were expected to capture both front row grid positions, and did so with ease. The Porsche number 6 of Sullivan, Haywood, Robinson and Pescarolo qualified third, while Britain's most famous sportscar champion, Derek Bell, was one of four drivers starting from fourth position in a privateer Nissan NPTI 90-03, turned out in striking Momo livery.

Chassis 990 as Jaguar number 3 in full flight. It went out with an oil leak after just 18 laps. (LAT Photographic)

The 1993 Daytona 24 hours not only marked the end of sportscar prototype racing for Jaguar, but it was also the beginning of the end of Camel-sponsored GTP racing in America, replaced in 1994 by the Exxon-sponsored World Championship open-topped series.
(Sutton Photographics)

The race started much as expected, the AAR Toyotas taking control at the front. They kept the lead for the first 258 laps, swapping over continuously with no other competitors getting a look in. The Jaguars started well, believing that the two leaders would fall victim to over-confidence and push too hard too soon. John Nielsen eased car 3 forward and passed Chip Robinson's Joest Porsche to take fourth but a faulty oil seal sent him back to the pits. After two hours' repair work the Jaguar was retired.

Jones had started Jaguar 32, completing a few laps as intended before returning to the pits, where it was pushed behind the wall, but with Jaguar number 3 out of action the new car was brought back into play. David Brabham took the first stint but his task was not destined to be an easy one. Unaccountably tricky handling problems, on top of having to spend more time in the pit to have a new ignition box fitted, ruled out all hopes of staying the course. The new prototype was withdrawn after 92 laps. For Jaguar it was now two down, one to go.

Jaguar number 2 was performing more in keeping with the Jaguars of old. While mishaps, incidents and blown engines were eliminating cars of all classes, it remained on the lead lap until 11.40pm. Scott Pruett was at the wheel, and eventually succeeded in taking the lead when Toyota 98 pitted for a new nose. The Fangio/Wallace/Acheson Toyota 99 had lost time in the pits and was now making a strong push to regain the lead partnership, but it never caught up with the Jaguar and finally went out much later in the race with a blown engine.

For the next 10 hours and 360 laps all eyes were firmly on the remaining Jaguar XJR-12 and Toyota Eagle, engaged in a nail-

biting duel. Of this total, the AAR car led for 284 laps, the Jaguar taking the lead no less than six times for a combined total of 76 laps. A little before 10am Pruett brought the Jaguar to a standstill with a broken gear linkage, which he managed to repair well enough to return to the pits. By coincidence the Toyota suffered a similar problem, so both leaders were in the pits being worked on. The Jaguar's problem was resolved quite speedily but for the Toyota it was a 75-minute operation.

Now well in the lead, Jaguar number 2 seemed set to take a win when a broken valve spring signalled the end for Jaguar in this race and in the entire TWR Jaguar prototype adventure. The Toyota 98 went on to win, while the Bud Light Jaguar number 2 was classified 10th. A pair of 6.5-litre Ford Mustangs took second and third places.

Venue: Daytona, Florida
Round 1, 30-31 January 1993
Race title: Rolex 24 at Daytona

Chassis type	Chassis no.	Race no.	Drivers	Grid pos.	Finish position	Laps
XJR-12D	190	2	Davy Jones, Scott Pruett, Scott Goodyear	6	10 - not running at the finish	618
XJR-12D	990	3	John Nielsen, David Brabham, John Andretti	7	DNF, oil leak	18
XJR-12D	193	32	Davy Jones, John Nielsen, David Brabham, John Andretti	8	DNF, handling	92

Race winner: All-American Toyota Eagle MKIII, drivers P J Jones, Mark Dismore and Rocky Moran, 698 laps

Chapter 17

XJR-15 JaguarSport Million Dollar Intercontinental Challenge

Demolition Derby?

XJR-15 was a typical example of Tom Walkinshaw's enterprise. It had become obvious, as the market for exotic and expensive cars peaked in the late 1980s, that there were wealthy customers who would like to have a Jaguar Group C race car of their own. These were not people who wanted to race the cars seriously, but enthusiasts who wanted to own and occasionally drive the ultimate Jaguar. Cars like Ferrari's F40 and Porsche's 959 had found a ready market, and Walkinshaw saw that the XJR series could also attract sufficient clients to warrant a limited production run. In creating the XJR-15, TWR took the basis of Tony Southgate's design and added elements that would make it even more appealing to the type of rich car enthusiast who had come to the fore on the wave of the 'supercar' boom. In place of the aerodynamics-led body of XJR-9, Walkinshaw commissioned

Peter Stevens to create a softer shape, more likely to appeal to a clientele attracted to Ferraris, Lamborghinis and other road-going exotics. Realising that the potential buyers were unlikely to appreciate the spartan cockpit of a Group C racer, TWR also made the car's interior more luxurious and comfortable.

Creating the XJR-15 did pose a political problem for TWR, since the car was a potential rival to the XJ220 which the company was turning into a production reality on Jaguar's behalf. In order to put distance between the two cars, the XJR-15 was a product of JaguarSport, the joint-venture company owned by Jaguar and TWR, and was badged as such. Although it seems likely that history will call the car a Jaguar, in fact it was not officially a Jaguar product. In a further move to distance XJR-15 from the production version of XJ220, which was conceived

Tom Walkinshaw demonstrates the JaguarSport R9R prototype XJR-15 during the Silverstone press launch in November 1990. (Zoom Photographic)

A splendid line-up of
XJR-15s at Silverstone
prior to the first race at
Monaco. (Sutton
Photographics)

Rare shot of an
XJR-9-based early
testbed for the
R9R/XJR-15 on
Enstone airfield. Initial
itentions to develop the
car on similar lines
proved impracticable.
(Ron Russel)

purely as a road car, XJR-15 was sold as a racing machine, a fact
underlined by the requirement for owners to sign up to participate
in a special race series.

During the late summer and early autumn months of 1990, the
motoring press abounded with rumours and speculation that
JaguarSport were about to launch a limited production street legal
road racer, based on the 1988 Le Mans winning Jaguar XJR-9
chassis. It was code-named 'R9R', and some claimed the car's
price tag would be around £700,000, which was roughly
equivalent to what Porsche were selling their 962C prototypes for.
Tom Walkinshaw dismissed this, stating that a more simplified
specification meant costs would be much lower. He also made it
quite clear that the cars were not intended for road use.

TWR arranged a press conference to take place at Silverstone
on 15 November 1990, when the car was shown to the public for
the first time. The car was given the name JaguarSport XJR-15,
an initial production batch of 30 cars was planned, and
Walkinshaw confirmed that total production would be strictly
limited to 50 cars. As a condition of sale, all new owners would
undertake to enter their cars in a highly prestigious one-make
series of races, planned to support three Grand Prix events in
1991. The first of these very exclusive races would take place
immediately after the Monaco Grand Prix in May, racing for a total

of 16 laps. Round two would take place on home ground at
Silverstone in support of the British Grand Prix. Here the cars
would race 20 laps but cover nearly twice the distance of the
Monaco race due to the lap distance being much greater. The
final race of the series would be programmed to support the
Belgium GP at Spa-Francorchamps in August.

The owners of the Monaco and Silverstone winning XJR-15s
would each receive a brand new £45,000 JaguarSport XJR-S 6-
litre. At Spa, the lucky owner of the winning car would receive a
cheque for $1,000,000, while the driver's National Sporting
Authority would receive a solid silver Challenge Trophy. The
winning driver of this particular event would get his own replica
trophy. All races would be subject to the usual practice and
qualifying sessions, and all participating drivers had to hold a
current FISA International Racing Competition Licence.

The stylish XJR-15 came in response to many requests from
privateers and would-be race teams to be allowed to buy
customer versions of the Jaguar XJR prototype race cars. Tom
Walkinshaw was not about to supply machinery identical to cars
currently being run in Group C and GTP racing, but TWR began
development work on a suitable alternative back in 1988. Fitted
with a modified 6-litre version of the V12 race engine, the new
model would be eligible for both Group C and GTP racing but
would have bodywork more akin to a road car. The beautifully
styled composite body came from the drawing board of Peter
Stevens, the stylist who had been responsible for the Lotus Elan
and who went on to design the McLaren F1 before becoming
design director of the post-BMW MG Rover Group. Only one
colour was available, listed as TWR blue. It suited the car's superb
lines perfectly, and presented an ideal background for sponsors'
decals and white race number roundels.

Under the skin, the general layout was similar to the V12
racers, with the rear uprights, dampers and springs designed to fit
inside the wheels, allowing more room for the underwing venturi
tunnels. The front springs and dampers were housed horizontally
above the driver's legs, much the same as on the XJR prototypes,

while the cockpit had many similarities including the position of the gear lever. The original R9R development car, driven by Tom Walkinshaw at the Silverstone launch, differed from later production XJR-15s in having a single NACA duct on the left side of the engine cover. It was also fitted with Goodyear tyres, but when the cars appeared in 1991, Bridgestone had become the main provider. Another smaller detail difference was mirrors fixed to the doors, whereas on the production cars they were stalk-mounted on the bodywork each side of the windscreen.

For the races, eight cars were entered by TWR on behalf of JaguarSport, piloted by drivers representing Europe, America, Australasia and Japan. The first names on the list were Derek Warwick and Vern Schuppan. Instead of £700,000, the purchase price of an XJR-15 was still very substantial at half a million pounds, but this also included full race preparation and back-up for the race series by a specialist team of trained mechanics and engineers from TWR, and body preparation from JaguarSport. Should damage occur during the races, the full cost of repairs would be borne by the individual owners.

Round one at Monaco saw only 16 XJR-15s entered, two of which were owner-driven. Most others were entrusted to a star-studded selection of drivers, many of them engaged in current SWC and IMSA GT Championship racing. Derek Warwick, David Brabham, Davy Jones, Armin Hahne and John Nielsen were past

or present Jaguar drivers, while Juan-Manuel Fangio II was one of TWR Jaguar's greatest adversaries in IMSA racing in his Toyota. Driving the XJR-15 proved very tricky at the best of times, and to be thrown in at the deep end on Monaco's narrow, twisty circuit with its unyielding metal and concrete barriers kept everyone on their toes, participants and spectators alike. As for entertainment, there was plenty.

Derek Warwick earned pole position, enabling him to run free of several spinners and barrier bashers behind. John Nielsen in car number 13 made it through lap one before hitting the barrier side on and then sliding on to a second more severe impact which caused considerable damage to his car. His race ended with him solemnly vowing never to race again in car number 13. The only other non-finisher was amateur owner-driver, record producer Matt Aitkin, who pleased the crowds with his gallant attempt to run with the big boys. He acquired his XJR-15 in exchange for a Group 44 XJR-5. To Matt, the opportunity to race at Monaco in front of massed Grand Prix spectators was irresistible, and even spinning out three laps from the end did not dampen his enthusiasm. Race winner was Derek Warwick, followed in by David Brabham, Davy Jones and Juan-Manuel Fangio II.

If Monaco's narrow street circuit had taken the blame for severely bent bodywork during round one, Silverstone, with its

Monaco's tight and tortuous circuit took its toll of the half million pound racers. (LAT Photographic)

Derek Warwick won the Monaco event but lasted no more than four laps in race 2 at Silverstone. (Sutton Photographics)

Juan Manuel Fangio II, Silverstone winner, on the podium with second-placed Bob Wollek and third-place man Ian Flux. (Sutton Photographics)

All five XJR-15LM variants lined up during a test session at Silverstone. Note the additional roof-mounted engine intakes. (Ron Russell)

prairie-like open spaces, should have been just the opposite. Once again 16 cars were entered, of which only five saw the race through without battle scars. Tom Walkinshaw in the XJ-S Pace Car led the field, intent on an orderly rolling start. Like sale day at Harrods the pack couldn't wait, charging by before he had had the chance to peel off. Away they went, almost five abreast at the first corner. Amazingly the first lap finished without major problems, but then the demolition derby commenced. John Nielsen and Davy Jones were the first to nudge each other, followed a little later by Derek Warwick turning in on Cor Euser. So it went on, with collisions, punctures and excursions on to the grass until the final lap saw just six of the half million pound cars

still running some semblance of a race. Monaco winner Derek Warwick lasted only four laps, while John Nielsen threw in the towel even earlier. Fangio won the race but missed seeing the flag and ran two extra laps before he realised it was all over.

The final round three at Spa-Francorchamps started badly for Tiff Needell in the Friday opening session when he crashed hard into the barriers near the top of Eau Rouge. Cor Euser took pole position and also completed fastest race lap of 2min 31.42sec. What made Spa different from the first two rounds was that no one was sure when the finish flag would drop. The only certainty was that there would be at least six laps. Cor Euser, Armin Hahne, Derek Warwick, Tiff Needell and Win Percy were amongst a small group starting well. The first three then moved ahead of the pack past the sixth lap hurdle and into lap eight. Euser then faltered, allowing Hahne to take the lead. Warwick also tried to take Euser but came to grief as his tail caught the wall. Now Percy was running third, but Hahne had moved too far in front for any possible change in this running order, particularly when the commentator announced that lap 11 would be the last.

Armin Hahne's first place came with a half share in the million-dollar prize money awarded to the car's owner. Euser finished in a good second place. The main consolation for other owners was that repair bills were not on the same level as in the two previous races. Whatever their feelings, they and JaguarSport had put on a unique show of racing which many will always regret not having witnessed. The XJR-15s, while not realising anywhere near their original price when they come up for sale, must surely one day become highly prized classics.

As a footnote to this particular episode, some time after the Intercontinental Challenge series five XJR-15s were fitted with 7-litre Group C engines and extensively rebuilt as fully fledged Le Mans contenders. In addition to being fitted with rooftop engine air intakes and much larger rear aerofoils, there were a number of subtle bodywork modifications. All five cars were bought by a Japanese investor and, as far as is known, have not been raced.

Cor Euser led the start
at Spa Francorchamps,
only to be beaten into
second place by Armin
Hahne. Win Percy
followed home in third.
(LAT Photographic)

Chapter 18

XJ220 Racing

Closing a chapter

XJ220 was an amazing paradox. It was one of the great cars of its time, a time when manufacturers vied to create what we have come to call 'supercars'. The late 1980s that gave birth to some of the most exciting sporting cars ever known will go down in history as one of the great eras of automobile history, and the XJ220 will perhaps be remembered as the most beautiful car of that period.

Commercially, however, the car did not live up to expectations. The conditions were against it, and despite the fact that the intention was to build 350 cars, that number was never reached. Nevertheless, among the owners who did collect their cars were some who wanted to prove the capabilities of the car on the track. It is inconceivable that Jaguar could produce a car with the potential of the XJ220 without some owners wanting to race it.

Tom Walkinshaw being interviewed on the stand after unveiling the XJ220C at the January 1993 Autosport Show in Birmingham. (LAT Photographic)

As a car-obsessed teenager I was compelled to journey by train into London to see a very special car displayed at the 1951 Earls Court Motor Show. This wondrous dream machine had taken the media by storm, and I had to see it in the flesh. The car in question was the fabulous Hooper coachbuilt 'gold' Daimler luxury limousine, built at the behest of that notoriously flamboyant couple, Sir Bernard and Lady Docker. Whatever they intended certainly worked, as alongside thousands of others I drooled and daydreamed - even today I get a lump in my throat reminiscing over this truly breathtaking masterpiece from one of the world's greatest coachbuilders. Many superb cars have come and gone since those heady days, but only one has come anywhere near to recreating that deep-felt longing. It resurfaced when the gorgeous Jaguar XJ220 concept car was unveiled to great acclaim at the 1988 Birmingham Motor Show. Like the Docker Daimler, it rocked the motoring world and, unlike the one-off gold car, Jaguar soon promised to put it into production for those lucky enough to afford the predicted £340,000 purchase price.

The production XJ220 differed from the ultra-heavy concept car in being slightly smaller, and in being fitted with a modified version of the 3.5-litre turbocharged V6 engine used in the Jaguar XJR-11 Group C Prototype racing cars. No sooner had the first customers taken delivery of their beautiful 200mph-plus supercats

than some were making enquiries about converting them for competition use. TWR wasted little time in coming up with a stunning race-prepared version, launched as the XJ220C at the Autosport Racing Car Show in January 1993. Designed expressly for racing in the newly revived GT categories, the new lightweight version made extensive use of composite materials. For instant access to the engine and other working parts the fully composite nose and tail sections were quickly detachable. The doors and sills were also changed to similar lightweight construction, and a single Kevlar seat replaced the plush leather seating of the road going cars. Substantial modifications were made to the transaxle, suspension, brakes and electronics, resulting in a highly sophisticated race machine capable of taking on and beating all comers in the GT class at Le Mans and elsewhere.

With the demise of SWC racing in 1992, a number of countries were setting up GT race series, each with their own set of regulations. What made this so exciting was the diversity of road-going sportscars eligible to compete in the different categories, including of course the mighty Jaguar XJ220.

In 1993, the Jaguar XJ220 raced on several fronts with some very encouraging early successes. The first round of the Italian GT Championship series was won by a Ferrari F40 only eight seconds ahead of a privately raced XJ220, one of two near-standard production cars in this Championship. The Ferraris were the most dominant competitors in this series but in round three at Vallelunga on 16 May 1993 Paolo Cutrera raced his XJ220 home to a convincing victory, 10 seconds ahead of a gaggle of the Maranello-built machines. The second Jaguar XJ220 driven by

Vincenzo Bianchi crashed out but the driver was unhurt. Throughout the Italian GT season the XJ220s gave a good account of themselves but were unable to prevent Marco Brand's Jolly Club F40 taking six wins in seven races.

On home ground the first Jaguar XJ220 to be seen in action by British race fans was a standard production car owned by Jaguar enthusiast and collector Allen Lloyd. Entered in the 100-mile Centurion Challenge race at Pembrey on 3 May 1993, driven by Rob Schirle, it started the race from pole position, holding out in second place until forced to retire on lap 27 due to a failed head gasket. With its beautiful Monza red paint finish, the crowds enjoyed a wonderful, albeit short-lived spectacle.

As a precursor to Le Mans one XJ220C was being made ready to race in the 1993 International GT Series organised by John Quenby of the RAC Motor Sports Association and Hugh Chamberlain Racing. In this there were three GT categories, firstly the FISA 1993 category which included the Ferrari F40 and XJ220. The second category conformed to the GT rules of the host countries, and the third was the ACO Le Mans GT group. Such was the confusion surrounding the diversity of rules that it is no wonder some race organisers experienced difficulties attracting entries.

Silverstone was the venue for round one of the International GT Race series. The XJ220C entered by TWR was in fact the beautiful yellow January launch car, which had been re-painted white for testing at Silverstone, then blue when in full racing trim for this particular event. The race had originally been intended to last three hours as a support event for the second round of the

This well-known pre-production XJ220, chassis 004, owned by Don Law, has won more races than any other. While on test at Fort Stockton in Texas during XJ220 development, Andy Wallace took an unofficial production car speed record of 217mph in this machine. (Linzi Smart)

Win Percy's comfortable win at Silverstone in 1993 was the first of his many outings racing XJ220s, including twice at Le Mans.(JDHT)

FISA International Formula 3000 Championship, but the small entry list forced the organisers into a major re-think, reducing it to two 20-lap heats and then finally settling for a single 10-lap race only. Win Percy was chosen to drive the Jaguar which, being the only starter in Class D, romped home to a stunning victory, lapping all but the second placed Porsche and the third placed Aston Martin

While the number of cars entered at Silverstone was disappointingly small, the Le Mans 24-hour race was a different kettle of fish. Just over half of the 50 cars due to take part were entered in the GT Class category 4. Of these, three were TWR-prepared works-entered Jaguar XJ220Cs. They raced as car 50, driven by David Brabham, John Nielsen and David Coulthard, 51 manned by Armin Hahne, Win Percy and David Leslie, and 52 with Paul Belmondo, Jay Cochran and Andreas Fuchs.

From the outset trouble was in store for the Jaguars. Way back in January it was rumoured that they would not be eligible for the GT Class. Confirmation that the XJ220Cs would take part came a few weeks later, and work began in earnest to prepare three cars for the event. At Silverstone, the rear wing was more or less standard, but for Le Mans the cars were fitted with a high-set adjustable aerofoil. Pre-race talk of running two cars in racing green and the third in Ecurie Ecosse blue with a trio of Scottish drivers came to nothing. All three cars were finished in the same attractive dark blue livery, as seen at Silverstone. Win Percy's

success at Silverstone no doubt helped Jaguar's parts distributor Unipart to confirm their willingness to become the team's main sponsor.

Many of the TWR proposed drivers were absent during the Le Mans test session held at the full 24-hour circuit on 19 May because of racing commitments elsewhere. However, David Brabham, Andreas Fuchs, Armin Hahne and Jay Cochran were there, and all four expressed confidence in the car's speed and reliability. David Brabham did most of the running and was clearly delighted with the car's performance. The main concern for some drivers in the faster Class 1 and 2 categories was the differential between their top speeds and those in the much slower GT Class. Observing lap times recorded this day it was inevitable that the top cars such as the Peugeot 905B and Toyota TS010 would lap the slowest cars once every three laps. The XJ220Cs' test lap times put them midway between the fastest and slowest groups.

The Jaguars passed scrutineering, but not before doubts had been expressed about their overall width being 4cm too great. This was soon sorted out but the real problem arose at the end of the first qualifying session. One of the race stewards, Alain Bertaut, noticed that the Jaguars were not fitted with catalytic converters and annulled their times. Tom Walkinshaw was far from happy, claiming the cars were within the rules. The team was eventually given the go-ahead to race pending an appeal. Final qualifying was much as predicted, with the three Peugeots and three Toyota 3.5-litre normally-aspirated cars taking the top six places. These six Group C cars were the only Class 1 entries. Their final appearance marked the end of a historic chapter in International Sportscar Racing.

There were no Ferrari F40s to challenge the mighty Jaguars, whose main threat in the GT Class was a single Porsche Turbo S LM, piloted by Hans-Joachim Stuck, Walter Röhrl and former Group 44 Jaguar driver Hurley Haywood. This car qualified in 21st place while the fastest Jaguar number 50 was 22nd, only 1.37 seconds slower. These were the fastest GT Class qualifiers, while the number 52 and 51 Jaguars were only a few seconds adrift in 24th and 25th places respectively.

The race got off to a reasonably good start in warm sunshine although slightly marred on the warm-up lap when Eddie Irvine, driving one of the Class 1 Toyotas, hit one of the GT cars, which was written off after spinning hard into the concrete wall. Irvine was able to continue but the other driver, Robin Smith, needed hospital treatment. Armin Hahne took first stint in the number 51 Jaguar but for only six short laps before returning to the pits with an overheated engine. The cause was found to be a blown head gasket. This was the first retirement of the race and Armin wryly joked: 'I thought this was a 24-minute race. I was waiting for the flag'.

As expected, the main race was dominated by the Peugeots, which were still given a good run for their money by the Toyotas. The number 3 Peugeot 905B of Geoff Brabham, Eric Helary and Christophe Bouchut shared most of the front running with the number 1 car of Yannick Dalmas, Thierry Boutsen and 1991 Jaguar SWC Champion Teo Fabi. These two cars finished one-two with third place taken by Peugeot number 2. Eddie Irvine's Toyota came fourth after leading very briefly in the first hour.

The progress of Jaguar number 52 through the first hours was reasonably uneventful, with all drivers taking double stints after the first two rounds of single stints. They had experienced a few spins without serious delays, and at one point led the GT class when the top running Jaguar number 50 was in the pits having a ruptured fuel tank replaced. At 4.40am on Sunday disaster struck when Andreas Fuchs lost control on the Mulsanne straight after collecting a puncture. He managed to get number 52 back on the track and return to the pits, but the car now fell victim to overheating and was retired.

All hopes now rested with Nielsen, Brabham and Coulthard in Jaguar number 50, which was running strongly again and leading the GT class. They might not have been so fortunate if the works Porsche of Stuck, Röhrl and Haywood had not been ousted by an accident on lap 79. This car led the class for the first hour and a quarter until a sticking throttle cost it five laps in pit repairs. When it got back into the race the Jaguars were well ahead, but with a lap time 1min 38sec faster the Porsche was soon making inroads into the leader's advantage. For five hours or so Jaguar's lead was whittled away until Walter Röhrl had the misfortune to plough into the back of a Debra Spyder at the first Mulsanne chicane. The

Launched at the NEC in 1993, XJ220C chassis 001 won at Silverstone before two appearances at Le Mans in 1993 and 1995. It is now owned by Allen Lloyd and is raced in the Group C Revival series. (Author)

*The victorious number
50 Jaguar XJ220C at
Le Mans in 1993.
(Jaguar)*

Porsche was seriously damaged. In spite of a ruptured oil tank Röhrl tried desperately to get the stricken car back to the pits but a seized engine forced abandonment.

Tension mounted in the Jaguar pits. With no other likely class rival to XJ220 number 50, everybody hoped the car would make it to the finish. Overheating had seen two Jaguars eliminated, and those involved with earlier Group C and IMSA programmes must have cast their minds back to the turbo era, when overheating had been a frequent problem. Now they were running the same basic engine for 24 hours, something not done before.

Of the three drivers in number 50, John Nielsen was one of the 1990 Jaguar winning team, so he knew the circuit very well. David Brabham had previous experience in Jaguar prototype racing, but David Coulthard was the new boy. One incident caused much amusement in the pits. A car had been dropped on David Brabham's foot during Wednesday's pre-race practice session. While he was resting in the pits, feet up, a bag of frozen peas was placed on the injured foot, duly marked 'David's foot - do not eat'.

Jaguar number 50 finished 15th overall and first in the GT class. To give some idea of the speed differences between Class 1 and the GTs in Class 4, the winning Peugeot completed 375 laps whereas the Jaguar's total was 306 laps. For Sir Jack Brabham, present in the pits to watch his two sons, Geoff winning in the Peugeot and David taking the class win in the XJ220C must have provided one of the proudest moments of all. However, the win was later disallowed, yet nothing could alter the fact that they had won and had produced a great result.

While events were unfolding at Le Mans, something rather different was taking place on the other side of the Atlantic. Tom Walkinshaw had entered his three XJ220C cars in the classic French 24-hour race in the IMSA GT category. An XJ220C was raced in the 1993 Camel GT Championship, but not until 11 July at Road America. Reported to have been the same chassis that Win Percy, Armin Hahne and David Leslie nearly drove at Le Mans (car number 51, which ran for six laps only), it was piloted here by Davy Jones and Jay Cochran. Entered by Snap-On Tools and Jaguar Inc., it put up an excellent performance, finishing 10th overall and first in the International GT class. As it was the only competitor in the class this was not that hard, but the 33 cars they beat to the flag included a formidable array of GTP, GTS, GTU and GTO competitors. However, if further IMSA outings had ever been intended for the XJ220C they seem to have come to nothing.

TWR's means of attracting interested buyers to take on the limited production XJR-15s by staging the Million Dollar International Challenge Series in 1991 repeated itself again in 1993 with the XJ220s. This time the format was rather different, involving an extraordinary list of 50 top drivers of Championship winning status, all over the age of 50. Divided into groups of 10, they were down to compete in five qualifying races, with the top two from each group competing in a final sixth race in which the winner's purse would be $100,000.

The series was titled the Fast Masters Championship, and while many of the drivers were better known in the USA than elsewhere, they boasted between them an incredible list of wins

Two years after the XJ220C class win at Le Mans, later disallowed, two of the cars returned to make a final appearance at the circuit in 1995. Entered as PC Automotive team cars, both failed to finish, but number 57, driven by James Weaver, Tiff Needell and Richard Piper moved up to fourth place overall before engine problems ended its endeavours on lap 135. (Richard Piper)

at Le Mans, Indianapolis, Daytona, Sebring and in all categories of racing including Sportscar, Indy Car, Nascar and IROC, etc. Brian Redman, Bob Wollek, Derek Bell, Henri Pescarolo, Guy Edwards, Bobby Unser and film star team-owner Paul Newman were listed, as well as many more legends of international motor racing.

Ten XJ220s were sent over from England and were managed by TWR Inc. engineers for the duration of the series. All races were staged at the Indianapolis Raceway Park on Saturday evenings. The original intention was to run one 10-lap oval heat, a second 10-lap heat on a modified road course, and finally 12 laps split into six on each of the two first circuits. Indianapolis Raceway Park circuit was not the easiest track for drivers handling these rather large and unfamiliar cars for the first time, so a few mishaps were to be expected. These did occur: round one saw a pair of XJ220s written off and others damaged, making it necessary to gradually pare down successive rounds, both in lap numbers and drivers taking part.

The winners of round one, Ed McCullough and Bob Akin, were joined for the final race by successive round winners Brian Redman, David Hobbs, Eddie Hill, Parnelli Jones, George Follmer, David Pearson, Bobby Unser and Johnny Rutherford. Whatever was originally intended for the final bash, it was reduced to a modest 10 laps around the 0.625-mile circuit. Even this was not without drama and accidents. Three times Indianapolis 500 winner Bobby Unser took the flag and the $100,000 winner's purse ahead of second place David Pearson. While the series may not have gone strictly to plan it attracted considerable media

interest including live television coverage on ESPN's prime time 'Saturday Night Thunder' programmes. American race fans were treated to a unique experience, seeing some of the sport's greatest heroes racing the world's fastest production cars.

The rather battered XJ220s were all shipped back to England, where work commenced on rebuilding some of them as XJ220S cars. This particular version had Le Mans-style removable nose and tail panels but retained the air conditioning system of the road-going cars and was fitted with more comfortable leather-covered competition seats.

Another XJ220 familiar to Intermark and Group C racegoers, pre-production chassis 009 first raced in the 1993 Italian GT series in the Group N class. Win Percy drove it to victory at Brands Hatch and Croft in 1999. (Ian Jones)

Chapter 19

Jaguars in Historic Group C Racing

The spirit lives on

Modern day Group C historic racing began not as a pre-planned series but as the direct result of a proposed one-off commemorative race organised to mark the 40th anniversary of Aston Martin's only Le Mans win in 1959. The Aston Martin Owners' Club Competition Chairman, Roger Bailey, had a vision of historic Aston Martin prototypes taking to the track once again, and this turned to reality at Donington Park in June 1999 as part of a special two-day Aston Martin Anniversary Meeting.

Don Law, the Stoke-on-Trent based Jaguar restoration specialist, took on the role of Group C race co-ordinator on behalf of the AMOC, using his considerable knowledge of Jaguar prototype racing and the mechanics of the cars involved. Jaguar fans fortunate enough to be present at the event were treated to a spectacle completely unimaginable only a year or two earlier. Could anyone have envisaged a turbocharged XJR-11 competing against its normally-aspirated would-be successor, the one and only XJR-17, or two of the JaguarSport limited production XJR-15s alongside a specially prepared XJ220 bidding to outrace

them. This extraordinary Jaguar combination lined up on the grid amongst a diverse collection of contemporary Group C rivals including two Porsche 956s, a lone Tiga and a distinctive Swiftair Ecosse C2. Aston Martin was represented by one of their EMKA racers while the rest of the grid comprised two Ferraris and several other Porsche variants. *which ?*

Two Jaguar XJR-11s were present, both owned by Paul Spires of AM Racing, but gearbox problems on race day kept one in the pit garage, leaving the other car to be driven to an easy victory by Paul. He set the trend for Jaguar to be at the forefront of Group C revival racing which has continued ever since.

2000 racing

Following the success of the Donington event, moves were made to establish a regular series devoted to these evocative racing machines. Roger Bailey, together with his equally enthusiastic son Brian, began organising a series of races for 2000 which would see the cars performing at the cream of British and European race

Paul Spires drove this XJR-11 to a runaway victory at the AMOC Group C Invitation race at Donington on 6 June 1999, the first of many wins by TWR Jaguar Prototypes in what soon became a regular Group C Revival Racing series. (Author)

circuits. The first race would be at Spa-Francorchamps in May 2000, followed by appearances at Donington, Silverstone and Brands Hatch, then back across the channel to visit the historic AvD Oldtimer meeting at Nürburgring in Germany. Everyone agreed that this was a most exciting year. The 2000 series was sponsored by JD Classics, another specialist Jaguar restoration company, based near Chelmsford in Essex. Derek Hood, the firm's owner, bought XJR-11 (590) in 2000, and has raced it under the JD Classics name ever since. He was also the owner of the 1985 XJR-6 (285) and two XJR-12s (990 and 193) before selling them on to the present lucky owners, who were equally eager to join in the fun.

In four out of the five first 2000 season races, one car and driver combination remained dominant. Ex-TWR Jaguar works driver Win Percy, in XJR-11 chassis 490, completed fastest race lap at Spa after qualifying on pole, only to be forced into retirement on lap eight after collecting a right rear puncture. From then on, Percy took runaway wins in the four remaining races, easily lapping the field on most occasions and completing fastest race laps in the process. As the season progressed, more and more important prototypes and invitation classics were brought out of retirement to join what had rapidly become established as a crowd-pleasing race series.

The final 2000 season race at the AvD Nürburgring Oldtimer meeting was given demonstration status by the organisers and was particularly interesting for Jaguar fans as the debut race for Neil Hadfield's V12-engined 1991 Silk Cut liveried Le Mans XJR-

12, chassis 990. This car had been present at Brands Hatch a few weeks earlier but had not raced. Another XJR prototype at Brands was Don Miles' ex-Group 44 XJR-5 in TWR green and white livery, brought along as a show car and not raced. Both raced at Nürburgring though, where the XJR-12 put on a very good show, leading for several laps and finishing in third place. The XJR-5 did not stay the course.

2001 racing

In February and March 2001 Don Law, accompanied by Win Percy, made a brave attempt to show the flag in America, shipping over an XJR-11 to compete in the Historic Sportscar Racers support races at the Daytona 24-hour and at the Sebring 12-hour classic. Racing former GTP and Group C cars has been

Another superb XJR racer: The Don Law-prepared turbocharged XJR-10 (389) in its original Castrol colours. (Ian Jones)

One year later, David Coplowe's beautifully presented 1985 XJR-6 (285) entered the series in the JD Classics Group C Invitation Race, also at Donington. Shortly afterwards it became one of the main Jaguar attractions at the 2000 Goodwood Festival of Speed. Here it waits to run up the hill alongside Bob Tullius in his group 44 XJR-5, brought over specially for the event. (Author)

popular on the other side of the Atlantic for a number of years, and the widely advertised appearance of the Silk Cut Jaguar was eagerly awaited, particularly at Sebring where local radio stations urged listeners to go along and see the famous 'Jag-wah' racing round the circuit. Regrettably on both occasions it was not to be. No one looked forward to it more than Win Percy who, in spite of many Touring Car Championship wins in Europe and Australia, had never raced on the American continent. A broken driveshaft, with no chance of finding a replacement, ended the team's endeavours at Daytona, particularly frustrating after Percy had made the fastest time in practice. At Sebring, serious water loss and overheating at the start of practice quickly ended any hope of making a run. After extraordinary levels of success during the previous season's Group C racing, these failures left all team members understandably dejected.

Win Percy was back on form during the first three 2001 Group C races, taking a hat trick of wins, this time in the superb Don Law-prepared Bud Light XJR-16 (191). As before, he made fastest lap times as well as capturing pole each time out. While the Group C turnout for the first meeting at Donington Park was disappointingly small, Jaguar fans must have marvelled at seeing the only three TWR prototypes entered, all finished in Bud Light Livery. The XJR-16 remained as raced in IMSA, as did the 1993 XJR-12D, which managed a few laps in this race prior to experiencing engine failure. The third XJR-chassis, looking most attractive in the Bud colours, was the XJR-17, which had never raced for Jaguar in this form.

The next event at Spa-Francorchamps should have seen the debut of another IMSA chassis, Don Law's Castrol-liveried XJR-10 (389). Technical problems kept it stationary in the pit garage

while Justin Law transferred to the team's white XJ220, coming home in fifth place.

The June Intermarque Classic Meeting at Donington Park involved 54 laps of racing for Group C and invitation class cars, split into Saturday and Sunday heats of 27 laps apiece. Out of 28 entries, no less than eighteen were Group C and IMSA racers, a clear indication of just how attractive the series had become.

Win Percy in the XJR-16 took the flag on Saturday a full lap ahead of Martin Koenig's Porsche 956. He did not enjoy such a comfortable margin in race two, flying over the line only milliseconds ahead of Nick Adams' Spice SE88C. To get some idea of the serious nature of this form of racing, Percy won on Sunday at an average speed of 103.77mph, with a fastest lap of 106.47mph. Even then he did not make fastest race lap, this going to Phillipp Brunn's Porsche 956 at 106.74mph. The previous day Win's best lap was at 107.84mph.

Racing for the first time on British soil, Don Miles's Group 44 XJR-5 did well on Saturday, finishing eighth, but gave fans a few anxious moments following set-up problems on Sunday. Paul Chudecki gained mastery of it though, finishing ninth on aggregate.

For the second visit to the famous AvD Oldtimer Grand Prix at Nürburgring, the Group C race was now given full race status. The quality of cars entered brought back memories of grids in the heyday of prototype sportscar racing. Porsche entries had been hard on the heels of the consistently victorious Jaguars for so long, particularly Siggi Brunn and son Phillipp in their 956. They won the first event, while the JD Classics XJR-11 raced to victory in the second event. On aggregate, the Porsche had the edge and claimed the trophy. Don Miles's XJR-5 driven by Paul

All three XJR turbo variants together as never seen before: Bud Light XJR-16 (191), unbranded Silk Cut XJR-11 (590) and Castrol XJR-10 (389). (Ian Jones)

Chudecki finished 10th in the first race and took eighth in the second.

Few people who attended the 2001 Silverstone Historic Festival will forget some memorable racing on the Saturday and on the August Bank Holiday Monday. The Saturday British Empire Trophy race was a full two-hour/two-driver affair in which five different Jaguar XJR prototypes, together with one of the Le Mans XJ220Cs, helped to make up a truly historic grid. To gain some idea of the high esteem this class of racing now enjoys, the cars were led to the grid by a modern successor, the fabulous Le Mans Bentley EXP Speed 8. Graham Hathaway and Gary Pearson took a hard-earned victory in the JD Classics XJR-11 after some exciting early lap duels with the Win Percy/Justin Law XJR-10. The Castrol car and the XJR-16 never made it to the finish, while the Grant/Rini Bud Light XJR-12D came home third.

A splendid one-two-three finish in the Bank Holiday Monday Bob Wollek Trophy race for the three turbocharged XJR prototypes crowned what had been a splendid weekend for the Jaguar marque. Nathan Kinch in the XJR-16 took the win, followed by Justin Law's XJR-10 and Graham Hathaway's XJR-11. The three remaining XJR-12, XJR-5 and XJR-6 Jaguars all finished, making this the best race so far. The late great Bob Wollek never raced for Jaguar although he tested XJR-12LM chassis 991 at Paul Ricard in May 1991. He was a great admirer of the TWR teams against which he competed in the Sportscar World Championships. There is no doubt he would have been thrilled to witness such a race in his honour.

For the 2002 season Roger Bailey continued the Group C Revival series with five races planned. New venues in France and Italy were added and races were organised on circuits as diverse

as Spa, Donington Park, Magny Cours, the Nürburgring and Monza - all of them historic battlegrounds for Jaguar Group C cars. Another complementary series of Group C races was scheduled by Roger Bennington of Heritage Racing. His intention was to hold Group C races as support events at some of the Green Flag saloon car Championship events. Four races were planned, all at UK venues - Brands Hatch, Silverstone, Snetterton and Donington Park. With a total of nine races in a closely-packed calendar from the end of April through to October, owners and drivers of Group C cars would have plenty of opportunities to exercises their charges, and fans across Europe were promised plenty of interest. With such high levels of interest, there is every hope that Group C sportscar racing will continue for many years to come, and hopefully the historic Jaguars will continue to shine in these events.

A fabulous line-up of Jaguar prototypes at the August 2001 Silverstone British Empire Trophy and Bob Wollek Trophy race meeting. From left to right, XJR-16 (191), XJR-12D (193), XJR-11 (590), XJR-10 (389), XJR-6 (285) and one non-TWR chassis, Don Miles' XJR-5 from the Group 44 stable. (Linzi Smart)

Not a TWR Jaguar prototype in the strictest sense but still based on the 1988 Le Mans winning XJR-9, Brian Wingfield's XJR-15, fitted with XJR-8 or IMSA-style wings, was a welcome addition to the field in 2000, racing in the Invitation Class. (Ian Jones)

Appendix

Individual Chassis Race Histories

Type: XJR-6   Chassis number 185

Build date: May-June 1985
First run: 2 July 1985, Snetterton, UK,
               shakedown by Martin Brundle
History: First Jaguar Group C car

Race history:

Date	Circuit	Race no.	Drivers	Grid pos.	Result
03.08.85	Mosport, Canada	51	Martin Brundle, Mike Thackwell	3	DNF, wheel bearing
01.09.85	Spa-Francorchamps, Belgium	51	Martin Brundle, Mike Thackwell	8	5
22.09.85	Brands Hatch, UK	51	Alan Jones, Jean-Louis Schlesser	5	DNF, engine
06.10.85	Fuji, Japan	51	John Nielsen, Mike Thackwell	19	Withdrawn, heavy rain
09.12.85	Shah Alam, Malaysia	51	Jan Lammers, John Nielsen, Mike Thackwell	4	2

Tested at Estoril, Portugal 3-6 February 1986 but not raced again. Converted to show car? Later restored to running order by TWR, retained in museum collection.

Type: XJR-6   Chassis number 285

Build date   May-June 1985
First run   1 August 1985, Mosport, Canada,
               shakedown by Hans Heyer and Jean-Louis Schlesser
History   Second Jaguar Group C car

Race history

Date	Circuit	Race no.	Drivers	Grid pos.	Result
03.08.85	Mosport, Canada	52	Martin Brundle, Jean-Louis Schlesser, Mike Thackwell	5	3
01.09.85	Spa-Francorchamps, Belgium	52	Hans Heyer, Jean-Louis Schlesser	11	DNF, handling
22.09.85	Brands Hatch, UK	52	Hans Heyer, Jan Lammers	6	DNF, engine
06.10.85	Fuji, Japan	52	Hans Heyer, Steve Soper	20	Withdrawn, heavy rain
09.12.85	Shah Alam, Malaysia	52	Brancatelli, Jan Lammers	5	DNF, puncture

Tested at Estoril, Portugal, 3-6 February 1986, but not raced again. Now privately owned and racing in Group C Revival series

Type: XJR-6   Chassis number 385

Build date   January 1986
First run   3 March 1986, Snetterton, UK,
               shakedown by Derek Warwick
History   1985 monocoque built to 1986 specifications

Race history

Date	Circuit	Race no.	Drivers	Grid pos.	Result
20.04.86	Monza, Italy	53	All - T car only		
05.05.86	Silverstone, UK	51T	All - T car only		
31.05.-01.06.86	Le Mans, France (as XJR-6 LM)	53	Gianfranco Brancatelli, Armin Hahne, Win Percy	14	DNF, driveshaft

Le Mans 1986 was the only race for chassis 385. Now privately owned and still in full 1986 Le Mans trim.

Type: XJR-6   Chassis number 186

Build date   February 1986
First run   17 March 1986, Silverstone, UK,
               shakedown by Eddie Cheever

Race history

Date	Circuit	Race no.	Drivers	Grid pos.	Result
20.04.86	Monza, Italy	52	Brancatelli, Jean-Louis Schlesser	9	DNF, fuel
05.05.86	Silverstone, UK	52	Brancatelli, Jean-Louis Schlesser	5	7
31.05.-01.06.86	Le Mans, France (as XJR-6 LM)	52	Hurley Haywood, Hans Heyer, Brian Redman	7	DNF, fuel pump
29.06.86	Norisring, Germany	52	Derek Warwick	6	3
20.07.86	Brands Hatch, UK	52	Jean-Louis Schlesser, Derek Warwick		Car did not race, switched to T car no. 53 (386)
03.08.86	Jerez, Spain	53	Brancatelli, Jean-Louis Schlesser	2	DNF, driveshaft
24.08.86	Nürburgring, Germany	53	Brancatelli, Jan Lammers, Derek Warwick	9	DNF, engine
14.09.86	Spa-Francorchamps, Belgium	51T	Eddie Cheever, Jan Lammers, Jean-Louis Schlesser, Derek Warwick		T car only
21.09.86	Norisring, Germany (non-championship race)	51	Eddie Cheever	3	1

Upgraded October 1986 to Le Mans specification, then tested at various circuits throughout the winter months as 1987 XJR-8 LM. Race history continued:

Date	Circuit	Race no.	Drivers	Grid pos.	Result
10.05.87	Silverstone, UK	6	Martin Brundle, John Nielsen	10	DNF, valve spring
13.06-14.06.87	Le Mans, France	6	Martin Brundle, Armin Hahne, John Nielsen	4	DNF, engine

Winter 1987-88, upgraded to XJR-9LM specification. Tested at Paul Ricard, France, 16-19 February 1988. Race history continued:

Date	Circuit	Race no.	Drivers	Grid pos.	Result
11.06-12.06.88	Le Mans, France	22	Kevin Cogan, Derek Daly, Larry Perkins	11	4

After 1988 Le Mans, chassis 186 was fully restored as it had raced in XJR-9 specification, and was then shipped to Jaguar Nederland, remaining in their ownership ever since.

Type: XJR-6   Chassis number 286

Build date   March 1986
First run   10 April 1986, Donington Park UK,
                   shakedown by Eddie Cheever
Race history

Date	Circuit	Race no.	Drivers	Grid pos.	Result
20.04.86	Monza, Italy	51	Eddie Cheever, Derek Warwick	6	DNF, driveshaft flange
05.05.86	Silverstone, UK	51	Eddie Cheever, Derek Warwick	3	1
31.05.-01.06.86	Le Mans, France (as XJR-6 LM)	51	Eddie Cheever, Jean-Louis Schlesser, Derek Warwick	5	DNF, suspension
29.06.86	Norisring, Germany	51	Eddie Cheever	4	2
20.07.86	Brands Hatch, UK	51	Brancatelli, Eddie Cheever	2	6
03.08.86	Jerez, Spain	51	Martin Brundle, Eddie Cheever	3	DNF, driveshaft
24.08.86	Nürburgring, Germany	51	Eddie Cheever, Hans Heyer, Jean-Louis Schlesser	3	DNF, driveshaft
14.09.86	Spa-Francorchamps, Belgium	51	Eddie Cheever, Jean-Louis Schlesser	4	5
05.10.86	Fuji, Japan	51	Eddie Cheever, Derek Warwick	13	3

Winter 1987-88, converted to XJR-8 LM specification, tested at Donington Park April 1987. Race history continued:

Date	Circuit	Race no.	Drivers	Grid pos.	Result
13.06-14.06.87	Le Mans, France	5	Jan Lammers, Win Percy, John Watson	5	DNF, accident

Severely damaged at Le Mans, subsequently rebuilt as 1986 sprint car although not fitted with the original gullwing doors. Now in private ownership in Japan.

Type: XJR-6   Chassis number 386

First run   23 June 1986, Silverstone, UK
                   shakedown by Win Percy
Race history:

Date	Circuit	Race no.	Drivers	Grid pos.	Result
29.06.86	Norisring, Germany	53	Jean-Louis Schlesser	8	17
20.07.86	Brands Hatch, UK	53	Jean-Louis Schlesser, Derek Warwick	3	4
03.08.86	Jerez, Spain	52	Jan Lammers, Derek Warwick	4	3
24.08.86	Nürburgring, Germany	52	Jan Lammers, Derek Warwick; Warwick crashed in qualifying		Did not race
14.09.86	Spa-Francorchamps, Belgium	52	Jan Lammers, Derek Warwick	5	2
05.10.86	Fuji, Japan	52	Brancatelli, Jan Lammers, Jean-Louis Schlesser	17	17
22.03.87	Jarama, Spain	4T	Used as T car by all the drivers		
29.03.87	Jerez, Spain	4T	Used as T car by all the drivers		
12.04.87	Monza, Italy	4T	Used as T car by all the drivers		
10.05.87	Silverstone, UK	4T	Used as T car by all the drivers		

Chassis 386 converted to show car, then upgraded to XJR-12 LM for 1991 Le Mans race, chassis re-numbered 991. For details, see chassis 991.

Note in file says it became IMSA test car after Silverstone. Maybe re-numbered (188)

Type: XJR-8   Chassis number 187

Build date   January 1987
First run   6 February 1987, Donington Park, UK,
                   shakedown by John Watson
History   First of two 1987 sprint cars
Race history

Date	Circuit	Race no.	Drivers	Grid pos.	Result
22.03.87	Jarama, Spain	5	Jan Lammers, John Watson	2	1
29.03.87	Jerez, Spain	5	Jan Lammers, John Watson	2	DNF, driveshaft
12.04.87	Monza, Italy	5	Jan Lammers, John Watson	4	1
10.05.87	Silverstone, UK	5	Jan Lammers, John Watson	5	2
28.06.87	Norisring, Germany	5	Jan Lammers, John Watson	7	DNF, transmission
26.07.87	Brands Hatch, UK	5	Jan Lammers, John Watson	1	3
30.08.87	Nürburgring, Germany	5	Jan Lammers, John Watson	4	DNF, engine
13.09.87	Spa-Francorchamps, Belgium	5	Jan Lammers, John Watson	3	2
27.09.87	Fuji, Japan	5	Jan Lammers, John Watson	5	1

For the 1988 season upgraded to XJR-9 specification. Race history continued:

Date	Circuit	Race no.	Drivers	Grid pos.	Result
06.03.88	Jerez, Spain	3	John Nielsen, Andy Wallace, John Watson	4	2
13.03.88	Jarama, Spain	3	John Nielsen, John Watson	4	3
10.04.88	Monza, Italy	1T	T car used in practice		
08.05.88	Silverstone, UK	2	Johnny Dumfries, Jan Lammers; T car replacing 488	6	DNF, fuel
10.07.88	Brno, CZ		T car only		
24.07.88	Brands Hatch, UK (with 4 valve engine)	3	Davy Jones, John Watson	8	DNF, engine timing

Chassis 187 in private ownership in UK.

Type: XJR-8   Chassis number 287

Build date   February 1987
First run   2 March 1987, Silverstone, UK
History   Regular sprint car for Eddie Cheever and
                   1987 World Champion Raul Boesel
Race history

Date	Circuit	Race no.	Drivers	Grid pos.	Result
22.03.87	Jarama, Spain	4	Raul Boesel, Eddie Cheever	1	3
29.03.87	Jerez, Spain	4	Raul Boesel, Eddie Cheever	4	1
12.04.87	Monza, Italy	4	Raul Boesel, John Nielsen	5	DNF, spin
10.05.87	Silverstone, UK	4	Raul Boesel, Eddie Cheever	4	1
28.06.87	Norisring, Germany	4	Raul Boesel, Eddie Cheever	4	4
26.07.87	Brands Hatch, UK	4	Raul Boesel, John Nielsen	2	1
30.08.87	Nürburgring, Germany	4	Raul Boesel, Eddie Cheever	2	1

Date	Circuit	Race no.	Drivers	Grid pos.	Result
13.09.87	Spa-Francorchamps, Belgium	4	Eddie Cheever, John Nielsen	4	4
27.09.87	Fuji, Japan	4	Raul Boesel, Johnny Dumfries	10	2

1988 and 1989, raced as XJR-9, race history continued:

Date	Circuit	Race no.	Drivers	Grid pos.	Result
11.06.-12.06.88	Le Mans, France (as XJR-9 LM)	3	Raul Boesel, Henri Pescarolo, John Watson	12	DNF, transmission
25.08.88	Donington Park, UK	Used for radial tyre testing			
04.09.88	Nürburgring, Germany	1T	T car only		
18.09.88	Spa-Francorchamps, Belgium	1T	T car only		
10.06.-11.06.89	Le Mans, France (as XJR-9 LM)	4	Alain Ferte, Michel Ferte, Eliseo Salazar	6	8
23.07.89	Brands Hatch, UK	1T	T car only		
29.10.89	Mexico City	2	Alain Ferte, Andy Wallace	10	5

Chassis 287 retained in TWR museum

Type: XJR-8   Chassis number 387

First run   15 May 1987, Le Mans, France, shakedown, John Watson

Race history

Date	Circuit	Race no.	Drivers	Grid pos.	Result
13.06.-14.06.87	Le Mans, France (as XJR-8 LM)	4	Raul Boesel, Eddie Cheever, Jan Lammers	3	5
05.07.87	Hockenheim, Germany (non championship race)	4	Raul Boesel	7	3
26.07.87	Brands Hatch, UK	4T	T car only		
30.08.87	Nürburgring	4T	T car only		
13.09.87	Spa-Francorchamps, Belgium	6	Raul Boesel, Martin Brundle, Johnny Dumfries	6	1

There is a document dated 21/12/87 suggesting this became chassis (388)

Type: XJR-9   Chassis number 188

Build date   July-August 1987
First run   20 August 1987, Silverstone, UK, shakedown, Jan Lammers
History   First IMSA specification XJR-9
Race history

Date	Circuit	Race no.	Drivers	Grid pos.	Result
30.01.-31.01.88	Daytona, Florida (as XJR-9 D)	66	Eddie Cheever, Johnny Dumfries, John Watson	4	3
28.02.88	Miami, Florida	66	Raul Boesel, Eddie Cheever	14	DNF, engine
19.03.88	Sebring, Florida	60T	Raul Boesel, Davy Jones	T car only	
10.04.88	Road Atlanta, Georgia	61T	Andy Wallace, John Watson	T car only	
24.04.88	West Palm Beach, Florida	61T	Davy Jones	T car only	

Shipped to UK for preparation to run in Le Mans 24-hour race in Silk Cut livery:

Date	Circuit	Race no.	Drivers	Grid pos.	Result
11.06.-12.06.88	Le Mans, France (as XJR-9 LM)	21	Price Cobb, Davy Jones, Danny Sullivan	9	16

Returned to the USA to continue racing in the IMSA series:

Date	Circuit	Race no.	Drivers	Grid pos.	Result
17.07.88	Road America, Wisconsin	66	Davy Jones, John Nielsen	T car only	
31.07.88	Portland, Oregon	66	Martin Brundle	T car only	
14.08.88	Sears Point, California	66	Jan Lammers	T car only	
04.09.88	San Antonio, Texas	60	Davy Jones, John Watson	7	2
02.10.88	Columbus, Ohio	60	Davy Jones, Jan Lammers, John Nielsen	5	10
23.10.88	Del Mar, California	61	Davy Jones, Jan Lammers	1	1
04.02.-05.02.89	Daytona, Florida (as XJR-9 D)	66	Derek Daly, Martin Donnelly, Patrick Tambay	8	Classified 67; DNF, accident
05.03.89	Miami, Florida	66	Davy Jones	T car only	
18.03.89	Sebring, Florida	66		T car only	
02.04.89	Road Atlanta, Georgia	66	Davy Jones; badly damaged in accident in week before race - sent back to UK for repairs		

Chassis 188 reported to have been restored to running order then sold by TWR

Type: XJR-9   Chassis number 288

Build date   September 1987
First run   15 October 1987, Donington Park, UK, shakedown, John Watson
Race history

Date	Circuit	Race no.	Drivers	Grid pos.	Result
30.01.-31.01.88	Daytona, Florida (as XJR-9 D)	60	Raul Boesel, Martin Brundle, Jan Lammers, John Nielsen	6	1
28.02.88	Miami, Florida	60	Martin Brundle, John Nielsen	3	2
19.03.88	Sebring, Florida (as XJR-9 D)	60	Raul Boesel, Martin Brundle, John Nielsen	3	Classified 60; DNF, engine
10.04.88	Road Atlanta, Georgia	60	John Nielsen, John Watson	1	2
24.04.88	West Palm Beach, Florida	60	Martin Brundle, John Nielsen	4	Class. 20; DNF, transmission
30.05.88	Lime Rock, Connecticut	60	Martin Brundle, John Nielsen	1	2
05.06.88	Mid Ohio, Ohio	60	Martin Brundle, John Nielsen	6	2
03.07.88	Watkins Glen, New York	60	Martin Brundle, John Nielsen	5	DNF, engine
17.07.88	Road America, Wisconsin	60	Martin Brundle, John Nielsen	2	4
31.07.88	Portland, Oregon	60	Martin Brundle, John Nielsen	6	3
14.08.88	Sears Point, California	60	Martin Brundle, John Nielsen	2	2
04.09.88	San Antonio, Texas	66	John Nielsen, Andy Wallace	3	Classified 10; DNF, brakes
02.10.88	Columbus, Ohio	66	Martin Brundle, John Nielsen	4	Classified 31; DNF, accident
23.10.88	Del Mar, California	60	John Nielsen; crashed during qualifying, badly damaged, tub sent to UK for repairs		

Date	Circuit	Race no.	Drivers	Grid pos.	Result
04.02.-05.02.89	Daytona, Florida (as XJR-9 D)	60	Raul Boesel, Davy Jones, Jan Lammers	2	Classified 43; DNF, engine
05.03.89	Miami, Florida	60	Davy Jones, Jan Lammers	3	DNF, accident
18.03.89	Sebring, Florida (as XJR-9 D)	60	Davy Jones, Jan Lammers	4	14
02.04.89	Road Atlanta, Georgia	60	Davy Jones, Jan Lammers	4	Classified 16; DNF, engine
23.04.89	West Palm Beach, Florida	60	Davy Jones, Jan Lammers	4	DNF, transmission

Shipped to UK for preparation to run in Le Mans 24-hour race in Silk Cut livery:

Date	Circuit	Race no.	Drivers	Grid pos.	Result
10.06.-11.06.89	Le Mans, France (as XJR-9 LM)	3	Derek Daly, Davy Jones, Jeff Kline	4	DNF, engine

Returned to the USA to continue racing in the IMSA series:

Date	Circuit	Race no.	Drivers	Grid pos.	Result
30.08.89	Heartland Park, Topeka, Kansas	66T	Michel Ferte, Davy Jones	T car only	
03.09.89	San Antonio, Texas	66T	Michel Ferte, Davy Jones	Practice session only	
10.09.89	Sears Point, California	60	Davy Jones, John Nielsen	5	3
01.10.89	Tampa, Florida	60	Price Cobb	6	1

Upgraded to XJR-12D specification for endurance racing:

Date	Circuit	Race no.	Drivers	Grid pos.	Result
03.02.-04.02.90	Daytona, Florida	60	Martin Brundle, Price Cobb, John Nielsen	9	2
17.03.90	Sebring, Florida	60	Price Cobb, John Nielsen	4	DNF, engine

Sent back to UK, upgraded to XJR-12LM specification for 1990 Le Mans 24 Hours, chassis re-numbered 1090. For details, see chassis 1090.

Type: XJR-9   Chassis number 388

Race history

Date	Circuit	Race no.	Drivers	Grid pos.	Result
30.01.-31.01.88	Daytona, Florida (as XJR-9 D)	61	Davy Jones, Jan Lammers, Danny Sullivan	2	Classified 26; DNF, engine
28.02.88	Miami, Florida	61	Davy Jones, Jan Lammers	7	6
19.03.88	Sebring, Florida (as XJR-9 D)	61	Davy Jones, Jan Lammers, John Nielsen, Danny Sullivan	5	7
10.04.88	Road Atlanta, Georgia	61	Davy Jones, Andy Wallace	3	4
24.04.88	West Palm Beach, Florida	61	Davy Jones, Jan Lammers	2	2
30.05.88	Lime Rock, Connecticut	61	Davy Jones, Jan Lammers	6	3
05.06.88	Mid Ohio, Ohio	61	Davy Jones, Jan Lammers	4	3
03.07.88	Watkins Glen, New York	61	Davy Jones, Jan Lammers	6	Classified 18; DNF, accident
17.07.88	Road America, Wisconsin	61	Davy Jones, Jan Lammers	4	5
31.07.88	Portland, Oregon	61	Davy Jones, Jan Lammers	5	4
14.08.88	Sears Point, California	61	Davy Jones, Jan Lammers	3	3
04.09.88	San Antonio, Texas	61	Davy Jones, John Watson; Jones crashed in qualifying, car severely damaged		Did not race

Car returned to UK for repairs. Not raced again in 1988. Race history continued:

Date	Circuit	Race no.	Drivers	Grid pos.	Result
04.02.-05.02 89	Daytona, Florida (as XJR-9 D)	61	Price Cobb, Jan Lammers, John Nielsen, Andy Wallace	7	2
05.03.89	Miami, Florida	61	Price Cobb, John Nielsen	5	2
18.03.89	Sebring, Florida (as XJR-9 D)	61	Price Cobb, John Nielsen	3	2
02.04.89	Road Atlanta, Georgia	61	Price Cobb, John Nielsen	2	2
23.04.89	West Palm Beach, Florida	61	Price Cobb, John Nielsen	6	2
29.05.89	Lime Rock, Connecticut	61	Price Cobb, John Nielsen	8	3
04.06.89	Mid Ohio, Ohio	61	Price Cobb, Davy Jones, John Nielsen	4	2
02.07.89	Watkins Glen, New York	61	Davy Jones, John Nielsen	6	Classified 18; DNF, engine
16.07.89	Road America, Wisconsin	61	Davy Jones, John Nielsen	1	3
30.07.89	Portland, Oregon	61	Davy Jones, John Nielsen	3	4
13.08.89	Heartland Park, Topeka, Kansas	60	Davy Jones, John Nielsen	2	5
03.09.89	San Antonio, Texas	60	Michel Ferte, John Nielsen	4	Classified 22; DNF, accident

Car badly damaged, sent back to UK for repairs, not raced again in 1989. For 1990 season, upgraded to XJR-12D specification. Race history continued:

Date	Circuit	Race no.	Drivers	Grid pos.	Result
03.02.-04.02.90	Daytona, Florida	61	Davy Jones, Jan Lammers, Andy Wallace	10	1
17.03.90	Sebring, Florida	61	Davy Jones, Jan Lammers, Andy Wallace	11	3

Chassis 388 retained in TWR museum

Type: XJR-9   Chassis number 488

Build date   January 1988
Race history

Date	Circuit	Race no.	Drivers	Grid pos.	Result
06.03.88	Jerez, Spain	2	Johnny Dumfries, Jan Lammers	2	DNF, transmission
13.03.88	Jarama, Spain	2	Johnny Dumfries, Jan Lammers	2	DNF, spin
10.04.88	Monza, Italy	2	Johnny Dumfries, Jan Lammers	5	DNF, spin
08.05.88	Silverstone, UK	2	Johnny Dumfries, Jan Lammers; car developed faults in practice, 187 used in race		Did not race

Date	Circuit	Race no.	Drivers	Grid pos.	Result
11.06.- 12.06.88	Le Mans, France (as XJR-9 LM)	2	Johnny Dumfries, Jan Lammers, Andy Wallace	6	1

After winning Le Mans the car was withdrawn from racing. Now in the Jaguar Daimler Heritage Trust collection. Regularly used in exhibitions and run at speed festivals etc.

Type: XJR-9   Chassis number 588

Build date	January 1988
History	The most successful Silk Cut XJR-9
Race history	

Date	Circuit	Race no.	Drivers	Grid pos.	Result
06.03.88	Jerez, Spain	1	Martin Brundle, Eddie Cheever	3	DNF, transmission
13.03.88	Jarama, Spain	1	Martin Brundle, Eddie Cheever	3	1
10.04.88	Monza, Italy	1	Martin Brundle, Eddie Cheever	4	· 1
08.05.88	Silverstone, UK	1	Martin Brundle, Eddie Cheever	2	1
11.06.- 12.06.88	Le Mans, France (as XJR-9 LM)	1	Martin Brundle, John Nielsen	4	DNF, head gasket
10.07.88	Brno, CZ	1	Martin Brundle, John Nielsen	3	2
24.07.88	Brands Hatch, UK	1	Martin Brundle, John Nielsen, Andy Wallace	6	1
04.09.88	Nürburgring, Germany	1	Martin Brundle, Eddie Cheever	5	2
18.09.88	Spa-Francorchamps, Belgium	1	Martin Brundle, Eddie Cheever; Brundle transferred to 688 after 588 retired	4	DNF, fuel pick-up
09.10.88	Fuji, Japan	1	Martin Brundle, Eddie Cheever	7	1
20.11.88	Sandown Park, Australia	1	Martin Brundle, Eddie Cheever	4	3
09.04.89	Suzuka, Japan	1	Jan Lammers, Patrick Tambay	3	DNF, fuel
21.05.89	Dijon, France	1	Jan Lammers, Patrick Tambay	7	DNF, fuel
10.06.- 11.06.89	Le Mans, France (as XJR-9 LM)	1	Jan Lammers, Andrew Gilbert-Scott, Patrick Tambay	3	4
25.06.89	Jarama, Spain	1	Jan Lammers, Patrick Tambay	3	2
20.08.89	Nürburgring, Germany	1T	John Nielsen		T car only
03.09.89	Donington Park, UK	1T			T car only
17.09.89	Spa-Francorchamps, Belgium	2T	John Nielsen, Andy Wallace		T car only
29.10.89	Mexico City	1	Jan Lammers, Patrick Tambay	5	6

588 upgraded and re-numbered as XJR-12LM Chassis no.990, for 1990 Le Mans. For details, see chassis 990.

Type: XJR-9   Chassis number 688

History	Not used until after 1988 Le Mans. Raced as car number 2 after chassis 488 was withdrawn from racing
Race history	

Date	Circuit	Race no.	Drivers	Grid pos.	Result
10.07.88	Brno, CZ	2	Johnny Dumfries, Jan Lammers	5	3
24.07.88	Brands Hatch, UK	2	Johnny Dumfries, Jan Lammers	4	DNF, electrics
04.09.88	Nürburgring, Germany	2	Johnny Dumfries, Jan Lammers	4	8
18.09.88	Spa-Francorchamps, Belgium	2	Martin Brundle, Johnny Dumfries, Jan Lammers; Brundle transferred to 688 after 588 retired	2	2
09.10.88	Fuji, Japan	2	Johnny Dumfries, Jan Lammers	6	DNF, accident
20.11.88	Sandown Park, Australia	2	Johnny Dumfries, Jan Lammers	3	4
09.04.89	Suzuka, Japan	2	John Nielsen, Andy Wallace	12	5
21.05.89	Dijon, France	2	John Nielsen, Andy Wallace	9	DNF, tyre
10.06.- 11.06.89	Le Mans, France (as XJR-9 LM)	2	Price Cobb, John Nielsen, Andy Wallace	8	DNF, head-gasket
25.06.89	Jarama, Spain	2	John Nielsen, Andy Wallace	4	6
23.07.89	Brands Hatch, UK	2	John Nielsen, Andy Wallace	11	DNF, accident

Not raced after the Brands Hatch accident. Chassis 688 retained in TWR museum.

Type: XJR-11   Chassis number 189

First run	8 February 1989, Donington Park, UK, shakedown, Jan Lammers
History	First Group C XJR-11 Turbo car
Race history	

Date	Circuit	Race no.	Drivers	Grid pos.	Result
23.07.89	Brands Hatch, UK	1	Jan Lammers, Patrick Tambay	1	5
20.08.89	Nürburgring, Germany	1	Jan Lammers, Patrick Tambay	3	10
03.09.89	Donington Park, UK	1	Jan Lammers, Patrick Tambay	5	DNF, electrics
17.09.89	Spa-Francorchamps, Belgium	1	Jan Lammers, Patrick Tambay	2	DNF, engine
08.04.90	Suzuka, Japan	3	Martin Brundle, Alain Ferte	8	DNF, engine
29.04.90	Monza, Italy		T car		
20.05.90	Silverstone, UK	3T	T car		
03.06.90	Spa-Francorchamps, Belgium		T car		
22.07.90	Dijon, France		T car		

Chassis number changed to 1390 in 1990. For details, see chassis 1390.

Type: XJR-11   Chassis number 289

First run	7 March 1989, Jerez, Spain, shakedown
Race history	

Date	Circuit	Race no.	Drivers	Grid pos.	Result
23.07.89	Brands Hatch, UK	3	Alain Ferte, Davy Jones	5	DNF, ignition
20.08.89	Nürburgring, Germany	2	John Nielsen, Andy Wallace	9	5
03.09.89	Donington Park, UK	2	Alain Ferte, Andy Wallace	6	DNF, fuel
17.09.89	Spa-Francorchamps, Belgium	2	John Nielsen, Andy Wallace	3	DNF, electrics
08.04.90	Suzuka, Japan	4	Jan Lammers, Andy Wallace	7	DNF, turbo
29.04.90	Monza, Italy	4	Jan Lammers, Andy Wallace	3	4

Re-numbered 590 for Silverstone race 20.05.1990. For details, see chassis 590.

Type: XJR-10   Chassis number 389

First run   31 March 1989,
                   shakedown, Andy Wallace

Race history

Date	Circuit	Race no.	Drivers	Grid pos.	Result
29 05 89	Lime Rock, Connecticut	60	Jan Lammers	2	2
04.06.89	Mid Ohio, Ohio	60	Davy Jones, Jan Lammers	2	Classified 16; DNF, cooling
02.07.89	Watkins Glen, New York	60	Price Cobb, Jan Lammers	2	Classified 16; DNF, puncture
16.07.89	Road America, Wisconsin	60	Price Cobb, Jan Lammers	2	2
30.07.89	Portland, Oregon	60	Price Cobb, Jan Lammers	1	1
13.08.89	Heartland Park, Topeka, Kansas	61	Price Cobb, Jan Lammers	5	3
03.09.89	San Antonio, Texas	61	Price Cobb, Davy Jones	3	Classified 25; DNF, engine
10.09.89	Sears Point, California	61	Price Cobb, Jan Lammers	1	4
01.10.89	Tampa, Florida	61	Jan Lammers	2	Classified 9; DNF, accident
22.10.89	Del Mar, California	60	Jan Lammers	7	1
25.02.90	Miami, Florida	61	Price Cobb, John Nielsen		Did not race
01.04.90	Road Atlanta, Georgia	61	Price Cobb, John Nielsen	1	2
22.04.90	West Palm Beach, Florida	61	Price Cobb, John Nielsen	6	3
06.05.90	Heartland Park, Topeka, Kansas	61	Price Cobb, John Nielsen	7	5
28.05.90	Lime Rock, Connecticut	61	Price Cobb, John Nielsen	4	1
03.06.90	Mid Ohio, Ohio	61	Price Cobb, John Nielsen	5	Classified 19; DNF, engine
01.07.90	Watkins Glen, New York	61	Price Cobb, John Nielsen	4	4
15.07.90	Sears Point, California	61	Price Cobb, John Nielsen	8	6
29.07.90	Portland, Oregon	61	Price Cobb, John Nielsen	6	Classified 20; DNF, engine
19.08.90	Road America, Wisconsin	61	John Nielsen	4	6
02.09.90	San Antonio, Texas	61	Price Cobb	4	Classified 14; DNF, accident
30.09.90	Tampa, Florida	61	John Nielsen	7	4
11.11.90	Del Mar, California	61	Martin Brundle	4	11
03.03.91	West Palm Beach, Florida	3	Raul Boesel	7	Classified 19; DNF, transmission
07.04.91	Miami, Florida	3	Raul Boesel	3	1

389 privately owned in UK. Active in Group C Revival racing. Painted in Castrol colours

Type: XJR-10   Chassis number 489

Race history

Date	Circuit	Race no.	Drivers	Grid pos.	Result
30.07.89	Portland, Oregon	66	Davy Jones	14	DNF, mechanical
13.08.89	Heartland Park, Topeka, Kansas	66	Price Cobb, Jan Lammers; practice only, not raced		
17.08.89	Grattan, Michigan		Price Cobb, Davy Jones	Testing only	

While being tested at Grattan, 489 crashed, caught fire and was completely destroyed.

Type: XJR-10   Chassis number 589

Race history

Date	Circuit	Race no.	Drivers	Grid pos.	Result
22.10.89	Del Mar, California	61	Price Cobb	4	7
25.02.90	Miami, Florida	60	Martin Brundle, Davy Jones	9	Classified 26; DNF, engine
01.04.90	Road Atlanta, Georgia	60	Davy Jones, Jan Lammers	5	7
22.04.90	West Palm Beach, Florida	60	Davy Jones, Jan Lammers	2	Classified 19; DNF, accident
06.05.90	Heartland Park, Topeka, Kansas	60	Martin Brundle, Davy Jones	8	6
28.05.90	Lime Rock, Connecticut	60	Davy Jones, Jan Lammers	8	Classified 23; DNF, engine/turbo
03.06.90	Mid Ohio, Ohio	60	Price Cobb, Davy Jones	4	Classified 17; DNF, engine
01.07.90	Watkins Glen, New York	60	Alain Ferte, Davy Jones	2	3
15.07.90	Sears Point, California	60	Alain Ferte, Davy Jones	9	4
29.07.90	Portland, Oregon	60	Davy Jones	2	1
19.08.90	Road America, Wisconsin	60	Davy Jones	3	2
02.09.90	San Antonio, Texas	60	Davy Jones	2	Classified 20; DNF, accident
30.09.90	Tampa, Florida	60	Davy Jones	4	Classified 12; DNF, driver fatigue
11.11.90	Del Mar, California	60	Davy Jones	3	2
03.03 91	West Palm Beach, Florida	2	Davy Jones	2	1
07.04.91	Miami, Florida	2	Davy Jones	2	Classified 22; DNF, engine
28.04.91	Road Atlanta, Georgia	3	Raul Boesel	2	3
05.05.91	Heartland Park, Topeka, Kansas	3	Raul Boesel	6	Classified 13; DNF, mechanical
27.05.91	Lime Rock, Connecticut		T car only; damaged in practice by Boesel	Did not race	

Chassis 589 offered for sale in UK in 2003 by JD Classics.

Type: XJR-12   Chassis number 190

Build date	1990
First run	28 February 1990, Silverstone, UK, shakedown by Andy Wallace
History	New chassis for IMSA

Race history

Date	Circuit	Race no.	Drivers	Grid pos.	Result
16.06.-17.06.90	Le Mans, France (as Silk Cut XJR-12LM)	4	Michel Ferte, Davy Jones, Luis Perez-Sala, Eliseo Salazar	7	DNF, engine
02.02.-03.02.91	Daytona, Florida (as Bud Light XJR-12D)	3	Kenny Acheson, Eddie Cheever, John Nielsen; crashed in practice by Nielsen		Did not race
16.03.91	Sebring, Florida (as Bud Light XJR-12D)	3	Raul Boesel, Davy Jones, John Nielsen	5	5
30.01.-31.01.93	Daytona, Florida (as Bud Light XJR-12D)	2	Scott Goodyear, Davy Jones, Scott Pruett	6	Classified 10; DNF

Chassis 190 retained in TWR museum

Type: XJR-12   Chassis number 290

Build date	January 1990
History	New chassis for IMSA

Race history

Date	Circuit	Race no.	Drivers	Grid pos.	Result
16.06.-17.06.90	Le Mans, France (as Silk Cut XJR-12LM)	2	Franz Konrad, Jan Lammers, Andy Wallace	17	2
02.02.-03.02.91	Daytona, Florida (as Bud Light XJR-12D)	2	Raul Boesel, Davy Jones, Scott Pruett, Derek Warwick	2	Classified 30; DNF, engine
16.03.91	Sebring, Florida (as Bud Light XJR-12D)	2	Crashed in practice by Davy Jones, did not race		
22.06.-23.06.91	Le Mans, France (as Suntec XJR-12LM)	36	Jeff Krosnoff, David Leslie, Mauro Martini	28	DNF, gearbox

Type: XJR-10   Chassis number 390

History	Listed as XJR-10 for IMSA.

No information available. No race history available. However, this car may have been a spare chassis intended to replace 489.

Type: XJR-11   Chassis number 490

History	New 1990 chassis

Race history

Date	Circuit	Race no.	Drivers	Grid pos.	Result
29.04.90	Monza, Italy	3	Martin Brundle, Alain Ferte	4	3
20.05.90	Silverstone, UK	3	Martin Brundle, Alain Ferte	2	1
03.06.90	Spa-Francorchamps, Belgium	3	Martin Brundle, Alain Ferte	3	DNF, wiring fire
22.07.90	Dijon, France	3	Martin Brundle, Alain Ferte	2	5

Re-numbered to 1190 for remainder of 1990 season; for details, see chassis 1190. 1991: Chassis number reverted to 490; raced in All Japan Sportscar-Prototype Championship, sponsored by Suntec.

Date	Circuit	Race no.	Drivers	Grid pos.	Result
05.05.91	Fuji, Japan	18	Jeff Krosnoff, Mauro Martini	9	DNF, engine
21.07.91	Fuji, Japan	18	Jeff Krosnoff, Mauro Martini, John Nielsen	7	DNF, turbo
25.08.91	Suzuka, Japan	18	Jeff Krosnoff, Mauro Martini, John Nielsen	7	DNF, electrics
15.09.91	Sugo, Japan	18	Jeff Krosnoff, Mauro Martini, John Nielsen	9	6
06.10.91	Fuji, Japan	18	Jeff Krosnoff, Mauro Martini	7	7

2005- Oppenheimer USA.

Type: XJR-11   Chassis number 590

History	Former XJR-11 chassis 289 re numbered to 590. See chassis 289 for previous race history.

Race history

Date	Circuit	Race no.	Drivers	Grid pos.	Result
20.05.90	Silverstone, UK	4	Jan Lammers, Andy Wallace	3	2
03.06.90	Spa-Francorchamps, Belgium	4	Jan Lammers, Andy Wallace	4	2
22.07.90	Dijon, France	4	Jan Lammers, Andy Wallace	4	4

For the rest of the 1990 season, this chassis was re-numbered to 1290, for details see chassis 1290. For 1991, the chassis reverted to 590 and was the spare car in All Japan Sportscar-Prototype Championship, sponsored by Suntec:

Date	Circuit	Race no.	Drivers	Grid pos.	Result
05.05.91	Fuji, Japan		Spare car only		
21.07.91	Fuji, Japan		Spare car only		
25.08.91	Suzuka, Japan		Spare car only		
15.09.91	Sugo, Japan		Spare car only		
06.10.91	Fuji, Japan		Spare car only		

Type: XJR-10   Chassis number 690

History	Listed as XJR-10 for IMSA

No information available. No race history available. However, this car is reported to be privately owned in Germany.

Type: XJR-12? Chassis numbers 790 and 890

These two numbers appear on a list of TWR chassis numbers of unknown origin found in the collection of the late Jaguar racing writer and historian Ken Wells. 790 and 890 are described as being XJR-12s for IMSA. It is not known whether these numbers were intended as 1990 numbers for newly up-graded IMSA XJR-9 cars 188 and 388, to be introduced at the same time as 288 and 588 were given new numbers (1090 and 990 respectively) for the 1990 Le Mans, or if two new chassis were built for which no information is available.

Type: XJR-12   Chassis number 990

History	Former Silk Cut XJR-9 588 upgraded to XJR-12 LM specification for 1990 Le Mans.
Note:	Not IMSA chassis 388 as reported elsewhere. See chassis 588 for previous history.

Date	Circuit	Race no.	Drivers	Grid pos.	Result
16.06.-17.06.90	Le Mans, France (as XJR-12 LM)	1	Martin Brundle, Alain Ferte, David Leslie	8	DNF, water pump
22.06.-23.06.91	Le Mans, France (as XJR-12 LM)	35	Raul Boesel, Michel Ferte, Davy Jones	18	2

30.01.-31.01.93	Daytona, Florida (as XJR-12 D)	3	John Andretti, David Brabham, John Nielsen	7	Classified 60; DNF, oil leak

990 now privately owned in the UK

Type: XJR-12 Chassis number 1090

Build date: March 1990
History: Former IMSA XJR-9 chassis 288 upgraded to XJR-12 LM specification for 1990 Le Mans. See chassis 288 for previous history.

Race history

Date	Circuit	Race no.	Drivers	Grid pos.	Result
16.06.-17.06.90	Le Mans, France (as XJR-12 LM)	3	Martin Brundle, Price Cobb, John Nielsen, Eliseo Salazar	9	1

This was the only race for chassis 1090. The car was retained in Tom Walkinshaw's museum, and has occasionally been seen at shows and speed festivals.

Type: XJR-11 Chassis number 1190

History: Former XJR-11 chassis 490 re-numbered to 1190. See chassis 490 for previous history.

Race history

Date	Circuit	Race no.	Drivers	Grid pos.	Result
19.08.90	Nürburgring, Germany	3	Martin Brundle, Alain Ferte	3	3
02.09.90	Donington Park, UK	3	Martin Brundle, Alain Ferte	4	3, disqualified
23.09.90	Montreal, Canada	3	Martin Brundle, Jan Lammers	3	DNF, driveshaft
21.10.90	Mexico City, Mexico	3	Martin Brundle, Jan Lammers	1	DNF, electrics

This car then reverted to chassis 490 for 1991, for details see chassis 490.

Type: XJR-11 Chassis number 1290

History: Former chassis 289, then 590 re-numbered to 1290. See chassis 289 and 590 for previous history.

Race history

Date	Circuit	Race no.	Drivers	Grid pos.	Result
19.08.90	Nürburgring, Germany	4	Jan Lammers, Andy Wallace	4	4
02.09.90	Donington Park, UK	4	Jan Lammers, Andy Wallace	7	8, disqualified
23.09.90	Montreal, Canada	4	Davy Jones, Andy Wallace	6	DNF, driveshaft
21.10.90	Mexico City, Mexico	4	Davy Jones, Andy Wallace	6	4, moved to 3

This car then reverted to chassis 590 for 1991, for details see chassis 590.

Type: XJR-11 Chassis number 1390

History: Former Chassis 189 re-numbered to 1390; spare car only? See XJR-11 chassis 189 for previous history.
Race history: Not known if this car attended any race meetings while listed as 1390.

Type: XJR-16 Chassis number 191

Build date: March-April 1991
History: The first turbo car developed and built by TWR at Valparaiso, USA.

Race history

Date	Circuit	Race no.	Drivers	Grid pos.	Result
28.04.91	Road Atlanta, Georgia	2	Davy Jones	1	1
05.05.91	Heartland Park, Topeka, Kansas	2	Davy Jones	1	2
27.05.91	Lime Rock, Connecticut	2	Davy Jones	2	7
02.06.91	Mid Ohio, Ohio	2	Davy Jones	3	1
16.06.91	New Orleans, Louisiana	2	Davy Jones	5	DNF, suspension
30.06.91	Watkins Glen, New York	2	Davy Jones	4	13
21.07.91	Laguna Seca, California	2	Davy Jones	3	1
28.07.91	Portland, Oregon	2	Davy Jones	3	5
25.08.91	Road America, Wisconsin	2	Davy Jones	1	1
13.10.91	Del Mar, California	2	Davy Jones	7	13
01.02.-02.02 92	Daytona, Florida	3	Scott Goodyear; Davy Jones qualified the car	2	Withdrawn, engine

Privately owned in the UK, active in Group C Revival racing with good results

Type: XJR-16 Chassis number 291

History: The second turbo car developed and built by TWR at Valparaiso, USA.

Race history

Date	Circuit	Race no.	Drivers	Grid pos.	Result
27.05.91	Lime Rock, Connecticut	3	Raul Boesel	15	6
02.06.91	Mid Ohio, Ohio	3	Raul Boesel	6	4
16.06.91	New Orleans, Louisiana	3	Raul Boesel	8	DNF, suspension
30.06.91	Watkins Glen, New York	3	Raul Boesel	6	DNF, accident
25.08.91	Road America, Wisconsin	3	Raul Boesel	19	4
13.10.91	Del Mar, California	3	Martin Brundle	8	4

Chassis 291 reported converted to non-turbocharged XJR-17 with no known chassis number.

Type: XJR-14 Chassis number 591

Phil Bennett's

Build date: February 1991
First run: 20 March 1991, Silverstone, UK, shakedown by Derek Warwick
History: First of the new 1991 formula 3½ litre non-turbo, normally-aspirated V8 cars.

Race history

Date	Circuit	Race no.	Drivers	Grid pos.	Result
14.04.91	Suzuka, Japan	3	Martin Brundle, Derek Warwick	1	DNF, starter
05.05.91	Monza, Italy	3	Martin Brundle, Teo Fabi, Derek Warwick	2	1
19.05.91	Silverstone, UK	3	Martin Brundle, Derek Warwick	2	3
22.06.-23.06.91	Le Mans, France (as XJR-14 LM)	3	Andy Wallace		Did not race
18.08.91	Nürburgring, Germany		T car only		
15.09.91	Magny Cours, France		T car only		
27.10.91	Autopolis, Japan	3	Derek Warwick; taken as T car, but used in race when tank failed in 791	4	2

switched in race, so not named on car Non Tobacco

Non Tobacco

Then transferred to the 1991 All Japan Sportscar-Prototype Championship (Suntec) for the final race only:

Former 1991 WSC Championship-winning XJR-14 (691), rebuilt as a Joest Porsche WSC95, won the Le Mans 24 hours race in 1996, then took a second win in the classic one year later. The distinctive side radiator intakes are about all that is recognisable as XJR-14. (LAT Photographic)

Date	Circuit	Race no.	Drivers	Grid pos.	Result
03.11.91	Sugo, Japan (AJS-PC)		Taken as T car, but some running by David Brabham		

1992: Raced in IMSA Camel GT Championship with Bud Light sponsorship:

Date	Circuit	Race no.	Drivers	Grid pos.	Result
19.07.92	Laguna Seca, California	3	Arie Luyendijk	6	4
09.08.92	Road America, Wisconsin	2	Davy Jones		Crashed in warm-up, did not race

Chassis 591 restored by TWR, sold to American buyer in 2003.

Type: XJR-14 Chassis number 691 — *Joest Porsche*

Build date	March 1991
First run	2 April 1991, Silverstone, UK, shakedown, Teo Fabi
History	Teo Fabi's 1991 World Championship winning car.

Race history

Date	Circuit	Race no.	Drivers	Grid pos.	Result
14.04.91	Suzuka, Japan	4	Martin Brundle, Teo Fabi	6	DNF, electrics
05.05.91	Monza, Italy	4	Martin Brundle, Teo Fabi	1	2
19.05.91	Silverstone, UK	4	Teo Fabi, Derek Warwick	1	1
22.06.-23.06.91	Le Mans, France (as XJR-14 LM)	4	Andy Wallace; taken for qualifying only		
18.08.91	Nürburgring, Germany	4	David Brabham, Teo Fabi	1	2
15.09.91	Magny Cours, France	4	David Brabham, Teo Fabi	4	3
06.10.91	Mexico City, Mexico	4	David Brabham, Teo Fabi	5	Did not race, oil leaks
27.10.91	Autopolis, Japan	4	David Brabham, Teo Fabi	1	3

Then transferred to the 1991 All Japan Sportscar-Prototype Championship (Suntec) for the final race only:

Date	Circuit	Race no.	Drivers	Grid pos.	Result
03.11.91	Sugo, Japan (AJS-PC)	17	David Brabham, Teo Fabi	1	1

1992: Raced in IMSA Camel GT Championship with Bud Light sponsorship. Chassis number changed to 192. For details, see chassis 192.

Type: XJR-14 Chassis number 791 *Aaron Hsu*

Race history

Date	Circuit	Race no.	Drivers	Grid pos.	Result
18.08.91	Nürburgring, Germany	3	David Brabham, Derek Warwick	2	1
15.09.91	Magny Cours, France	3	David Brabham, Derek Warwick	5	5
06.10.91	Mexico City, Mexico	3	David Brabham, Derek Warwick	4	6
27.10.91	Autopolis, Japan	3	David Brabham, Derek Warwick; car not raced, tank failed; they used the spare car 591 instead		

Then transferred to the 1991 All Japan Sportscar-Prototype Championship (Suntec) for the final race only:

Date	Circuit	Race no.	Drivers	Grid pos.	Result
03.11.91	Sugo, Japan (AJS-PC)	18	Jeff Krosnoff, Mauro Martini	2	9

1992: Raced in IMSA Camel GT Championship with Bud Light sponsorship:

Date	Circuit	Race no.	Drivers	Grid pos.	Result
23.02.92	Miami, Florida	2	Davy Jones	1	DNF, spin
26.04.92	Road Atlanta, Georgia	2	Davy Jones	1	1
26.05.92	Lime Rock, Connecticut	2	Davy Jones	1	DNF, accident

Chassis 791 retained in TWR museum

Type: XJR-12 Chassis number 891

Build date	Spring 1991
First run	May 1991
History	New chassis for 1991 Le Mans.

Race history

Date	Circuit	Race no.	Drivers	Grid pos.	Result
22.06.-23.06.91	Le Mans, France (as Silk Cut XJR-12 LM)	33	John Nielsen, Andy Wallace, Derek Warwick	24	4
01.02.-02.02.92	Daytona, Florida (as Bud Light XJR-12 D)	2	David Brabham, Scott Goodyear, Davy Jones, Scott Pruett	7	2, and 1 in GTP Class
21.03.92	Sebring, Florida (as Bud Light XJR-12 D)	2	David Brabham, Davy Jones	10	4

Chassis 891 retained in TWR museum

Type: XJR-12   Chassis number 991

Build date   Spring 1991
First run   24 May 1991, Silverstone, UK, shakedown
History   Former chassis 386 upgraded to XJR-12 LM
          specification for 1991 Le Mans.

Race history

Date	Circuit	Race no.	Drivers	Grid pos.	Result
22.06.- 23.06.91	Le Mans, France	34	Kenny Acheson, Teo Fabi, Bob Wollek	27	3

Type: XJR-14   Chassis number 192

History   XJR-14 chassis 691 re-numbered for IMSA racing
          in 1992. See chassis 691 for previous history and
          other information.

Race history

Date	Circuit	Race no.	Drivers	Grid pos.	Result
31.05.92	Mid Ohio, Ohio	2	Davy Jones	1	1
14.06.92	New Orleans, Louisiana	2	Davy Jones	2	4
28.06.92	Watkins Glen, New York	2	Davy Jones	1	3
19.07.92	Laguna Seca, California	2	Davy Jones	3	3
26.07.92	Portland, Oregon	2	Davy Jones	3	DNF, mechanical
04.10.92	Phoenix, Arizona	2	Davy Jones	3	2
11.10.92	Del Mar, California	2	Davy Jones	2	3 - not running at the finish

XJR-14 chassis number 691/192 was subsequently converted to a Porsche
WSC95 Spyder car in late 1994, raced at Le Mans in 1996 and 1997 by Joest
Porsche, winning the race on both occasions. It is now in Reinhold Joest's
private museum.

Type: XJR-12   Chassis number 193

Build date   Late 1992
First run   15 January 1993, Silverstone, UK,
          shakedown by David Brabham, John Nielsen
History   New chassis for Le Mans - raced only once, and not
          at Le Mans, but at Daytona as XJR-12D. There are
          reports that this car was listed as chassis 790 while it
          was being restored for sale in the late 1990s.

Race history

Date	Circuit	Race no.	Drivers	Grid pos.	Result
30.01.- 31.01.93	Daytona, Florida	32	John Andretti, David Brabham, Davy Jones, John Nielsen	8	DNF, handling

193 now in private ownership in UK, and active in Group C Revival racing

The reader must understand the difficulty of tracing historic racing cars, which
during their working life are subject to continuous development and even
changes of identity. Inevitably, with the passage of time this may lead to
occasional confusion.

Postscript

As this book was being prepared for publication, news emerged
that TWR's Kidlington base and workshops, where most of the
racing activities detailed in this book originated, was placed in
administrative receivership in February 2003. Some weeks later, the
business was sold to MC Technology, an American company
involved in the Indy racing League series. The initials MC stand for
John Menard and ex-TWR racing driver Eddie Cheever.

TWR's entire collection of historic race cars was also placed in
receivership, including no less than eight historic Group C and IMSA
prototypes, and a single Group A XJ-S. The list of Group C and
IMSA cars in this collection was as follows:

1985 XJR-6 chassis 185
1987 XJR-8 chassis 287
1988 IMSA XJR-9 chassis 388
1988 Group C XJR-9 chassis 688
1988 IMSA XJR-9 chassis 288 later re-numbered 1090
      and winner of 1990 Le Mans
1990 XJR-12 LM chassis 190
1991 XJR-14 chassis 791
1991 XJR-12 chassis 891

At the time of going to press, all of these cars were being restored
to full running order prior to being offered for sale.

The list of chassis numbers is the result of extensive research
carried out over several years. Cars re-numbered in 1990 or later to
which an original number was subsequently re-allocated may not
now bear the number that was assigned to them when first built.

Acknowledgements

It gives me great pleasure on behalf of the Jaguar Daimler Heritage Trust to thank first and foremost Leslie Thurston, the leading expert in the field of the XJR racing cars, for having so diligently researched all the minutiae concerning these cars and their racing histories, and for having put all his knowledge down on paper in this book which we are proud to be associated with. As the charitable trust concerned with preserving Jaguar's heritage, we are extremely conscious of our responsibility not only to mantain our fine collections of cars and archive material, but also to educate, by publishing books such as this.

Ian Norris, who was very much on the scene at the time when the XJRs ruled the world of sportscar racing, has contributed introductory pieces to the book and to individual chapters, which help to create the context as a background for all the detailed information which follows. Roger Putnam, my ex-boss, who was also deeply involved at the time, has since gone on to greater things but keeps his interest alive, not least through being Chairman of Trustees for the Jaguar Daimler Heritage Trust, and he enthusiastically agreed to write the foreword.

Alan Hodge of Jaguar and the eminent Jaguar historian Paul Skilleter, editor of *Jaguar World* magazine and author of many erudite books on our marque, both read and commented on the typescript. Many photographs came from our JDHT archive, but were also contributed by other photographers who generously agreed to let us use their work.

Amongst JDHT staff, our chief archivist Anders Ditlev Clausager and our volunteer Penny Graham - herself deeply interested in motor sport history and involved in historic motor sport, particularly as it concerns Jaguar - took on the task of editing the book to make it ready for publication. The actual process of producing the book was expertly overseen by the experienced publisher Charles Herridge. I thank all who have been involved with this challenging project.

John Maries
Executive Director
Jaguar Daimler Heritage Trust

The author would like to express his gratitude to the many former personnel associated with the TWR Jaguar racing programme who kindly helped in the quest to make this book as comprehensive as possible. Special thanks go to race car designer Tony Southgate, the late Ron Elkins, Jaguar Racing Manager, and two other company stalwarts deeply involved with the teams at the time: Alan Hodge and Colin Cook. Also thanks to Win Percy, one of the sport's true gentlemen, in particular for the two-lap ride enjoyed with him around Le Mans in the 1988 winning XJR-9. I also thank Norman Wells, brother of the late Ken Wells, whose books on the same subject are a joy to read because of his unique style of journalism. Howard Davies of the JDHT, Neil Smith of XK Engineering, Don Law, Gary Pearson, Derek Hood, Steve Carr and many more Jaguar prototype owners and racers in the Group C Revival Series have all been of considerable help. My thanks go not least to Irene Day for all her secretarial work, helping to convert my scribbled notes and recordings into a readable manuscript. Finally, I and the JDHT are very much indebted to the many photographers, car owners and fans who have kindly supplied photographs to ensure that the book is fully illustrated. As far as possible, photos have been individually acknowledged where they appear. While every effort has been made to trace the origin of photos used in the book, we apologise for any unintended infringement of individual copyright.

Leslie F Thurston